Adam, Eve, and the Genome

Adam, Eve, and the Genome

The Human Genome Project and Theology

Edited by Susan Brooks Thistlethwaite

FORTRESS PRESS
MINNEAPOLIS

ADAM, EVE, AND THE GENOME
The Human Genome Project and Theology

Unless otherwise noted, biblical quotations from the New Revised Standard Version are copyright © 1989 by the Division of Christian Education of the National Council of the Churches of Christ in the United States of America and are used by permission.

Cover art: *Fall of Man* by S. E. Bottex (20th century. Haiti) Coll. Manu Sassoonian, New York, N.Y., U.S.A. Copyright Manu Sassoonian/Art Resource, N.Y. Used by permission.

ISBN 0-8006-3614-7

The paper used in this publication meets the minimum requirements of American National Standard for Information Sciences — Permanence of Paper for Printed Library Materials, ANSI Z329.48-1984.

Manufactured in the U.S.A.

07   06   05   04   03   1   2   3   4   5   6   7   8   9   10

To our three sons, James, Bill, and Doug,
now adults, who have each contributed,
from his own unique intellectual perspective,
to my understanding of the complexity
of the relationship of religion and science
through spirited family debates ⌁ *SBT*

Contents

About the Contributors   *xi*
Preface   *xiii*

Introduction: Liberation Theology in Dialogue with
   the Human Genome Project
SUSAN BROOKS THISTLETHWAITE   1

   A Beginning Point   5
   Different Questions, New Insights   12

Part One: The Science of Genetics

1. Setting the Context: A Brief History of Science
   by a Sympathetic Theologian
   LAUREL C. SCHNEIDER   17

   Aristotle and Plato   18
   Islamic Science   25
   Medieval Science in the West   28
   The Reformation and the Renaissance   31
   Descartes   33
   Newton   36
   Darwin   44
   Freud   47

2. An Introduction to Mendelian Genetics
   LAINIE FRIEDMAN ROSS   52

   Gregor Mendel and Peas   52
   DNA   53
   Autosomal Recessive Conditions   54
   Autosomal Dominant Conditions   61
   X-Linked Conditions   63

3. From Peapods to the Human Genome Project:
Post-Mendelian Genetics
LAINIE FRIEDMAN ROSS   69

   Chromosomal Variations   70
   Clinical Genetics   77
   Ethical and Policy Issues   83

Part Two: Being Human

4. Theological Anthropology and the Human Genome Project
THEODORE W. JENNINGS JR.   93

   Theology and Science   94
   Bringing Theology to the Human Genome Project   98
   Redemption and Resurrection   102
   Imago Dei   109
   Reflections on Romans   110

5. Adam, Eve, and the Genome
KEN STONE   112

   The Genome as "Text"   112
   The Quest for a "Gay Gene" as "Etiological Text" 115
   The Story of Adam and Eve as "Etiological Text"   117
   Who Asks Etiological Questions?   121

Part Three: Critical Issues

6. Dreaming the Soul: African American Skepticism
Encounters the Human Genome Project
LEE H. BUTLER JR.   129

   Racism in American History as a Feature of the American Dream   132
   A Way out of the Nightmare: A Different Dream of Being Human   136
   Dreaming of Freedom   139
   The New Dream   141
   On Being Human   143

7. **A Gene for Violence? Genetic Determinism and Sin**
   SUSAN BROOKS THISTLETHWAITE   145

   A Short History of the Doctrine of Sin   145
   Genetic Determinism   148
   Flies Who Rape?   149
   Flawed Science   151
   Human Freedom and Genetics   152
   Human Dignity/In the Image of God   153
   Social Sin and Human Violence   155
   To Sin Rationally   157

8. **The Chemistry of Community**
   SUSAN BROOKS THISTLETHWAITE   161

   The "Case" of Hypertension in African Americans   163
   The "Case" of Breast Cancer   165
   Grace   167
   Soul/Body Dualism   171
   The Grace of Community   173

Notes   *175*
Glossary   *188*
Index   *194*

About the Contributors

LEE H. BUTLER JR. is Associate Professor of Theology and Psychology at the Chicago Theological Seminary. He is an African American pastoral theologian whose primary research emphasis is on African American identity formation. He is the author of *Loving Home: Caring for African American Marriage and Family* (Pilgrim Press, 2000).

THEODORE W. JENNINGS JR. is Professor of Biblical and Constructive Theology at the Chicago Theological Seminary. He is the author of numerous books and articles. His most recent books include *The Insurrection of the Crucified: The Gospel of Mark as Theological Manifesto* (Exploration Press, 2003) and *The Man Jesus Loved: Homoerotic Narratives from the New Testament* (Pilgrim Press, 2003). Jennings research interests include Christian doctrine, biblical theology, gay studies, and contemporary late modern philosophy. He also writes, particularly in Spanish, on Wesleyan theology.

LAINIE FRIEDMAN ROSS is an Associate Professor in the Department of Pediatrics at the University of Chicago and an Assistant Director of the MacLean Center for Clinical Medical Ethics at the University of Chicago. Dr. Ross's research interests are ethical issues in pediatrics, genetics, and human experimentation. Her first book, *Children, Families, and Health Care Decision Making* was published by Oxford University Press in 1998. Her current research in genetics, "Ethical Analysis and Public Policy Recommendations Regarding the Genetic Testing of Children," is supported by a Harris Foundation Grant. This study involves focus groups with the public and interviews with health care professionals regarding their attitudes and beliefs about genetic testing of children, for conditions that present in childhood and beyond, for conditions that are and are not treatable. She has also just begun a project, "Newborn Genetic Screening: For Whose Benefit?" which is funded by the National Institute of Children's Health and Development. The goal of this project is to understand what has been done right, what has been done wrong, and what we should do differently as we consider expanding newborn screening programs.

LAUREL C. SCHNEIDER is Associate Professor of Theology, Ethics and Culture at the Chicago Theological Seminary. In addition to articles and chapter contributions in feminist theology, queer theory, and race, she is author of *Re-Imagining the Divine: Confronting the Backlash against Feminist Theology* (Pilgrim Press, 1998) and has co-taught courses on the history of science with Nancy Peterson, Associate Professor of Chemistry at North Central College.

KEN STONE is Associate Professor of Hebrew Bible at the Chicago Theological Seminary. He is the author of *Sex, Honor, and Power in the Deuteronomistic History* (Sheffield Academic Press, 1996) and editor of *Queer Commentary and the Hebrew Bible* (Sheffield Academic Press, 2001), which won a Lambda Literary Award. Currently he is completing a book on food, sex, and biblical interpretation.

SUSAN BROOKS THISTLETHWAITE is the eleventh President of the Chicago Theological Seminary and a Professor of Theology. She is the author or editor of eleven books and has been a translator for two different translations of the Bible. Her works include *Casting Stones: Prostitution and Liberation in Asia and the United States* with Dr. Rita Nakashima Brock (Fortress Press, 1996) and *The New Testament and Psalms: An Inclusive Translation* (Oxford University Press, 1995). In 1999, Orbis Press published the tenth anniversary edition of *Lift Every Voice: Constructing Christian Theologies from the Underside*, a work Thistlethwaite edited with Mary Potter Engel. This is the third most widely used textbook in the U.S. to teach theology. She works at the intersection of theology and culture.

Preface

Susan Brooks Thistlethwaite

The full report of the President's Council on Bioethics, *Human Cloning and Human Dignity,* is 350 pages long. Despite the parity in the title, there is no section that explicitly defines "human dignity." Less than two pages out of 350 are devoted to statements about human beings.[1] While science today is confronted with extraordinary ethical challenges, very little attempt is made to achieve anything like the precision of scientific definitions for the often-used category "human dignity." Yet, as is clearly the case in the President's council report, the basis of the decision-making rests on an assumption that there is such a thing as human dignity.

This volume is an attempt to provide theological reflection on the human being by means of a dialogue with the newer advances in human genetics, the Human Genome Project. The chapters included in the volume began as lectures given in a course called "God, Adam, and Eve: Theology and Science in the Genome Age."[3] My colleague Dr. Laurel C. Schneider and I designed this course and received generous grant support for it from the Center for Theology and the Natural Sciences (CTNS). CTNS deserves not only our thanks for their financial support but also the thanks of the students at the Chicago Theological Seminary and at the Division of Biological Sciences at the University of Chicago for making possible this addition to the curriculum. Dr. Lainie Friedman Ross, the pediatric geneticist at the University of Chicago Medical Center, agreed to team-teach with us, and we had students from both institutions take the course in the fall of 2001. The presence of both theology students and science majors made the class discussions very rich. An additional plus was that Dr. Ross, an Askanazi Jew and a deeply religious as well as philosophically trained person, managed, even with her incredible schedule, to participate in the whole course. We unexpectedly taught a course in Jewish/Christian theologies and the Human Genome Project.

One thing that quickly became apparent to Dr. Schneider and me as we began to draft the course design was that we were not going to be able to cover all the theological loci, so we narrowed our focus to theological anthropology. We were aided in this endeavor by the participation of faculty colleagues from the Chicago Theological Seminary. We benefited from the perspectives on theological understandings of the human from Dr. Theodore W. Jennings Jr. (Constructive Theology and Biblical Studies), Dr. Ken Stone (Hebrew Bible), and Dr. Lee H. Butler Jr. (Pastoral Care). It is a testimony to the intellectual curiosity and energy of this faculty that so many colleagues would take the time to read several books and prepare a lecture relating their field and its insights on the human to this emerging branch of science. Their chapters are edited versions of their original class presentations.

As the class progressed, we were able to witness the benefit of the progressive interaction of the scientific information with the various theological disciplines. Dr. Schneider began with a thorough survey of the history of the relationship of religion and science. For most of recorded human history, religion and science have not been separated by a huge intellectual gulf as is often the case today. Indeed, as Dr. Schneider's chapter shows, the history is rather one of inseparability.

Dr. Ross then introduced us to the science of genetics through its clinical application. The field of genetics not only poses enormous challenges for the human future, it poses enormous challenges as well as benefits to individuals and families today. Often patients and their families are left to sort out the challenges without informed aid from their religious communities.

Dr. Jennings began the search for an understanding of the human being from his perspective in historical and biblical theology. Theologians from the early centuries of the church did not divide up the human being into compartments of soul and body: their comfort with and insight into the creaturely nature of the ensouled human being is an important lesson as we try to build bridges over today's chasms dividing body and soul.

The Human Genome is actually a text, albeit a chemical one, notes Dr. Ken Stone, and those who investigate it try to answer questions. This is much like the way biblical scholars are coming to interrogate the text of the Hebrew and Christian scriptures. Frequently, the answer sought is to the question, "Who is the human being?" These different kinds of texts can be more similar than perhaps we had thought.

Dr. Butler offers a cautionary tale. Those who have been exploited in the history of science, in the history of the field of genetics itself, are not sanguine that this research will be done with sufficient attention to the ways in which the social construction of science is part of the history of American racism. Religion is equally complicit in this racist history, as Dr. Butler also makes clear. It is only through the complete inclusion of those who have been excluded can science and religion find a new ways to understand the complexity of questions about who gets to be counted as human.

In my two concluding chapters, I look at what might be considered a traditional approach to theological reflection on the human being under the topics of sin and grace. As many who have been excluded in religion in the past have done theological reflection on the human, these doctrines are changing. They change even further when placed alongside the insights gained from the Human Genome Project.

Thanks for support and inspiration are owed, more deeply than I can put into words, to my husband, Dr. J. Richard Thistlethwaite Jr., Professor of Surgery and Immunology at the University of Chicago. Without his encouragement and support, I never would have attempted to teach a course, much less edit a volume, on religion and science.

I have also learned a tremendous amount from being, through my husband, Dick, an observer of the organ transplant community. As a transplant surgeon and immunologist, Dick works with a community of both scientists and community leaders to wrestle with the difficult ethical issues that make organ transplantation possible. Human organ transplantation has become not only possible but a routine choice for the treatment of certain diseases. This is both because of scientific advances, and because patients, their families, donor families, and the wider community work together to educate society and to solve the intricate problems of organ procurement and allocation.

Organ transplantation, while different from genetics, illustrates several key insights of this work on theological anthropology and the Human Genome Project. All humanity is one: we can literally become one another as we share our organs. Each human being is unique: the immune system of each individual is particular to him or her and not easily bypassed. And finally, community is part of healing: without commitment to the well-being of the whole human community, organs for transplant would not be donated. I have been privileged to witness, through Dick, the amazing commitments of lay members of the organ transplant community as well as its medical scientists, like Dick, who work with them to find cures for dreadful diseases and literally save lives.

I would also like to thank the students of our class for their engagement with the material and their final project, a draft web course summarizing the class material. This was the first time I had assigned designing a web-based course for a course requirement. It worked very well and was an integral part of the engagement of the students with the material. I would like to thank Dr. Julia Speller of the Chicago Theological Seminary faculty for leading that section of the course and helping us understand how to teach in this format. The basic glossary included at the end of this volume was compiled by the students of our class as part of that assignment.

Far more work needs to be done to repair the breach between religion and science that opened after the Enlightenment. This volume is a very preliminary step. Yet even this step took imagination and courage from all involved. The information revolution has brought us access to more facts than anyone can possibly assimilate. It is tempting to burrow down into one's own narrow field and never poke one's head above the surface. The intellectual community then resembles a prairie dog city when a predator comes near. It's a barren plain with a lot of holes.

In this volume, several of us have taken the risk of sticking our heads up and taking a look around. As we climbed out on to the landscape, danger lurked. We could be risking superficiality. We could look like idiots when we step out into a field of knowledge not our own. But the risks to the whole human community of not poking our heads up are even greater. Knowledge of great potential for harm and for good is being created. All of us need to engage this knowledge. We are considering a huge and important question: what does it mean to be human? As we seek answers, everybody gets a say. The greatest danger comes when the answer to that question comes only from a few. We invite you, the reader, into this conversation. We need you, too.

Introduction

Liberation Theology in Dialogue with the Human Genome Project

Susan Brooks Thistlethwaite

The mapping of the human genome, the information on human heredity stored in our cells, is a momentous achievement. If the nineteenth century was the industrial age and the twentieth the digital age, it is now clear that the twenty-first century is the biological age. We are told that the next great leap in information storage may be bacteriological; future generations of computers will perhaps be organic.

How are we to understand such a profound shift in human history? Pivotal moments in human history are often imaged in religious terms. When Robert Oppenheimer witnessed the splitting of the atom in the first nuclear test in Alamogordo, New Mexico, he quoted a Hindu text, the *Bhagavadgita:* "I am become Death, the Shatterer of Worlds." Harvard molecular biologist and Nobel laureate Walter Gilbert has called the genome "the Holy Grail."[1] Connecting the two across more than fifty years, the Human Genome Project has been called the "Manhattan Project for biomedicine."[2] But whereas the invention of the atomic bomb potentially heralded the "death of death," the possibility of complete extinction of all life on the planet, the Human Genome Project is very much about the origins of life and its yet untapped potential.

What is equally remarkable, from an explicitly religious perspective, is how the Human Genome Project offers a way to overcome long centuries of opposition between religion and science. For the genome may be, as one *NOVA* television program labeled it, "The Book of Life."

In his best-selling book *Genome: The Autobiography of a Species in 23 Chapters,* Matt Ridley makes the religion/science gulf disappear as though it had never existed. He accomplishes this feat with an extended metaphor. Ridley explains that the genome is actually a text.

There are twenty-three chapters, called CHROMOSOMES.
Each chapter contains several thousand stories, called GENES.
Each story is made up of paragraphs, called EXONS, which are
interrupted by advertisements called INTRONS.
Each paragraph is made up of words, called CODONS.
Each word is written in letters called BASES.[3]

This book is as long as 800 Bibles, Ridley goes on to say.[4]

Now, indeed, *metaphor* may not be exactly the right term to describe
Ridley's message, since *metaphor* denotes an indirect description, not a
literal one. And the genome *is* actually a text, says Ridley. Exactly like
computer code, whose sequences of zeros and ones make up the patterns of digital information, the genetic code is written in four letters, A,
C, G, T (which stand for the chemical bases adenine, cytosine, guanine,
and thymine).

Ridley offers this statement:

> In the beginning was the word. The word proselytized the sea with
> its message, copying itself unceasingly and forever. The word discovered how to rearrange chemicals so as to capture little eddies in
> the steam of entropy and make them live. The word transformed
> the land surface of the planet from a dusty hell to a verdant paradise. The word eventually blossomed and became sufficiently
> ingenious to build a porridgy contraption called a human brain
> that could discover and be aware of the word itself.[5]

It is no accident, of course, that Ridley echoes John 1:1: "In the
beginning was the Word, and the Word was with God, and the Word
was God." We *are* actually a word, Ridley implies, and we have been a
word from the beginning. And suddenly it is as though Descartes had
never written and humanity had never dug a deep intellectual trench
between religious and scientific understandings of the human being.
Twenty-first-century genetic science tells us that John 1:1 is no more
than a literal description of the origin of all life.

Now it is also true that tremendous discoveries are neither all
benign nor all destructive. The splitting of the atom also enabled radiation therapies and other medical interventions, which have now
probably saved more lives than were destroyed in Hiroshima and
Nagasaki. The former does not justify the latter; it just helps complete

the picture. And the reverse is certainly true for the mapping of the human genome and the potential of genetic therapies and even genetic enhancements that might follow. Great good can come of these investigations—the capacity to relieve suffering and improve human life—and there is also enormous potential for abuse and discrimination.

This may be why approximately 3 to 5 percent of the National Institutes of Health budget for the Human Genome Project has been set aside to address the ethical, legal, and social implications of this work. In the words of one scholar, "It represents the largest expenditure of money for biomedical ethics and health law in the country."[6]

But even such a large commitment of funds may not be sufficient to fully examine the ramifications of issues such as human cloning, stem cell research, genetic engineering, the possible social stratifications arising from "imperfect" or "deviant" genetic material, the economic disparities that prevent access to new genetic diagnosis and treatment, and the potential traffic in human genetic materials.[7] Where even to begin to sort through such a bewildering maze of problems?

Many conferences and published collections of papers have focused on the specific ethical challenges posed by a medical science that can map and manipulate the genome.[8] And while it is critical to examine ethical issues case by case, often the decision-making rests on whether one or another proposed avenue of research or treatment is deemed in accordance with "human dignity." Human dignity, however, is not defined in these discussions and becomes then merely the well into which unresolved questions are dropped.[9]

One way to explore the meanings of "human dignity" is to consider what we mean today by "human." As the science of genetics suggests a different human biology, and indeed planet biology, than has commonly been assumed, so too has the field of theology been reexamining the nature of the human.

Theological anthropology is the discipline in theology that considers the nature of the human being. Several of the many volumes that view the Human Genome Project from a religious standpoint do, in fact, posit an essential human nature.[10] This is the influence of Protestant evangelical/reformed perspectives,[11] or the Roman Catholic.[12] Process theology—the Christian theological field that has been influenced by the work of scientist and philosopher Alfred North Whitehead[13]—takes a less essentialist view of human nature and at least opens the door to the concept that human nature can and does change.

Liberation and feminist theologies have been conspicuously absent from dialogues between religion and science. Women in general have been disproportionately underrepresented in the sciences.[14] The same is true in the theological disciplines. Feminist theologies, then, are rarely presented by women theologians or requested by women scientists, for such women are so scarce.

Liberation theologies are missing from the debate for several reasons. Many liberation theologians are not from the first world, where much of the research on the Human Genome Project has taken place. Moreover, the emphasis on the human being as an agent in history is so fundamental to liberation theology that many liberation theologians do not engage with contemporary science. Liberation theologians have been more interested in economics and political science. Also, the early liberation theologians, influenced by Karl Marx, have seen the human being as dominant over nature. Liberation theologians have been relatively silent on creation in general. But science, particularly the new genetics, needs the insights of liberation theology, particularly its epistemology of the oppressed. The methods of gene therapy, the mapping of the genome itself, stand to disproportionately affect vulnerable populations, both as unwitting objects of genetic research and perhaps shut out from receiving its benefits due to lack of access to healthcare.[15] Consider also the potential sociopolitical quagmire of insurance issues. What are the political and social implications if each person does not hold the "copyright" to his or her own genetic code? If you carry BRCA1 on chromosome 17 or BRCA2 on chromosome 13—these are the notorious "breast cancer genes"—and this information is not protected, what are your chances of being insurable, or being employable, *even if you never develop the disease?* Hence the attention to these ethical quandaries in the making.

Feminist theologies have emphasized the continuity of the human with the rest of creation. Like process theology in this respect, feminist theologies in general have opposed seeing the human as static and a unique "lord of creation." And genetic science certainly supports the feminist view. Ridley notes, "The three-letter words of the genetic code are the same in every creature. CGA means arginine and GCG means alanine—in bats, in beetles, in beech trees, in bacteria. . . . Wherever you go in the world, whatever animal, plant, bug or blob you look at, if it is alive, it will use the same dictionary and know the same code. All life is one."[16]

A new genetic science may be more open to innovative theological dialogue partners as fresh and challenging theoretical and practical problems emerge.

A Beginning Point

In chapter 4 of this volume, theologian and biblical scholar Theodore Jennings Jr. suggests a rubric for thinking about the relationship of theological anthropology and the Human Genome Project that helps to begin the constructive conversation. He suggests there are several theological/biological categories that help us get into the material. They are more fully fleshed out in chapter 4.

Species Solidarity: What Human Beings Have in Common with Other Creatures

One of the inescapable learnings from the evidence of the Human Genome Project is that human beings are deeply creatures in the most basic sense. As humans we share 90 percent of our genes with mice. We share 98.4 percent of our genes with chimpanzees, while chimpanzees share 97 percent of their genes with gorillas. Thus, chimpanzees have more in common genetically with humans than with gorillas. Human beings have approximately 30,000 genes. The eukaryote plant has 25,000 genes. How far are we genetically from wild asparagus? Not all that far, as it turns out.

Too often classical theological anthropology has interpreted the image of God to mean there is an unbridgeable gulf between the human being and the rest of creation. Coupled with a body/spirit dualism, which, as Rosemary Radford Ruether definitively has shown, is the linchpin of patriarchalism, this has placed man—and I do not use the word generically—at the top of a pyramid with women, children, and those deemed of lesser races below. The image of God, a symbolically male deity, has been held to primarily reside in reason, especially a reason conceived as disinterested objectivity.

Some of the most deeply held tenets of feminist theology are dramatically supported by insights from the Human Genome Project. The connectedness to nature is amply documented by the remarkable similarity, across the creation, in how genetic material functions.

Certainly feminist theologians derive this conviction in part from the feminist critique of the symbolic association patriarchal dualism makes between women and nature. It was Susan Griffin's book *Woman and Nature* that first extensively documented this symbolic identification and made an effort to both claim this connectedness and critique the framework of dominance in its then current sociopolitical setting. In her later work *Pornography and Silence* she wrote, "We are inseparable from all other beings in the universe."[17] Albeit in more passionate and inflated rhetoric, this is essentially the same point developed by Mary Daly in her work *Pure Lust:* "Thousands of women struggle to remember our Selves and our history, to sustain and intensify a biophilic consciousness."[18] Carol Christ, Margaret Atwood, Starhawk, the women of Greenham Common—all have poignantly tried to raise the theological point that human beings are connected to the creation. Starhawk and the Greenham Common women in particular have made the political connection to militarism and environmental degradation that is sometimes missing in other feminist analyses of the relation of women and nature.

As womanist theologians have lifted their voices, African American women have cogently critiqued the theological justification of the exploitation of those who are symbolically "the creature," including, therefore, nondominant races. They curse those who exploit the powerless and who exploit the planet that sustains life. Their curse condemns the exploiters ultimately to stew in the chemical juices in which they marinate the planet.

In chapters 1 and 6, by Laurel C. Schneider and myself respectively, we suggest that a constructive feminist and liberation perspective must take into account: that the human being is *both* body and soul. The human being understood as a unity of body and soul binds humanity to the whole of creation. This unity also strengthens the human community itself. We can see more clearly that our social arrangements either bring healthy humanity into being, or warp, distort, and ultimately destroy healthy human beings, their communities, and the planet.

Species Unity:
What Human Beings Have in Common with Each Other

The early work of psychologists such as Carol Gilligan, Jean Baker Miller, and Nancy Chodorow has grounded feminist theory in relationality and connection. Asian theologians such as Chung Hyun Kyung make a similar argument.[19] Another profound learning from the Human Genome Project is that at the genetic level racial distinctions are so minor as to be almost negligible. Human begins are profoundly related one to another. Genetically speaking, we are deeply connected. We are more than 99.9 percent the same.

This book is based on a course team taught by Chicago Theological Seminary professor Laurel C. Schneider, pediatric geneticist Lainie Friedman Ross, and myself. In chapters 2 and 3, Ross illustrates the profound relationality of humanity through basic genetics. Beginning with her realization, at a family wedding, that a cousin she had never met could be a carrier for cystic fibrosis—and that therefore, given their common ancestry, so could she—Ross reveals in practical medical terms how genetic science documents that we are inextricably, physically connected as a human community. In one anecdotal example, a rabbi volunteers as a bone marrow donor to help some Jews in his local community in New Jersey only to finally be matched with a young boy in Italy as his closest tissue type. Indeed, the "human family" is not just a metaphor.

Our course included a laboratory session for DNA fingerprinting. We used a polymerase chain reaction to pick out a repeating DNA sequence, in which copies of a single, short repeated unit lie next to each other on a chromosome, rather like boxcars on a train. They do not code for any protein. We spit into test tubes, added some chemical separators, spun the glop around in a centrifuge, and sent the resulting material to a lab to be run through a gel and mapped. The map of my DNA fingerprint showed that each allele was different.[20] I was, given my polyglot ancestry, heterozygous: the gene that I inherited from my father was not the same in this sequence as that from my mother. Ross is an Ashkenazi Jew, a member of a very small and tightly knit European population. She was, of course, homozygous. Her two alleles were identical because members of the Ashkenazi Jewish population are genetically very similar. We also compared images of our gel-separated genes with those of other such genes from different populations: Asian, African, Latin American, and European. In this short DNA sequence, I most closely resembled the Asian genetic profile. This is probably due to my distant Russian ancestry passed to me through my Hungarian forebears. I am, genetically speaking, most closely related to Asian populations. In my physical appearance, what genetic science calls my phenotype, I look Anglo-Saxon. But my DNA denies it.

One of the meanings of this genetic unity of humanity from a liberation perspective, says Jennings, is that "at the immediate practical level . . . race [is] a category invented by early modern Europeans [and] is a complete fiction, a fabrication of the will to domination. One of the most interesting and alarming and instructive inventions of modernity and of modern science has been white supremacy. From a theological perspective, this has always been unspeakable heresy that makes utter nonsense of the most basic affirmations of Christian faith."[21] It is utter nonsense judging by the data of the new genetics as well. But before we can dream of the unity science can document, we must confront the nightmare of racism head on, as Lee Butler argues in chapter 6.

But this genetic unity does not mean that a single genome is repeated again and again in every individual, however. Your genome is completely unique unless you are an identical twin. What the Human Genome Project has done is to average about two hundred anonymous individuals in forming its version of the human genome. These individuals were drawn from employees of the National Institutes of Health; while this group is actually quite diverse in terms of race and ethnicity, if not gender, it is scarcely representative of the whole planet.

To provide information on human genetic variation throughout the globe, the Human Genome Diversity Project has been seeking since 1993 to collect genetic material from four to five hundred geographically isolated or culturally unique populations. But the HGDP has been plagued from the beginning with a host of concerns about racial exploitation, as well as difficulties in obtaining genuine consent from the populations to be studied. There is fear that the project could be a vehicle for biopiracy and biocolonialism. Given the worldwide history of exploitation of land and of labor, the suspicion of the exploitation of biology is not unfounded.

As of 2003, the Chinese Human Genome Diversity Project is the one furthest along. After collecting cell lines from its official ethnic groups, it has begun preliminary analysis of its data. The CHGDP has showed a distinct genetic difference between northern and southern Chinese ethnicities. In addition, the study has reached the conclusion that the majority of the current gene pool in East Asia originates from Africa. So while one perspective the human community is profoundly one, the social constructions of racism endure. They even structure the scientific research into the human genome itself.

Indeed, the social construction of sin, as emphasized by theologies of liberation, is very apt at this point. We do not approach scientific investigation with a theological tabula rasa. The accumulated individual sins that co-conspire to structure large and enduring evils such as racism, sexism, or colonialism must be taken into account as we evaluate the potential for any endeavor to work toward human betterment or human subjugation, a point taken up in chapter 7, on genetic determinism and sin.

Individuation: How Each Human Being Is Unique

Today, the field of criminology conducts the most practical measures of our individual distinctiveness in genetic terms. The DNA fingerprint test has certainly freed many from prison, often from death row, when DNA evidence has been obtainable. The test is simple; it is the one we ran in our class lab. As we novices finished up twenty-five or so DNA fingerprints, one student suddenly asked, "If this is so easy to do, why does it take up to six years for people in prison to get their DNA results?" Why, indeed? Taking the "view from below" in liberation perspective, we should be wary of any Justice Department plan to have every person accused of a crime—not even convicted of a crime—DNA tested and their results kept on file. In the *Brave New World* future this suggests, the state DNA fingerprints everyone at birth and files the results. Hollywood has already imagined this future for us.

But if our uniqueness is not limited to our criminal potential, how then are we to understand it theologically? Feminist liberation theologies have approached the issue of the uniqueness of the human being in several ways. In contrast to theologians such as Reinhold Niebuhr who held that the sin of pride—the selfishness of hubris—is the besetting sin of humanity, Valerie Saiving and then Judith Plaskow have held that "sin for women" is better described as the failure to be a self. A peculiar temptation for some, often white women, is to dissolve the uniqueness of their individuality and become soluble to the needs and desires of others. The temptation to fail to be an individual is facilitated by the Niebuhrian separation of the public arena of politics and male activity, where a justice ethic rules, from the private sphere, the realm of women and the family, where love is the guiding ethic. Freedom and equality do not apply to the private sphere, the world of women, according to Niebuhr.

This soluble self has been less of a preoccupation for womanists—they have not been accorded the dubious privilege of living solely in the private sphere. It is a strong concern of Asian and African feminists, however. What remains constant is that the issue of individuality for women is always rooted in the social constructions of power in any context.

For the purposes of this discussion, however, the theological emphasis falls on the unique and fundamental irreplaceability of any one of us. Even cloning will not achieve duplication, as we are uniquely the product of the interactions of our genetic heritage with our changing environment. No one's life history can be duplicated.

Thus the unique value of each individual is not only asserted spiritually, but physically. Feminist theology strongly asserts that the physical must not be ignored or denigrated. Bodies matter, as the title of Naomi Goldenberg's book *Returning Words to Flesh* would tell us.[22]

On the other hand, we should problematize the concern for individual uniqueness and the implications of the new genetics. If spitting into a test tube is all it takes, genetic testing will increasingly become routine; it may be included with amniocentesis, for example.

A recent study, "The 50 Million Missing Women," notes that "an epidemic of gender selection is ravaging countries like China.[23] With China's one-child-per-couple policy, amniocentesis is done to determine the baby's sex, and female children are frequently aborted. Prenatal sex determination and abortion of female fetuses threatens to skew the sex ratio" in all southeast Asian countries.[24] We are not that far from a genetically engineered future in which the sex of a child can be changed in utero. Certain societies could see the elimination of female births.

The discovery in 1993 of Xq28, the so-called "gay gene," was at first greeted with celebration by GLBT persons and their supporters. A T-shirt sold in gay and lesbian bookstores in the mid-90s bore the message "Xq28—Thanks for the genes, Mom." To yield this result, molecular biologist Dean Hamer and his team at the National Institutes of Health had tested forty pairs of homosexual brothers to see if they shared a trait: specifically, a certain segment of the X chromosome.[25] The discovery of an 83 percent commonality of Xq28 led to this insight.

What is the theological status of this finding? Does it imply that homosexuality is part of the unique biological heritage of some individuals and therefore has all the moral complexity of brown eyes, or, as Ted Peters labels it in his book *Playing God*, is this a "gay gene defect"? Are these men sinning genetically?

From the field of biblical studies, Ken Stone looks at both the Hamer and Peters material and offers a unique interpretive lens. He sees a parallel between the ways in which biblical texts and scientific texts are constructed to answer questions about human nature. When science asks the question, "Why are some people gay?" the researchers need to use critical theory to examine their own interest in finding an answer to this question. Indeed, Peters's suggestion that this gene might be a "defect" illustrates very well the pejorative interpretation that can lie behind such investigations. And like the risk of abortion for undesired female fetuses, so too can a test for undesired gay and lesbian fetuses introduce an enormous ethical problem into the already over-problematized issue of abortion.

Dean Hamer has said, "I think that discriminating against people based on their genetic makeup is wrong. . . . The 'wrong' genes should never be used as a basis for terminating a pregnancy." Hamer opposes the idea of developing prenatal tests for homosexual orientation. If he eventually isolates the gene, he plans to patent this knowledge as intellectual property and use his patent rights to prevent the development of tests to determine if a fetus is gay. But patent life is now only seventeen years. At best, in about two decades it would again be legally and scientifically possible to test for "gayness" and abort fetuses that carry the gay gene, or again, intervene in utero and eliminate the gay gene.

This is not to suggest that all aspects of one's unique genetic heritage are to be off-limits for gene therapy. Applied knowledge of genetic factors can help avoid many inherited diseases, among them retardation, sickle-cell anemia, Tay-Sachs, and various cancers. Even today, it is routine, if one has these types of devastating inherited diseases, to do genetic family planning, as Lainie Ross indicates in chapters 2 and 3. Clearly, gene therapy in these and other cases is much to be desired. The elimination of unnecessary human suffering is a way to value the uniqueness of each human life.

Different Questions, New Insights

Since its inception, the discipline of genetics has been a highly contested field of scientific endeavor. From phrenology as applied to criminals and prostitutes to the eugenics movement to Nazi doctors, the Tuskegee syphilis experiments, and the Bell Curve, knowledge of genetics has had more than its share of dubious applications to social policy. Perhaps this is inevitable, given the fact that its subject matter is almost too close for comfort. For genetics attempts to answer the question, "Who is the human being?" As geneticist Ruth Hubbard notes:

> In the case of human genetics and molecular biology, we must expect the value our society attaches to genealogy and heredity to influence every stage of research and discussion. Societal values are automatically coded into scientific meanings of terms like "inherited traits" and "genes." This is not to say that scientists deliberately misrepresent what is happening in nature or that their descriptions are necessarily wrong. But, especially in areas that touch closely on cherished beliefs about ourselves, about our society, and about other living beings—and genetics does all of that—science is likely to reflect those beliefs.[26]

One of the reasons religious knowledge is also so highly contested, and so frequently used to support dubious sociopolitical movements, is that it too has the huge agenda of answering the question, "Who is the human being?" Religious scholars representing racial/ethnic and sexual minority groups, among others, have worked to develop theories that can expose the unconscious beliefs that underlie commonly accepted religio-social assumptions and cast them into relief. Feminist and liberation theologies—with their attendant analyses of institutional power arrangements, gender, race, and class—and the intellectual resources of postmodernism also have much to contribute to the constructive work society must do with rapidly changing scientific research. These newest scientific findings, like those of the twentieth century, are making enormous claims about who human beings are and how science can improve human life. It is true that applied genetics has the potential to relieve human suffering. But without partnering with those who ask different and critically informed questions about the beliefs that underlie both the research and proposed interventions, science will make decisions in a conversation with science. Neither science nor religion can any longer afford to be isolated in this way. Only by opening themselves to new questions and insights can each provoke and learn from the other about the infinite permutations of human creativity and destructiveness.

In the beginning was the word
It came from the sea and proselytized the earth
The words flowed out from the ones born of the word
And flowed back into the sea with their toxins
Be careful of the words you speak
The word is also speaking you
And someday you will have to listen

PART ONE

THE SCIENCE OF GENETICS

1

Setting the Context: A Brief History of Science by a Sympathetic Theologian

Laurel C. Schneider

For most of recorded history, the relationship between what we today call "religion" and "science" has been intimate and productive. Indeed, what distinction we can meaningfully make between these two areas of human life and knowledge is relatively recent, a feature of modernity and the rise of disciplinary knowledge.[1] The separation of knowledge of the world and knowledge of the spirit is a curious result of the scientific revolution, which itself cannot be understood apart from church history and the politics of late medieval Christian theology.

We may in fact decide, along with some contemporary scientists and theologians, that the historical split between knowledge of the world (science) and knowledge of the spirit (theology) is a product more of political expediency than of some natural difference between the two realms of inquiry. The split itself makes little sense when viewed through a historical lens. For many centuries, for example, many if not most major funding for research into the natural world came from church bodies, and most of the scientific advances in the West until the eighteenth century were made by priests and monks with access to libraries and the training and time to use them. These were "natural philosophers" who sought a deeper understanding of God through God's greatest work: the world. Even with the advent of secularism in the late sixteenth century, and with Galileo's discoveries accelerating a decline in ecclesial authority concerning things worldly or planetary, the foundations upon which modern science is built remained deeply theological.

Aristotle and Plato

As is Confucius to the East, so are Plato and his student Aristotle to the West. These are the thinkers who, building on the earliest Greek philosophers' attempts to describe "fundamental reality, the basic stuff of which the universe was made or out of which it emerged,"[2] set the terms for our continued quest to understand the world and ourselves today. In tracing the history of science and theology in the West, it is impossible not to look at Plato and his famous student together. They disagreed on a fundamental aspect of reality—whether it is at heart idea or matter—and this disagreement has echoed down the millennia in the form of a very productive and sometimes problematic tension that shapes the history of science and of Christian theology.

Plato, a self-described student of Socrates, was born in 427 B.C.E. into a wealthy Athenian family; he grew up interested in politics and philosophy. He opposed the ideas of earlier thinkers who posited a mechanistic universe of simple cause and effect, one in which nonmaterial ideas ("forms") had little relevance or place with the basic structure of material reality. Plato was convinced that something other than matter and motion lay at the heart of reality. In the context of his famous Athenian Academy, he constructed a powerful philosophical approach to the question of reality that started with abstract ideas instead of matter; indeed, Plato granted to the nonmaterial realm of ideas the greater share of effective power and of substantive reality. His reasoning goes like this: That which is true must be perfectly true. Perfect truth is not subject to decay or degradation, and so it cannot change; it must therefore be eternal. That which is real must also be true. So that which is real also cannot change. Matter always changes (a tree, stone, building, or person will eventually completely decompose or be changed into something else, as will everything on earth). So that which is truly real cannot be made of matter. What things are not made of matter? Ideas! The perfect, eternal thing is its form abstracted from matter. And so, the form or idea is, for Plato, the true reality.

Although challenged almost immediately by his brilliant student Aristotle, Plato's idealist influence can be traced throughout the history of Western science and theology, particularly in the Christianity of medieval times, when so many endeavors that we would today call scientific were pursued exclusively by theologians. As Charles Singer has pointed out, Plato's thought "was dominated by the ethical motive [because he was] convinced, like Socrates, that Truth and Good exist and that they are inseparable."[3] This made his ancient Greek approach to questions of reality and creation particularly salient to later Christian thinkers such as Plotinus, Augustine, and Anselm who wanted to account for God's role in creation. As we shall see, it is Plato's influence on Aristotle, and Aristotle's revision of Plato that creates a dialectic between the material and the ideal—a dialectic that is particularly important in tracing the history of the relationship between scientific and theological questions in the West, questions that continue to influence our approach to science and theology today.

Born in 384 B.C.E. in the northern Greek town of Stagira, Aristotle was the son of the Macedonian king's physician and so had the extensive literary and gymnastic schooling typical for sons of the rich. At seventeen he left home and joined Plato's Academy in Athens, where he studied for twenty years until Plato's death around 347. Several years of travel then afforded him an opportunity to make comparative studies of plants and animals, an experience that would go further than any other in fueling his modifications of Plato's reliance on ideas over material things. He eventually returned to Macedonia, where he reputedly became the tutor of the young Alexander the Great. When Athens fell under Macedonian rule, Aristotle eventually returned to that city and taught until his death in 322. Jonathan Barnes has painted the following picture of Aristotle:

> He was a bit of a dandy, wearing rings on his fingers and cutting his hair fashionably short. He suffered from poor digestion, and is said to have been spindle-shanked. He was a good speaker, lucid in his lectures, persuasive in conversation; and he had a mordant wit. His enemies, who were numerous, accused him of arrogance. His will, which has survived, is a generous document. His philosophical writings are impersonal; but they suggest that he prized both friendship and self-sufficiency, and that . . . he was properly proud of his own attainments. As a man he was, I suspect, admirable rather than amiable.[4]

At the time of his death at sixty-two, Aristotle was at the height of his power. A tireless scholar and teacher, he remains unrivaled not only for his systematic thought, but for the breadth of his inquiries. He is said to have lectured on a vast range of subjects including logic, physics, astronomy, meteorology, zoology, metaphysics, theology, psychology, politics, economics, ethics, rhetoric, and poetics. Over the course of his life, he wrote down and edited these lectures into a vast body of literature. One contemporary scholar notes, "However, still more astounding is the fact that the majority of these subjects did not exist as such before him, so that he would have been the first to conceive of and establish them, as systematic disciplines."[5] An ancient biographer lists 150 works by Aristotle, but unfortunately only about one-fifth of these, or thirty books, survive.

As might be expected, Aristotle and Plato had a difficult, brilliant, and complicated relationship. Aristotle loved Plato like a father but disagreed with him on several key philosophical points, leading Plato to call Aristotle "the foal," because a foal kicks its mother when it has had enough milk.[6] But because Plato's influence on Aristotle was so substantial, it is helpful to think about them together in order to understand the influence of their thought on later theology and science.

Plato reflected deeply on the unity of the sciences. He saw human knowledge as a potentially unified system, not as a random amassing of facts. Because he began with the philosophical assumption of the primary existence of ideas, and particularly of the inseparability of the key ideas of the Good and the True, Plato sought to organize the facts before him into a deductive, systematic account of the world and its phenomena. It might be possible to suggest that Plato was first a mystic and a poet, and that his commitment to the unity of knowledge stems from that source. Although he is often caricatured and misunderstood on this point, Plato was convinced that ideas are ultimately what are real and that the material world is a mere shadow of that enduring and perfect reality.

Aristotle, on the other hand, dismissed the purity and primacy of ideas, although he made a place for them in his basic systemic approach to the causes of things. He amassed facts. He was an empiricist and, in effect, found that Plato's deductive approach failed to account sufficiently for difference and change in the world. Aristotle, in one sense, came at reality from the opposite direction. In Plato's world, ideas, or forms, give shape to matter but do not depend on matter for existence. Using an everyday metaphor, we might imagine a waffle iron giving shape to a waffle. Plato might argue that the waffle iron is the perfect idea of the waffle and both pre-exists and post-exists the waffle itself. The waffle iron holds the key to true and perfect waffles. Actual waffles come and go, none of them quite as perfect as the idea contained in the design on the iron. But Aristotle argued that ideas rely at some level on matter for their very existence and cannot ultimately be separated from matter. The perfect waffle for Aristotle, in other words, requires batter. And while no two waffles are alike and so no waffle can ever be perfect (if perfection denotes immutability, as it did for both Plato and Aristotle), Aristotle essentially argued that perfection is not the only determinant of true reality. Aristotle was convinced that matter is indispensable from anything that is real. Eternal, perfect ideas and forms are important, but only insofar as they establish the variety and shape of differences in the world. They do not determine the entirety of its reality.

Whether one is a philosopher, a scientist, or a theologian, one cannot make claims about what is true or real without establishing first one's method of attaining and testing one's conclusions. Plato was a logician. For him the beauty of mathematical formulas—particularly those formulas that function entirely apart from reference to material things— lies in their function as the basis of knowledge, and so of science and theology. Aristotle refined his teacher's approach to logic so that, while still the basis of knowledge, logic is not the totality of *understanding*, which requires reference to worldly facts. The best knowledge, to Aristotle, consists in the understanding that links information to meaning. At its root the Greek word for knowledge, *episteme,* can mean a science: an organized body of systematically arranged information.

You can see Plato's influence at work in Aristotle's contributions to logic. Both accepted that systematic arrangements of knowledge take the form of a chain of syllogistic deductions, preferably in universal affirmations called axioms. For example, if we know that all Bs are Cs, and all As are Bs, then it is a necessary truth that all As are Cs. To have *scientific* knowledge, then, is to have an axiomatic explanation for a given piece of empirical fact or information. Scientific knowledge does not consist merely in "knowing" a fact incidentally, or in simply asserting that such-and-such is true. It means being able to know *why* something is true, based on key axiomatic premises taken to be true.

Here is another example: we know that humans are mortal because we see humans die. "Humans are mortal" is a discrete fact. But to *understand* that fact scientifically as a property for a class of objects (all humans are mortal) is to explain the dependence of that property (mortality) on some other property (being a mammal, let's say): all humans are mortal because they are mammals. This can be demonstrated syllogistically: all humans are mammals; all mammals are mortal; so all humans are mortal. By linking human mortality to some other property, greater understanding is achieved.

Aristotle took the logic of the syllogism a step further in his effort to establish certainty and understanding in knowledge. The syllogism alone is not enough to truly explain why humans are mortal, and therefore it cannot offer real understanding. The only way to achieve understanding, for Aristotle, is through proper classification. And this requires observation and study. Humans must be mortal because they belong to some classification of mortal things. They are mammals, and all mammals are mortal. Is that it? No, there is a higher class of mortal things: "mammals" are only a subset of animals, which are a subset of biological life. Aristotle claimed that only the highest, most comprehensive class could be taken as explanatory. You arrive at explanatory knowledge only when you have exhausted all attempts at classification. A maple leaf does not fall from a tree in winter just because all maple leaves fall in winter; although true, this is not sufficiently explanatory, according to Aristotle. It falls because maple trees are deciduous, and all deciduous trees shed leaves in winter. Only the biggest possible classification provides meaningful explanation for the smallest events.

This classificatory condition for real knowledge allowed Aristotle to search for relationships between seemingly different things—such as maple trees and humans, for example. And it foreshadows a contemporary challenge in postmodern science. Aristotle admitted that explanation is always intentional; you pick the data that appears relevant to you and place it within interpreted classes. It does not explain itself to you without interpretation. But where Aristotle saw himself as merely identifying appropriate, actual classifications in the world, postmodern science recognizes the vital handprint of human imagination.

Classification depends on the senses, however, and Plato knew that the senses can deceive. How can one ever be sure? Where is certainty in the world of embodied things? Aristotle could never fully answer this critique; therefore Plato's vision did not fully disappear. Plato's doctrine of ideas is counterintuitive (the book in your hands seems real, does it not?) but he is persuasive when one really considers the fallibility of the senses, the changeability of the world, and thus the uncertainty of conclusions based on sensory, empirical perception. Plato explains this metaphorically in his famous illustration of the cave in the fifth book of *The Republic*. He describes the material world as a cave with a fire burning in the center. People sit in chains, restrained so that they can see only the wall of the cave in front of them. Outside of this dim cave and just out of their view, the world of eternal purity exists in brilliant light and casts alluring but flickering shadows on the cave's interior wall. Humanity, chained in ignorance, mistakes these shadows for the real things themselves. The world that we think is real—this book in your hands, for example—is merely a shadow on the wall of the cave because it is not eternal. It is an imperfect copy of the perfect and ideal book, which exists just beyond your limited view. The philosopher, of course, is the one who casts off the chains of delusion and is not deceived by the shadows, but looks out of the cave to the realm of the ideas.

As we have noted, Aristotle rejected Plato's notion of ideas as the ultimate reality; indeed, perhaps it was this rejection that felt the most to Plato like a foal's kick. For Aristotle, his teacher's theory did not account sufficiently for the world at hand, or for understanding differences in it, how things change, grow, and move. Reality—and the investigation of reality, that is, science—exists in the material world and cannot be understood apart from it. Ideas and matter exist in symbiotic relationship. Understand that, Aristotle believed, and you begin to understand reality itself. Matter alone is incomprehensible, amorphous, and meaningless. Ideas alone require the denial of the senses and so of the world in which they occur.

To investigate the world more rigorously, to take its form and substance seriously *and* to account for motion and change, Aristotle developed a theory of four interrelated causes for reality, each of which applies to every thing and event. Find the four causes to any one thing and you reach true understanding of that thing, according to Aristotle. He calls the four causes the "material," "prior," "formal," and "final" causes. Their names are somewhat self-explanatory but become clearer with illustration.

The material cause of a thing is the stuff, quite literally, of which it is made. In the case of a small dog named Missy, her material cause is flesh: blood, bone, cells, and so forth. The prior cause of a thing is the mechanical "domino effect" of conditions that bring a thing into being. Missy's prior cause is all of the events that conspired to bring her into existence: her ancestors, her breeder, the availability of food, a willing human to keep and feed her now, and so forth. Missy's formal cause, according to Aristotle, is her dogness, or canine classification. This includes her dog shape and character, her long, sensitive nose, her interest in treats, her four legs and sharp ears, all of which fit the form of dog. Lastly, Missy's final cause is the inevitable end and growth toward which she moves, the blueprint perhaps, of her life. This includes a certain life span and process of growth and change from fertilized egg to puppy to full-grown dog and eventually to old age and death. Missy cannot grow up to be a tree—although her final cause of healthy old age might be thwarted, just as any of the four causes can be distorted in some way by external circumstances.

It should be obvious how Aristotle's scheme of causality has been amenable both to late Christian theological claims about the nature of the human, its purpose and aim, and to contemporary assumptions about the role of genetic material in human life. Although Aristotle's writings fell into obscurity in the tumultuous period after the fall of Athens, were for centuries preserved only in the great libraries of the Islamic world, and were only later returned to Western thought through the work of Saint Thomas Aquinas, it was this understanding of causality that enabled Aquinas to posit a "great chain of being" with God as its ultimate cause.[7]

Aristotle's influence on classical theology and on contemporary science is incalculable. His division of knowledge into three major classes—the productive, the practical, and the theoretical—form the basis of the academic disciplines today. Productive knowledge refers to the making of things and knowing how things function *(technē)*; practical knowledge is concerned with effective human action, such as ethics or politics; and theoretical knowledge concerns itself with ultimate or absolute truth and rationality. Everything we today call science is contained within this last class of theoretical knowledge, which for Aristotle covered both mathematics and the natural sciences. But significantly, the so-called disciplines of theology and philosophy fall within the same class of knowledge, especially to the ancient mind. It is only in modernity that the distinction between these areas becomes politically important to both.

Islamic Science

After the fall of the Roman Empire in the fifth century C.E., Latin philosophy, scientific inquiry, and education in the classical tradition declined precipitously in the West. It was most likely during this period that the bulk of Aristotle's writings were lost, and certainly all of them fell completely out of circulation in the Latin West. Although the eastern half of the old Roman Empire also experienced upheaval, invasions, and economic distress, "that the city of Constantinople (present-day Istanbul) did not fall to invaders before 1203, while Rome was sacked as early as the fifth century, tells us something about the relative levels of stability," as one scholar puts it.[8] Thus in Byzantium, the transmission of Aristotelian natural philosophy continued, if on a much smaller scale. Even in the Greek East the early medieval intellectual fashion favored platonic abstractions and unified theological systems over observation of the world at hand. Eventually, it was the countries under Islamic rule—from Pakistan to Spain, the Persian Empire, Syria, and Egypt—that primarily preserved and advanced Aristotle's approach to scientific knowledge.

The founding text of Islam, the Qur'an, was revealed to a young man named Muhammad. He was born around 570 C.E. to caravan traders in Mecca, in what is now Saudi Arabia. Orphaned by the age of six, he was raised by a Bedouin foster mother. His accomplishments as founding prophet of Islam and military leader are remarkable. Before his death at sixty-two or sixty-three, the Islamic faith had spread far beyond both Mecca and Medina, and Muhammad's armies had taken over the Arabian peninsula. Within one hundred years those armies had gained control of all of the Alexandrian empire in Asia, North Africa, and the Middle East, including Syria, Palestine, Persia, and Egypt, as well as the whole of Spain. Within a few generations, therefore, all of the surviving intellectual traditions of the Greek world were incorporated into the Arab world, where they were energetically translated into Arabic, studied, and improved. Islamic scholarship, particularly in natural philosophy, bloomed; indeed, it may not be an exaggeration to suggest that the first outline of our modern concept of science was born.

There can be no doubt of the profound influence of this period of intellectual development and innovation, from the sixth to the twelfth century C.E., on the emergence of both science and of philosophy in the West. It is an unfortunate consequence of later Christian parochialism, when Islamic fortunes were declining after the Crusades, that Renaissance historians played down or ignored the depth of Muslim influence on emergent Western science—and this despite the obvious adoption of Arabic symbolic writing in mathematics and theory.

It was during the centuries of Islamic rule that the concept of a distinct category of knowledge called science, based in empirical study, truly emerged. Research facilities modeled on Alexandria (taken by the Muslims in 642) were created in Baghdad. The persecutions of pagans by Christians in the West also forced some proto-scientists to emigrate to Arab lands where they found both tolerance for their religious beliefs and a thriving interest in theoretical questions of natural philosophy. Situated at the intersection of trade routes linking the East and the West, the majority of Islamic cities in the latter half of the first millennium became a meeting point for Greek, Egyptian, Indian, and Persian thought and Chinese technology. This was a remarkable multicultural and multi-epistemological crossroads rivaling the environment of many contemporary cities for its diversity.

A number of critical advances in scientific method were made in the Islamic world during these centuries. The experimental method, so important to the development of the natural sciences, was perfected during this period with the introduction of multiple iterations for establishing proof. Researchers recognized that one attempt at an experiment is never enough to establish proof. As observations became increasingly complex, the scholars working at the height of Islamic wealth and advancement of science realized that error is a real and constant threat to the certainty of scientific inquiry. And not only the experimenter, but also the method the experimenter uses, can cause error in the results. So multiple iterations of single experiments, sharing of information among scientists, and cross-checking methods became widespread and generally assumed practices of study.

The introduction of Chinese paper to the Arab world in Samarqand in the early eighth century greatly facilitated the recording, dissemination, and preservation of scientific work. Like the impact of the computer in the twentieth century, the use of paper allowed ideas to flourish through wide distribution and comment by various scientists.

Moreover, the Arabic language was and is conducive to emergent scientific inquiry because of its flexibility, lending itself to new words and terminologies suited to the demands of new scientific and artistic discoveries. Beginning in 800 C.E., Hunayn Ibn Ishaq and his students translated thousands of texts of Greek philosophers and of Indian and Persian scientists. These writings became available and were preserved in libraries throughout the Islamic urban world.

Some historians have suggested that it was interest in the medical libraries of the Greeks, especially the writings of Hippocrates and Galen, that spurred urban Muslim interests in research and translation. Quite possibly, the Qur'an's religious emphasis on purity meant that diet and personal hygiene were a priority; this might tend both to improve public health and heighten the value of medical science. Whatever the cause of the widespread scholarly interest, the combination of general prosperity, religious tolerance, and relative peace in the great centers of the Muslim world were a boon to research in general. In particular, medical diagnosis became systematized, hospitals were invented, and candidates for medical degrees examined patients, opening the way to a professionalization and standardization of medical practices. Medical scholars focused on observation and experimentation, leading inexorably to the invention of medical specialties and disciplines. And due to the widespread influence of texts by Aristotle, empiricism remained central to Islamic scientific and medical research.

One example of the early medieval difference between the Christian West and Muslim East is the medical work of Galen. Galen, who lived from about 130 to 200 C.E., was a Greek-educated student of Hippocrates' texts and physician to Roman gladiators. He used both Plato's deductive and Aristotle's inductive philosophies to study the human body. Rejecting Roman epicurean notions of an irrational or random nature, Galen assumed a system of bodily organs that functioned teleologically. He postulated the principle of a "pneuma," a flow of heat, air, spirit, and blood through the body. Seeking unity in his understanding of the body, he took Aristotle's four causes and argued for four bodily "humors": air, earth, water, and fire.

Galen's creative emphasis on empirical study of the human body combined with a concern for the body's unity was almost completely unknown in the West of the Middle Ages. Medicine, as it was developing in the Muslim East and as it would eventually come to be known in modernity, was still nonexistent in the Christian West outside of the often highly effective but idiosyncratic practices of women herbalists and witch-healers. It is important for us to remember that it was Arabic scholars such as Abu Bakr Mohammad Ibn Zakariya al-Razi and Abn Ali Al Hosain Ibn Abdallah Ibn Sina (called Avicenna by the Latins) who actively studied Aristotle. They also studied Galen's 129 books on medicine and wrote extensively on their own medical research as a result. Modern Western medicine and perhaps Western philosophy as a whole are profoundly dependent upon their work. Avicenna, for example, foreshadowed Francis Bacon and René Descartes by half a millennium when he claimed, as one translation has it, that "*intellectus in formis agit universalitatem,* that is, the universality of our ideas is the result of the activity of the mind itself."[9]

After the twelfth century, when the centers of Islamic culture were worn down by war and Muslim libraries had been plundered by Crusaders, the writings of the Greek and Arabic philosophers traveled west, and Galen's view of the balance of the humors, Avicenna's commentaries on Aristotle, and Ibn Roschd Averroes's legal theories held sway in Western culture until the seventeenth century. But as with Aristotle, the work of the ancient empiricists such as Galen were preserved in the Muslim world throughout the violent and anti-intellectual rise and fall of Rome, and were only returned to the West in the late Middle Ages.

Medieval Science in the West

With the Crusades and with the gradual social and political changes in the religious empire of Latin Christianity in Europe, Christian scholars began eagerly to study the "new" writings of Aristotle and the Greeks coming to them from the East by way of Muslim philosophers such as Avicenna and Averroes. Saint Thomas Aquinas in particular took Aristotle as the basis for a whole new approach to Christian theology and thereby to Christian science. In his massive systematic *Summa Theologica,* he argued prodigiously for "natural theology": a study of the natural world in the style of "the philosopher" (his shorthand for Aristotle) that would expose God's purposes and meaning in creation.

The academic world of the twelfth-century West was lodged entirely in ecclesial bodies and monasteries where the emphasis on study had been mystical on the one hand and focused on abstract principles of divinity on the other. Following Thomas meant that Christian scholars could read the pre-Christian, pagan Aristotle, open the doors of the church, and begin again to take account of empirical data without risking theological censure. This deceptively simple change in focus ushered in a new era of scholarship, one that would eventually explode into the heavens and begin what the West calls the scientific revolution.

Islamic science, for all of its contributions to modernity, has been faulted for not overthrowing the geocentric system, though it did improve substantially upon the Ptolemaic framework. The scholars of early medieval Islam surpassed the Greeks in optics and in astronomical measurement and instrumentation. They constructed the astrolabe and introduced Hindu astronomical notation, all of which enabled them to correct specific problems in the complicated Ptolemaic system. Despite the fact that the heavens cooperated less and less with the predictions that the Ptolemaic system imposed upon it, the system worked well enough most of the time for the common uses of astronomy. Perhaps no one questioned the centrality of the earth in the cosmos, or perhaps the political and religious labor of displacing it was reason enough to put up with the existing system and its occasional errors.

Between the times of the first-century Egyptian Claudius Ptolemy, whose geocentric universe held sway for 1,600 years, and the sixteenth-century Polish priest Nicolaus Copernicus, who posited a heliocentric universe (against Christian teaching), scientific advancement in both East and West wandered generally between concepts of a unified cosmos and a divided one. Aristotle had posited a rigid distinction between heaven and earth, imposing on each a different set of rules and principles. In other words, for Aristotle the cosmos was not unified by principles or forces applied to all heavenly and earthly bodies. This was supported both by empirical evidence—looking at the stars—and by general theological ideas that granted to the gods a home in the heavens and freedom from the rules and principles that govern earthly events.

The Roman philosopher Lucretius (99–55 B.C.E.), on the other hand, had argued for a unified, atomistic view of all of reality in heaven and on earth. All motion everywhere, he claimed, is ultimately random and any apparent design in the cosmos is the product purely of chance. Several generations later, born within fifty years of Jesus' death, Ptolemy had also perceived the cosmos as unified in a single system, but not a random one. The heavens, he argued, can be deciphered according to principles of motion observable from earth and so exist in some continuity with rules of motion on earth. Ultimately the empirical evidence favored Ptolemy over Aristotle on this subject and the Ptolemaic system held sway throughout the Muslim and Christian empires. Earth, for Ptolemy, was the central point of reference for the observable motion in the heavens, and so earth was the center of the universe.

From the beginning, the Ptolemaic synthesis of heaven and earth was persuasive, in part because it was useful in politics as well. Early Christian rulers, under Constantinian mandate, were concerned principally with unifying a Roman Empire of widely disparate peoples, with equally disparate native beliefs, who came to Christianity as much by force as by persuasion. The Aristotelian separation of heaven and earth, which supported popular Roman religious ideas about divinity, along with Ptolemaic geocentrism, which supported the work of empire, were useful to Roman purposes. A separate sphere of the gods was intelligible to most of the non-Christian ancient world, making evangelism and persuasion to a consistent worldview a little easier to attain. And geocentrism satisfied imperial rhetoric that positioned Rome at the center of the earth.

Empires need certain conditions and practices to survive and prevail: stability, unity, universal communication—and coercion. A strong military helps, but an easily communicable unified ontology and cosmology that structurally supports the primacy of the emperor helps enormously. A three-tiered universe with Rome at its center; a heaven above, a hell beneath, and an earth modeled on a hierarchical heaven with the threat of hell for social control, is a powerful combination. Despite the fact that the three-tiered universe both predates and contradicts the philosophical efforts of the Greeks, the Arabs, and modern science, it has lasted into the twenty-first century for many Christians. Not only was it useful to first-millennium political rulers, it continues to last today because of its sheer mythic and narrative strength.

This mythic cosmology took firm root in Western thought in large part because of the cultural environment of Rome prior to Constantine, and of the related cultural environment of Roman Christendom after. And because it was closely allied to theology, scientific thought in the early medieval West was also influenced by Roman culture, in particular its anti-intellectualism and gendered emphasis on practice over theory.[10] Latin scholars such as Irenaeus, Tertullian, and Lactantius actively polemicized against the classical Athenian tradition of thought, claiming it to be effete and that it made men "soft." They considered Greek (pagan) philosophy to be part of a morally dissolute world. The world is not redeemed by reason, they argued, but only through the second coming of Christ.

The most influential early Latin thinker, Augustine of Hippo, had a more complex attitude toward philosophy and the Greeks; indeed, he makes it wrong to suggest that theoretical reflection on the world was completely nonexistent in the West from the fall of Rome to the thirteenth century when Saint Thomas Aquinas read Aristotle and Avicenna. Augustine had seen Plato's views as a necessary but transient stage in Christian education, parallel to the education of the world itself. In the history of thought, said Augustine, the world had to progress from the Greeks to the Romans to the clear light of the Christian empire. That this path for the world paralleled the route Augustine himself took in his own intellectual life, from Greek philosophy and rhetoric to Christian faith and the three-tiered universe, is probably not accidental.

In the end, while Muslim scholars were transforming science into the basic shape it would later take in the West, the primary contributions of the Latin Christian Middle Ages to emergent Western science were long simmering in the geocentric image of the world and a Roman distaste for theory. Saint Thomas Aquinas's reintroduction of Aristotelian theory to Christian thought opened the doors to empirical observation on the one hand but solidified the three-tiered universe on the other. This tension erupted into a full conflict by the sixteenth century, when the observable heavens began resolutely to contradict their assigned relationship to earth, and more specifically, to Rome.

The Reformation and the Renaissance

The late Middle Ages in Europe were hard. Plagues, warring popes, poor harvests, and increasing economic disparities made the old answers to big questions less persuasive and made the primary purveyor of knowledge about the world in the West—the Roman church—less effective. For the people who managed to stay out of harm's way as papal armies crashed across Europe and disease emptied the urban centers, nothing really changed but the seasons and the quality of crops. Gradually, however, change and disruption reached even the furthest edges of Christendom.

Between the thirteenth century, when Saint Thomas Aquinas was introducing Aristotle into Christian thought, and the sixteenth century, when Martin Luther tacked his Ninety-five Theses to the Wittenberg door in Germany, western ecclesial centers faced social and political upheaval from without and theological innovation from within. The character of the Latin priesthood was shifting, due in part to Thomas's *Summa Theologica* with its Socratic investigative style into the nature of things, and to an influx of writings from Arabic natural philosophers, whose texts spoke to Europe's real and present need for medical innovation. Gradually, the Latin priesthood became a community of scholars who struggled to make sense of a world that increasingly did not seem to fit the traditional teachings about it.

It is no secret that the "scientific revolution" that officially began with Kepler's and Galileo's seventeenth-century challenge to the geocentric universe came about because of political and cultural changes in Europe linked with erosion in the authority of the church—an erosion that actually dates back much further. While individual ideas can appear to have the quality of lone meteors that effect massive climate change, the history of ideas is a history of many processes that are social, political, economic, religious, and geographic. They all go together to make possible what appears in hindsight to be sudden massive change.

Martin Luther's challenge to the authority of the Catholic Church began over the issue of corruption, but it led inexorably to the dissolution of the church's authority over all questions of truth. The impact of this challenge cannot be overstated, nor can its importance in setting the scene for the eventual separation of science from theology. When Luther wrote, "He who sees a man in need, and passes him by, and gives [his money] for pardons, purchases not the indulgences of the pope, but the indignation of God" (Forty-fifth Thesis), he made clear that the authority of the church did not extend to knowledge of God, nor did the power of the church extend to divine power.

The real significance of this challenge is difficult to grasp in the twenty-first century. Luther lived in a time when knowledge of all kinds was completely dominated by the authority of a church that was modeled directly on the political structure of early imperial Rome. Without the teaching of the priests, there was no formal education. There were no alternative universities or alternative access to new research for the average person, literate or illiterate. So Luther's assault on the knowledge and power of the church meant, for those who agreed with him, that some other source of knowledge would have to be identified, if it did not reside in the pope and his priesthood. Here a subtle but most important turn in the history of Western thought occurred. Luther and the reformers identified the Bible as the source for ultimate truths—which included all truths—and that individual study of this source was necessary for individual conversion based upon individual comprehension (understanding!) of God's grace. This was a new theological anthropology—one that insisted on individual relationship to God and on a certain individual capability to reach understanding of God's will, a synonym for truth.

The invention of movable type and the resulting Gutenberg Bible gave technological support to the theological anthropology of Luther and his followers, who argued for a "priesthood of all believers." Individual reading and study of the Bible seemed logical outgrowths of this preaching, leading to a more general value on literacy and mass education. But more importantly for science, this theological innovation— the priesthood of all believers—made the search for truth begin from individual study and observation (of the Bible), opening the door to a more democratic process to knowledge. Thomas had already opened the study of the world to the Christian. This, combined with Lutheran anthropology and the influence of Islamic views of science, made the scientific revolution inevitable.

Descartes

René Descartes (1596–1650) and Isaac Newton (1643–1727) are probably the principal contributors to what we call the scientific revolution, although both depended heavily on the ideas and practices of others throughout the Renaissance. Educated primarily in Aristotelian logic, their primary question was not, as it still is for many people in the contemporary theology and science debate, "How do I make science fit the Bible?" but "How might we attain both clarity and certainty about the world that God made"? The excessive persecutions that the Catholic

Church had meted out on their recent forebears diminished the ultimate authority of that body in both men's minds, and they both sought to assist in the overall reformation project of locating a source for divine revelation outside of doctrine and church tradition. Both modified Aristotle's extreme empiricism with a platonic concern for universal unity, a unity achievable in abstract mathematics. For Descartes, therefore, the extra-ecclesial source of truth, or certainty, was the human mind and its reasoning power; for Newton it was the magnificent unity of mathematics and universal, observable, and testable physical laws.

Why was Descartes so concerned with the problem of certainty? His concern was not so different from that of many people today. He lived in a time after the demise of church authority and after the violent upheavals of the Protestant reformations. Protestantism was already showing its radically democratic approach to theology by splintering into many different and competing groups, each with different and competing claims. The Catholic counter-reformations did much to eliminate corruption in that church but did nothing to restore confidence in it as arbiter of knowledge about the world. Explorers were also returning to Europe and Northern Africa with wild tales and ships full of evidence that the world was much larger, and much less certain in its substance, than anyone from the Thames to the Northern Nile had previously assumed. These natural philosophers, nascent modern scientists, had no intention of dethroning God but thought that they could restore to God a *certainty* of place that no amount of ecclesial mismanagement, error, or prejudice could undo. Modern science was born in this search for a new foundation for certainty in a rapidly changing world.

Francis Bacon (1561–1626), a contemporary of Descartes, took a radical approach to the problem of certainty. While we do not know if he and Descartes were aware of each other's work, it is interesting that both gave voice to similar approaches to truth, although they were quite different in the details. Bacon argued that certainty only comes from the immediate senses. *Everything* else is presupposition. Even memory, Bacon claimed, is supposition regardless of how clearly I may hold a thing in my mind. As soon as it passes out of sight, sound, smell, and touch, a thing in memory no longer exists in certainty. He called everything except immediate sense perception an idol of the mind.[11]

Descartes saw the limitations of such radical empiricism. How can we be absolutely certain of sense perception when our senses sometimes deceive us? He pointed out that even in dreams we are persuaded of sense perception, at least for the duration of the dream. And no one can be absolutely certain in any given moment that he or she is not in fact dreaming. So Descartes sought certainty elsewhere. He sought it in radical doubt. Anything that can rationally be doubted, he argued, cannot be certain. So he set out to discover whether there was anything at all that could withstand doubt, and upon that one certain thing he would rebuild knowledge. Given that the existence of everything around him, including his own body, could be the result of hallucination or dream, the one certainty Descartes was able to convince himself of was his own thought, present even in dreaming. And thought, he argued, required a source of thought. *Cogito, ergo sum* was his famous conclusion: I think, therefore I am.

After doubting the existence of everything except the one certainty of his own thought, Descartes believed that he could reconstruct certain knowledge piece by piece, such that doubt would not be allowed to creep back in. If thinking means that I exist as thinker, then I, or at least my mind, must also arise from somewhere: this is how Descartes arrives at God as the source of the mind.[12] Whether his proof for God's existence is persuasive—and ultimately in modernity it has not been—is less important than the persuasiveness of his method for attaining knowledge.

Although a devout Catholic and despite the fact that he dedicated his *Meditations* to the faculty of the Sorbonne, which at that time was the divinity school of the University of Paris, Descartes knew that he was posing the strongest philosophical challenge to traditional ecclesial authority yet. Skepticism about all preconceived notions necessarily entailed skepticism about the teachings of the church. Whether Descartes actually believed that his method would make the claims of the church stronger (which is what he said that he intended) or whether he was simply wise enough in an age of church reprisals to cover his tracks, he hoped to show that real knowledge is possible *based on* skepticism and, more particularly, that a mathematically based scientific knowledge of the material world is possible.

For Descartes, then, what we have is in effect a resuscitation of Plato. Mathematical ideas are the only real certainties, and for God to be certain God must also exist primarily in the realm of the ideal rather than the physical realm of change and possible deception. What is real is the unmovable, unchangeable idea. This certainly fit with late medieval ideas of divinity as an unmovable, abstract Other, even as it allowed for a separation of ecclesial authority from real knowledge. Anyone truly interested in the rigors of skeptical philosophy, Descartes believed, would eventually get at knowledge of both the real world and of God. Descartes, and Plato before him, did not start from physical reality because that is the thing we can be *least* certain of. They started from those things that we together determine are absolutely free of doubt, and for these thinkers those things are ideas. Ultimately Descartes argues we can deduce the entire universe from the abstract, immovable God.

Eventually modern science dispensed with Descartes's notion that we can deduce the entire universe from God. But what modernity has not dispensed with is a more subtle and important point that he asserted. Because we can deduce the universe from God, according to Descartes, and God is one, it follows that the universe—reality—is one. What follows from that point is that there is a single, universal science. A single universal science is a completely contemporary presupposition. The way in which we build our understanding of the world is based on universalizable principles. And the significance of that assumption for our purposes here is that it introduces the notion that, in order for us to make sense of something *scientifically,* it has also to fit universal applicability. And universalism is, first and foremost, a theological claim.[13]

Newton

Born in the year Galileo died, Isaac Newton lived in England one generation after Descartes. Like his French predecessor, he believed that mathematics is the way to certainty, and so to truth. In his preface to the *Philosophiae Naturalis Principia Mathematica,* Newton makes plain his assumption that from math he can derive knowledge of all natural phenomena:

> The whole burden of philosophy seems to consist in this: from the phenomena of motions to investigate the forces of nature and then from those forces to demonstrate the other phenomena. . . . for by

the propositions mathematically demonstrated we there derive from the celestial phenomena the forces of gravity with which bodies tend to the sun and other several planets. Then, from these forces, by other propositions which are also mathematical, we deduce the motions of the planets, the comets, the moon and the sea.[14]

What is significant here is that Newton brings together all of the fields of inquiry of his time, claiming that the same principles apply to all things regardless of their differences over time and space. Again more Platonic than Aristotelian, Newton built on Descartes's turn to mathematical principles to establish a standard epistemological foundation for all scientific investigation. Newton was convinced, and may well be correct, that the cosmos functions in obedience to certain universal laws. This assumption allows the observer to apply rules that work in any one place to all places.

The Mechanistic Universe

Despite his massive specific contributions to many fields of scientific inquiry (physics, mathematics, optics, astronomy, and so forth) perhaps Newton's greatest impact on all of modern science is in his twofold insistence on the universal application of theory, which we will discuss below, and his depiction of the cosmos and all things within it as a great machine. Newton was a Christian who believed that he was serving theological purposes in revealing the mechanics of the universe. We can well imagine that when he prayed the Lord's Prayer he thought that the words "Thy will be done on earth as it is in heaven" refer quite literally to laws of motion, dimension, and time that he claimed are universal and applicable to things heavenly as well as earthly. He was also intelligent enough to know that the work he was doing could prove to be the demise of prior understandings of God.

The mechanistic universe as Newton described it represented a real conceptual shift away from earlier understandings of the cosmos itself as a place of disorder and willful powers. A mechanistic view of human bodies in particular, accepted wholesale in modern Western medicine, is quite different from the more mystical medieval view of the body and its processes. It is a mistake, however, to suppose that premodern organic notions of humors, balance, and spiritual powers were either ineffective or entirely wrong. Premoderns relied on medical experts who used theories that, for the most part, work. The difference lies in their views of the human being and of the world that give substance and credence to the theories, as well as to the methods and expectations of the practitioners. While contemporary scientists and theologians are beginning to recognize the limits of the mechanistic model, it has yielded massive amounts of information about the individual parts and the mechanical interconnections between parts in both human and other kinds of bodies.

A mechanistic view of the things requires, in one sense, a manual for understanding the various parts and their causal interactions. If your car's tires keep blowing out and you don't have a ritual expert (mechanic) around to fix the problem, it helps to have a manual that tells you how much air pressure you should maintain in the tires and how much weight they can normally bear. Neither you nor a mechanic needs to do special tests on *your* tires to answer these questions. There are certain rules of physics that apply generally to all rubber, air-filled tires. Or, if you are a golfer, it helps to know that, no matter how strong or skilled you are at hitting a golf ball, certain weights in clubs will allow for greater or lesser distance when you hit the ball, and that this factor applies to all golf balls all the time and under all circumstances.

While Newton was by no means the first to apply mathematics to mechanics, he made possible the final shift in science to a completely mechanistic view of the entire universe by way of mathematics. Newton's unification of all study under mathematical principles reverberates today in the contested astrophysical proposal that there is one unifying "theory of everything" (dubbed T.O.E.).[15] In one sense, Newton is the father of the "uni" in universe because—possibly more than any other principle—he demonstrated persuasively the possibility of a rational, universalizing theory for all of reality. This demonstration took hold in the West, and modern science, in all of its permutations, came into its own. Within one hundred years of Newton's life, Immanuel Kant took Newton's penchant for rational, universalizing theory and applied it to morality, an application that today governs the judicial and ethical systems of most industrialized countries.

It is important to understand that despite the fact that Newton was concerned first and foremost with explaining the material world that he observed in front of him every day, he also saw his work organized and shaped by a particular theological framework. The epistemological principles he invoked related ultimately to a rational God as author of the unity of the physical universe.[16] Newton started from the assumption that rationality is the perfect form of reality. Being perfect, God is also perfectly rational and so created the world by means of perfectly rational physical laws. Rationality is accessible to the (rational) human mind, and while Newton could see that both Aristotle and Thomas were in error over the three-tiered universe and its attendant separations in realities, he did believe along with both of them that close observation of the world would yield the mind of its creator. Such an audacious claim is possible, Newton argued, because no rational deity would break universal laws that he created in perfect rationality.

Newton's *Principia Mathematica* provided the strongest basis yet for modern empirical methods. Because he rejected Aristotle's premise of different natures for different classes of being in favor of a unified existence in which all specificity and particularity exists in subordination to universally governing physical laws, he set up a more unified science. Study of one phenomenon in the world can, theoretically, yield information about any other phenomenon as well. Therefore it follows that empirical study of the smallest class of thing—say, protons—should follow the same basic rules as study of the largest—say, black holes.

Four primary principles, Newton argued, should be applied in all scientific study. Doing so, he argued, will afford the scientist the greatest level of certainty. A quick review of these principles reveals their contemporary, foundational relevance for science and, interestingly enough, their dependence on some theological assumptions.

Parsimony

The first of Newton's principles is the rule of parsimony, sometimes called "Ockham's razor." Newton argued that in the event of multiple plausible explanations for a given phenomenon, the scientist should always opt for the simplest one. "Nature," he claimed, "is pleased with simplicity and affects not the pomp of superfluous causes."[17] Nature here is the reflection and image of God, since God—being rational, unified, and One—is simple. When contemporary science has to adjudicate between competing claims, it is to this principle of parsimony that it turns. Thus a fundamental rule by which science makes decisions originates theologically in the simplicity of God. Simplicity, in this sense, is a philosophical term denoting the unity and oneness of reality and of the originating force of that reality, which for Newton is God. The number one is also the simplest of all numbers. Thus, for Newton, the mathematical is also here a theological claim.

Same Effects, Same Cause

The second rule is a consequence of the first. Sometimes the rule of parsimony is inadequate for determining the true and sufficiently explanatory cause when two effects are the same. For example, as Newton puts it, there is "respiration in man and in beast—now, man and beast are not the same so how do we deal with same effects in different circumstances?" He also noted that "there is the descent of stones in Europe and there is the descent of stones in the New World. Do they descend from the same stones? Likewise, there is the light of our culinary fire, and there is the light of the sun. There is reflection of light in the Earth and there is reflection of light in the planets."[18] What should the scientist infer from identical effects in different situations? The scientist, Newton claimed, should always infer that where the effects are exactly the same, the cause is the same. It is noteworthy that Newton lived two hundred years before Darwin when he established that humans and animals are materially subject to the same causes.

Universality

We have already discussed Newton's concern for the universalizability of all of his theories, but it is good to place that concern squarely within his method for science. This third rule is set up by the first two and allows Newton to make his decisive move toward a cosmos absolutely unified in all of its parts by original design rather than by intrusive divine agency. He wrote that the "qualities of bodies which admit neither intensification nor remission of degrees and which are found to belong to all bodies within the reach of our experiments are to be esteemed with universal qualities of all bodies whatsoever."[19] If I find that a particular piece of granite has a particular hardness and weight per square inch, and that every other piece of granite within my reach has similar weight and hardness, I can make the claim that all granite everywhere will have the same weight and hardness per square inch. This rule enabled Newton to make a universalizing claim from a reasonable sample without having to test every single instance. It set him up for making his famous claim about gravity and its applicability not only to pieces of granite but to stars and galaxies.

Moreover, this rule enabled Newton, once and for all, to dispense with the idea of a three-tiered universe (heaven, earth, and hell below) as a reasonable and therefore godly picture of the universe. The Newtonian problem with the three-tiered universe was that it places God in a specific location that does not obey the physical laws applicable elsewhere. In addition, Newton's foundation for science disallows the existence of a rational deity who is both perfect and who breaks perfectly rational physical laws. Miracles that disrupt the laws of nature are, for Newton, both undesirable and inconceivable in a rational God. The "miracle" is an error in human perception, a point that David Hume argued at great length at the end of the eighteenth century.[20]

What is more, God the Creator cannot be perfectly rational and yet break the rational rule of parsimony. It is far simpler to posit a single-tiered, created universe governed by laws that apply equally everywhere, including heaven, than it is to posit a more complex theory of multiple and conflicting realities, requiring different and conflicting physical laws.

Refutability

Finally, Newton's fourth principle for science states that a workable theory should stand, and be assumed to be true, until after careful testing it is proven false by empirical evidence. The Ptolemaic geocentric system, for example, was a workable theory until empirical evidence against it, aided by the invention of telescopes, grew sufficiently to undermine it. Certainly, the memory of Galileo's persecution at the hands of the church must still have been fresh, and Newton wanted to make a strong case for empirical evidence over and against any political or traditional pressures or prejudices. No matter how popular (or well funded) it may be, Newton claimed, no theory can be viable if the *physical* evidence, parsed through the rules of parsimony, similar effects, and universality, does not support it.

In setting up this fourth principle, Newton was deeply indebted to Descartes's method of radical doubt, which privileges observation over attractive or politically useful theories and traditional knowledge. Descartes had written in his *Discourse on Method* that the long chains of simple and easy reasoning, by means of which geometrists are accustomed to reach the conclusions of their most difficult demonstrations, led me to imagine that all things, to the knowledge of which man is competent, are mutually connected in the same way, and that there is nothing so far removed from us as to be beyond our reach, or so hidden that we cannot discover it, provided only we abstain from accepting the false for the true, and always preserve in our thoughts the order necessary for the deduction of one truth from another.[21]

For Descartes, and later Newton, to argue that nothing is beyond the reach of human understanding—nothing is "so hidden we cannot discover it, provided only we abstain from accepting false for true"—was revolutionary in that it insisted on the availability and ultimate comprehensibility of all that is. This marks a decisive step in the West: a step away from a story about the universe that allows for forces and phenomena intelligible only to a mysterious deity and toward a story of a great cosmic machine. What divinity there is in this machine is wholly rational, orderly, and ultimately comprehensible to the human mind.

Newton had no doubt that sufficient reason, observation, and testing of observed phenomena would ultimately yield absolutely true (and unchanging) knowledge about the world by yielding the eternal (and unchanging) laws that govern the world. It is not that he considered human beings to be incapable of error; quite the contrary. Newton believed the human gift of reason to be the imago Dei, the image of God, and that through reason error can slowly be eliminated through rigorous search, experimentation, and testing. And what is revealed, after all error is removed, is the perfect (and reasonable) truth of universal laws that govern the natural world. The world changes according to these laws, but the laws are unchanging. They are, Newton would say, the mind of God.

In this faith, Newton was more like Plato than Aristotle: the mathematical equations that most consistently explain worldly phenomena are the true fruits of science; they are the eternal truths that only this kind of rational science can reveal. By virtue of the principles of parsimony and universality, Newton could claim that the observations of scientists can be applied everywhere not only as explanatory *descriptions* of what occurs, but more importantly for this discussion, as laws or *prescriptions* for what God both designed and intends in creation.

It is difficult to remember, even in the twenty-first century, a time of unprecedented postmodern questioning of our pictures of reality, that the "laws" Newton discovered are theories that continue to be persuasive to us, rather than absolute truths that will persuade all future generations. Hypotheses, equations, theorems, and laws work to describe and even to predict what we see, or think we see, in and around the world. They are our best attempts at one kind of story for what is happening and we stick to them so long as we find their results persuasive. Because Newton's theory of gravitation works so well to explain the motion of inter- and intra-planetary bodies, it is a good example of the fine line between so-called objective, absolute truth and creative interpretation.

Stories do not have to possess some kind of absolute objectivity to work and so to be regarded as true (and so, in effect, to *be* true in a meaningful way). Stories—physical laws in this case—are true because they work, because they fit our current data, not because they are either eternal or unchanging. When a hypothesis becomes a law, the distinction between human story and absolute truth tends to muddy. Theories that *work* sufficiently to explain a phenomenon in the world, such as gravity, can easily become mistaken for the kind of absolute and eternally certain truth that Plato, Aristotle, Aquinas, Newton, and Descartes sought, and that even some scientists today still seek. It is hard to remember that working theories, and the mathematical equations that express them, are still stories subject to change.

Ever since the scientific revolution came into its maturity with Newton, the resulting story of modern science in the West has yielded discoveries about the continents, the seas, the weather, the stars, planets, animals, cells, atoms, light, and so forth, all based upon the principles Newton set out for scientific inquiry. This evolution of thought has had massive effect on theology, and its effect on theological views of the human is equally great. Before we look more closely at the theological issues raised by that one aspect of being human—the genome—let us turn to two more scientific figures who concerned themselves particularly with investigating the existence, composition, and meaning of human beings. Charles Darwin and Sigmund Freud did not significantly alter the shape of scientific inquiry as did the other figures discussed in this chapter. But, influenced by modern science, they have contributed significantly to contemporary Western conceptions of the human. So a brief description of each will help us complete the task of orienting ourselves in the present as we take up the contemporary theological question of the human in the age of genetic research.

Darwin

Charles Darwin's name is often used synonymously with the theory of biological evolution. After spending five years in the 1830s as unpaid naturalist on the HMS *Beagle's* scientific expedition to the Pacific coast of South America, Charles Darwin wrote and eventually published his famous book *On the Origin of Species by Means of Natural Selection*. Published in 1859, it outlined his nascent theory that all of biological life on earth is descended by means of natural selection, or evolution, from a relatively few originary sources. The controversy surrounding this theory, of course, had to do with the theory's inevitable linkage of humans with animals and indeed with all other life on earth. This constituted a massive challenge from Newtonian science to the heretofore relatively unchallenged field of theological anthropology, which assumed humans to be both fully formed and uniquely placed in God's creation.

Charles Robert Darwin, named after his uncle and father, was born on February 12, 1809, at the Mount in Shrewsbury, Shropshire, England. His father, Robert, was a physician, and his mother, Susannah Wedgwood Darwin, died when he was only eight years old. Charles's grandfather was Erasmus Darwin, a fairly well-known poet, philosopher, and naturalist. It is likely that Charles came by his own interest in the natural world through his family's occupational interests. Although chastised as a teenager by his father for his lack of interest in school learning, Charles demonstrated an interest in chemistry; at thirteen he had set up a chemistry lab in his father's toolshed with his brother Erasmus.

At age sixteen, Darwin left Shrewsbury and followed his older brother to study medicine at Edinburgh University. But while there, he reportedly became upset by the requirements of surgery, performed without anesthesia, and decided to leave medicine to enter the priesthood. So from Edinburgh Darwin went to Cambridge University to study theology for ordination in the Church of England. It is unlikely that he was at all convinced that the life of a clergyman was right for him, and in fact likely that he did not know what he wanted to do, because soon after earning his theological degree, he accepted an invitation to join the crew of the HMS *Beagle*. The ship left England for South America on December 31, 1831. Charles was twenty-two years old.[22]

The voyage was to shape Darwin's life. In the preface to his book entitled *The Voyage of the Beagle,* he wrote of his gratitude to Captain Fitz Roy, who had extended the invitation and who gave up part of his own accommodations to allow Darwin passage and a place to work on board. He wrote that "during the five years that we were together, I received from him the most cordial friendship and steady assistance."[23] The purpose of the voyage was, as Darwin himself put it, "to complete the survey of Patagonia and Tierra del Fuego, commenced under Captain King in 1826 to 1830—to survey the shores of Chile, Peru, and of some islands in the Pacific—and to carry a chain of chronometrical measurements round the World."[24]

The world in the early nineteenth century was fairly well mapped. The scope of the globe was known. But several centuries of exploration had yielded hugely varying accounts of the biological life of the world, and the *Beagle*'s surveying mission was an opportunity for Darwin to look for himself at the world outside of England. As the naturalist on board, he spent his time collecting and observing. It should come as no surprise that, trained as a theologian, Darwin was also looking for clues to an underlying or ultimate order of things in his observations. That is, he wanted to discern links between all of the strange and wonderful animal and plant differences that he encountered. His notebooks are full of questions relating to connections and similarities, leading to questions of origins and change. How is it, he wondered, that creatures can have some similarities, such as beak, wings, and hairless feet, and yet huge differences in size, shape, color, sound, habitat, and so forth? From his years of concentrated collection and observation aboard the *Beagle,* and then from a decade of reflection on his specimens thereafter, Darwin generated his controversial, but persuasive, theory of natural selection.

Darwin approached his evidence with an interest in finding a universalizable theory for biological life that also accommodates the reality of change and difference. His theory of natural selection, based upon ideas of scarcity and struggle for survival, worked for quite a while to explain the variation and mutation evident among and between species. While current theories of evolution have revised and in some ways rejected many of Darwin's own conclusions about specific processes of biological change, his theory of evolution eliminated any remnants of serious scientific support for Aristotelian notions of separately created species. (Needless to say, there remain to this day many vociferous religious supporters of the Aristotelian claim of separately created species because of its compatibility with their interpretations of the Bible, which is precisely what made Aristotle attractive to Saint Thomas in the twelfth century.) Darwin's rejection of Aristotelian naturalism provided yet more strength to the Newtonian view of parsimony and universality:

> Although much remains obscure, and will long remain obscure, I can entertain no doubt, after the most deliberate study and dispassionate judgement of which I am capable, that the view which most naturalists entertain, and which I formerly entertained—namely, that each species has been independently created—is erroneous. I am fully convinced that species are not immutable; but that those belonging to what are called the same genera are lineal descendants of some other and generally extinct species, in the same manner as the acknowledged varieties of any one species are the descendants of that species. Furthermore, I am convinced that Natural Selection has been the main but not exclusive means of modification.[25]

Darwin made clear that, faced with this vast and dizzying array of species difference, biological science need not resort to an anti-Newtonian conclusion of separate origins with separate teleologies. And for Darwin the theologian, who had studied the philosophical requirements for unity in the godhead, the theory of natural selection must have appeared more consistent with his own classical theological training as well. A God who is One creates a universe fundamentally unified, and so all change, difference, and diversity can be reduced to that simple unity. Newton's notion of God's basic rationality had taken hold throughout Western Christianity by the time Darwin studied theology, and so a theory clarifying the relationship of complex beings to one another in a created, rational order would have appealed not only to Darwin the naturalist, but to Darwin the theologian as well.

That human beings are animals was one shock to the public, but that we evolve by means of something called natural selection—a process shared by plankton—was an even greater shock. That the new science would make cousins of monkeys went beyond the pale for some, and the resulting controversy has entertained many others for the last century. Remarkably, those most opposed to evolutionary theory seldom notice that this theory in fact privileges humans to an inordinate degree. It privileges all thriving species by explaining their success in hindsight and thereby imputes to that success an assumed necessity and inevitability. If humans are still here, evolutionary theory goes, humans are more fit for survival and so must survive. Our survival becomes inevitable, rather than the result of chance. It is a small step from that to a theological anthropology that privileges humans in the scheme of things, a view that literal readers of Genesis 1–2 might appreciate.

The apparent similarities between species became, with Darwin and his followers, evidence of biological unity. Natural selection seemed most simply and elegantly to explain an apparently universal reality of difference within species and of similarity between them. Evolutionary theory did not explain the exact mechanical means of change and evolution, but it paved the way for thinking about it. Indeed, it spurred a search for that mechanism, which would turn out to be a tiny strand of proteins we call DNA.

Freud

To conclude a brief history of Western science in the early twentieth century with a Viennese doctor of neurology may seem a curious choice. For one thing, the history of contemporary science by no means ends there; in some ways it merely begins with Sigmund Freud. What we commonly think of as modern Western medicine, certainly itself a culmination of Newton's mechanistic view, was still in its infancy at the turn of the twentieth century, when Freud was generating his theories of consciousness. Most of the discoveries that would completely change the relationship of science to the human body, in terms of both diagnostics and treatment, had yet to be made. So what does a theory of the mind add to our discussion of theology, human being, and genetic science? The answer, for our purposes, is that the mind is both our greatest asset in scientific inquiry and our greatest liability, something Freud demonstrated more clearly and systematically than anyone had before.

In terms of science, Freud spanned more than one lifetime in his eighty-three years. He was born in 1856 in Moravia and raised in Vienna in a world of horse-drawn carriages. Freud was thirty years old before the first electric street lamp was lit, far from Vienna in New York

City. He died in exile from Nazi Vienna in England in 1939, when automobiles clogged London streets and physicists Lise Meitner and Otto Frisch published confirmation of the process they coined "nuclear fission." The Western world had, in some senses, completely changed during his lifetime.

Sigmund Freud was a medical doctor and psychologist who today is sometimes called the father of psychoanalysis. Through close observation of his patients and in particular through study of extreme cases of delusion and hysteria, he articulated a structure of the human mind that posited and clarified a place for the nonrational unconscious in individual human life and in communal life as well. Meaning, he argued, is a human artifact of the mind, and it relies on both cognitive processes (Newton's precious rationality) and on symbolic and noncognitive processes that give shape to meaning. The human mind, he argued, has a three-part structure—ego, id, and superego—all the parts of which are necessary to survival and healthy functioning. In this work Freud made accessible a kind of scientific exploration of human thought and established persuasive theories, consequently, of human existence. It is probably fair to say that all contemporary Western ideas and theories about human identity, memory, childhood, sexuality, and, most generally, of the production of meaning have been shaped in relation to—and at times in opposition to—Freud's work.

Freud's influence on the birth and growth of psychoanalytic theories of mental health and treatment is profound and deserves high stature in any history that includes medical science.[26] However, it is what Freud himself perhaps did *not* intend to contribute to modern science that makes him especially important to this discussion. He discerned the function of the unconscious in human life and in so doing created a solid place for fantasy, delusion, and nonrational projection. This element of human consciousness relies on the fabrication or adoption of a story or stories that connect sensory experiences to an emergent sense of self, so that the self may exist within a coherent realm and succeed in daily survival. Not only is this story-making aspect of human consciousness fully functional, but it is necessary to the completion of the human mind and so, perhaps, to the world that the human mind perceives.

By itself the possibility of a zone of nonrationality and even irrationality in human existence might not make Isaac Newton roll over in his proverbial grave. However, the Freudian discovery that human consciousness necessarily functions on the basis of at least partially fabricated meaning and potential delusion certainly would make him do so. The human capacity for meaning-making through the symbolic projection of fantasy, which is then taken as descriptive of actual reality, is fine as a theory of mental disorder. It does not as such disrupt or challenge modern Newtonian science's dependence on assumptions of a human rational capacity to distinguish objective reality in and of itself from fantasy. But to suggest, as Freud did in several of his more general works on the psychology of culture, that stories of reality are necessary projections for *all* humans, not just the mentally ill—this throws some doubt on modern science's claim to objective certainty in its findings. Indeed, Freud's questions about communal perceptions of reality, which he developed in a brief essay on religion entitled *The Future of an Illusion,* were focused on human beings' capacity to be duped by religious myths despite what contrary material evidence may be present. But Freud's argument applies, of course, to all myths and not just to so-called religious ones.

In his later thought, Freud applied his interest in the power of the unconscious as much to collective human life as to individual life. Moreover, his depiction of the human mind as a process of sensory interpretation, meaning making, and self-production through symbols and stories, opened the door to a deeper questioning of the mechanistic myth posited by Newton and his followers. Most troubling of all, Freud may have exposed Descartes's quest for absolute certainty as an unattainable fantasy.

Freud's fundamental work on the structure of consciousness serves both as an apex of modern Newtonian science and a limit of that science at the same time. So he represents, in one sense, both the culmination of modernity and a foreshadowing of what we call postmodernity. While a mechanistic model for biological science continued apace during and after Freud's work achieved prominence, and we might even say that Freud himself was offering a more or less mechanistic view of the mind, the content of that view has created room for a science that sees the limits of the machine model both for the universe and for the human body/person. The multiplicity inherent in the human mind itself suggests that a reductive view of the human as, for example, a mechanical series of chemical processes directed by a few proteins called DNA, is perhaps insufficient to a full *scientific* understanding of that perceived reality we call human being.

The twentieth century, following Freud's introduction of complex consciousness, has yielded a dramatically evolving story in Western science. Albert Einstein was a contemporary of Freud's; his astrophysical theories cast much of modernity into a new frame for the boldest of scientists. The very possibility of relativity as a new narrative for the relationship of time, space, and matter makes many of our inherited views of the universe once again in need of new metaphors and new stories. A purely mechanistic view cannot carry us all the way to Einstein. And it cannot carry us all the way to an understanding of genetic codes either. Thirteen years after Freud exploded modernity's reliance on a story of mind that can empirically work its way, experiment by experiment, past all delusion and fantasy, the first X-ray image of DNA was created by Rosalind Franklin. Her work revealed the molecule's helical shape and enabled two brash young scientists to brag the next year to patrons of the Eagle Pub in Cambridge, England, that they had "found the secret of life."[27]

Whether Rosalind Franklin, James Watson, and Francis Crick in fact discovered the secret of life in the chemical structure of DNA is a matter for debate; indeed, it lies at the heart of the question before us. Watson and Crick thought they had, and many continue to think that this chemical structure in itself is a reductive blueprint for the whole of human life on the one hand and the key to human destiny on the other. Structurally speaking, the human genome is without doubt the mechanism by which human life is replicated and renewed. Can the science of human life be reduced to a mechanical process? Or does our metaphoric frame of the machine now need to change as profoundly for the field of biology as it has already changed in astrophysics? This is a part of the debate that we, as scientists and theologians together, are endeavoring to explore.

The history of Western science and theology has been a history of our human search for certainty about the world in which we live and whose patterns and meanings we struggle to discern. The question "What is human?" is both a scientific and a theological one. From Plato and his rebellious student Aristotle to the best thinkers of today, the questions of what the human really *is*, where we come *from*, what we are here *for*, what makes us *do* what we do and toward what *end* we are headed, are ones that occupy both scientists and theologians, albeit with different emphases and methods. Despite our differences, however, it is increasingly clear to all of us that the ancient, merely old, and even relatively recent stories are insufficient to the complexity, relativity, multiplicity, and mutability that we are discovering daily in our scientific and theological inquiries into the human condition, including its genetic map. This inquiry, for theologians, is about divinity as well as humanity. For scientists it is about scope, meaning, and method as well as empirical observation and inductive reasoning.

Indeed, it is not a new phenomenon under the sun for scientists and theologians to inquire together—or even to inquire at the same time and in the same person—into the meaning of a thing, with hopes that the collective view may yield greater clarity to both perspectives. But it has been a relatively long time since scientists and theologians have seen each other as companions rather than as adversaries. That fact makes our own time a pivotal and revelatory one in the histories of both Western science and of Western theology.

2

An Introduction to Mendelian Genetics

Lainie Friedman Ross

Gregor Mendel (1822–1884), an Augustinian monk from Austria, is considered the father of genetics, the study of the science of inheritance. Mendel published his two laws of inheritance in 1865, but their importance was not appreciated until 1900, sixteen years after his death. We now know that his laws were only partly correct, but here we will focus on what is right in Mendelian genetics.

Gregor Mendel and Peas

Working with pea plants, Mendel discovered that hereditary traits could be explained by the action of certain invisible but predictable "factors." Mendel studied seven seed and plant characteristics: (1) plant height, (2) pod shape, (3) pod color, (4) flower position, (5) flower color, (6) seed shape, and (7) seed color. Observing the plants and their progeny, Mendel noted that each plant inherited two copies of each factor—one from each parent plant. (We now call these factors genes.) He realized that some factors were dominant: only one copy was necessary for the characteristic to express—that is, to be physically observable in the plant. Other factors, however, were recessive: two copies were necessary for the characteristic to express. If the plant had only one copy of a recessive factor, the trait would remain latent but still could be passed to the next generation. Mendel's first law, therefore, states that each individual carries two factors for every trait, while gametes—reproductive cells—carry only one factor. The second law states that each pair of factors segregates independently—meaning that plant height, for example, was inherited independently from pod shape such that one could not infer pod shape from height or height from pod shape.

DNA

In the 1950s, biologists Francis Crick and James Watson deciphered the structure of DNA (deoxyribonucleic acid), a double-stranded molecule consisting of a string of chemicals called nucleotides. There are four types of nucleotides—adenine, cytosine, guanine, and thymine—and they bond to each other according to a strict set of rules. The DNA serves as code for genes, which are sequences of nucleotide bases containing instructions for making proteins.

Most human DNA is found in the cell nuclei, carried by paired, threadlike bodies called chromosomes. Most normal human cells contain 46 chromosomes, paired into 23 sets. Of these 23 sets, 22 are "somatic pairs," also known as autosomes, which carry genetic information from both parents. Then there are the sex chromosomes, conventionally called X and Y. Females have two X chromosomes (XX), while males have an X and a Y (XY). Human gametes—the sperm and ovum cells—each have 23 chromosomes so that offspring inherit one set of chromosomes from each parent. Although Mendel did not know about chromosomes, his basic insight into the inheritance of traits was accurate.

DNA, then, is composed of an ordered sequence of nucleotide bases that encode genetic information in the form of genes, which are found in specific locations along the chromosomes. Chromosones also carry a lot of extra DNA between the genes; these areas are known as "junk DNA." Most of the genome is so-called junk DNA, which may serve regulatory and other functions.

The Human Genome Project (HGP) is a worldwide research effort whose numerous goals including mapping the entire human DNA. Begun in 1990 with a three-billion-dollar budget, it yielded a "completed" draft that was published in February 2001—under budget and ahead of schedule. It is calculated to include over 3 billion nucleotide bases, the backbone of the DNA molecule. The average gene consists of about 3,000 bases, but sizes vary greatly, and the largest gene has 2.4 million bases. In humans, the total number of genes is approximately 30,000, much lower than expected. Compare this to the fruit fly, with 13,000 genes, the roundworm with 19,000, and rice—which has over 40,000 genes. This fact alone is revolutionary. Just as humans had to accept that the earth was not at the center of the universe, we now have to accept that we do not have the most genes. Furthermore, we share 90 percent of our genes with the mouse and 98.4 percent with the chimpanzee. In fact, we are more similar genetically to the chimp than the chimp is to the gorilla! This certainly bears on our understanding of the uniqueness of the human species.

While we are similar to other animals, we are even more similar to each other. In fact, 99.9 percent of nucleotide bases are exactly the same in all people. It was the homogeneity of *homo sapiens* that led geneticists to study fruit flies: fruit flies display much more diversity than people do. Fruit flies have one different nucleotide base in every hundred bases, whereas humans have only one different nucleotide in every thousand bases. So until we had large enough computers, the study of human genetic diversity was inaccessible.

Although much of modern genetics is "post-Mendelian," plenty of ethical issues are raised simply by our knowledge of Mendelian inheritance. Let's start there.

The diseases known as Mendelian conditions are rare and can be classified in three groups. For *autosomal recessive* conditions such as cystic fibrosis and sickle-cell anemia, the person must have inherited *two* copies of that gene—two "abnormal" alleles—in order to actually be symptomatic. *Autosomal dominant* conditions, such as Huntington's disease, inherited breast cancer, or achondroplasia (dwarfism) only require one abnormal allele. X-linked recessive conditions such as Duchenne muscular dystrophy and hemophilia, are conditions whose genes are found on the X chromosome. Since a boy has only one X-chromosome, if the allele is abnormal, the boy will inherent the condition. In contrast, his sisters who have two X-chromosomes will usually be healthy asymptomatic carriers. In reality, Mendel did not know about X-linked conditions, but that is because he was studying pea plants and not humans.

Autosomal Recessive Conditions

Let's look at two of the best-known autosomal recessive conditions: cystic fibrosis (CF) and sickle-cell anemia (SCA). Cystic fibrosis is associated both with pulmonary (lung) abnormalities and gastrointestinal abnormalities. In children, symptoms can range from foul-smelling diarrhea to a general failure to thrive. Pulmonary problems usually cause the most morbidity in these children: lung infections and progressive lung damage are very likely. Eventually individuals with CF will either need lung transplantation or will die from the pulmonary damage. It is most common in the Caucasian community; among Caucasian children it is the most common autosomal recessive condition.

Sickle-cell anemia, on the other hand, is most common in individuals with African ancestry, although it is also found in those of Greek and Italian origin. SCA presents in several distinct ways. People with SCA, particularly young children, are at increased risk for certain types of infections. Individuals of all ages are at risk for vaso-occlusive crises (VOC) when the micocirculation of blood is blocked by sickled red blood cells causing injury to the organ because of decreased oxygen supply. Pain is the most common complaint during these episodes, which frequently involve the bones but can involve the lungs (for example, acute chest syndrome) and be life threatening. SCA can also lead to splenic sequestration, a life-threatening condition in which a substantial portion of the blood volume is sequestered in the spleen, and aplastic crisis, in which the bone marrow stops or slows its production of red blood cells, possibly resulting in severe anemia. This, too, can be life-threatening.

Both CF and SCA are associated with a shorter life expectancy, although improved treatments means that those with CF typically die in their forties, those with SCA in their mid-sixties.

How are these diseases inherited, and what makes a person exhibit them? As autosomal recessive traits, two abnormal alleles (copies of the gene) must be inherited in order for a person to be affected. With just one abnormal allele, a person is a "healthy carrier," not diseased, but still capable of passing the abnormal allele to the next generation. We cannot tell by appearance who is a carrier. (And in the case of SCA, there is actually benefit to being a carrier. One copy of the sickle cell gene provides individuals with resistance to malaria—an important advantage historically, which explains why it was such a common mutation.)

Let's imagine yourself as a counselor in a prenatal clinic. A couple comes in with a question. The female partner is a known carrier of an autosomal recessive disease, CF, for example. She is a carrier but does not have the condition herself—meaning that she has just one abnormal allele. The couple wants to know their likelihood of having an affected child.

Their risk will be the product of the woman's risk and her male partner's risk. The possible outcomes can be displayed in a Punnett square, familiar to many of us from high school biology. The capital letter "A" refers to a healthy allele; in this case it is dominant (meaning that you only need one A to be healthy). A small "a" refers to a diseased allele; in this case it is recessive (meaning that you need two a's to be affected by the disease). We know that Mom is "Aa," as she is healthy but a carrier. To answer the question, "What's our risk of having an affected child?" we need to know Dad's allelic inheritance. In this case, the man does not know. Let us consider the three possible scenarios:

Scenario A: He is a healthy carrier (Aa).
Scenario B: He is a healthy noncarrier (AA).
Scenario C: He is affected by the disease himself (aa).

Scenario A: Both partners are healthy carriers.

| | | Carrier partner | |
		A	a
Carrier	A	AA	aA
Partner	a	Aa	aa

The middle squares in the diagram show the possible outcomes for a child of these two parents. We see three possible outcomes, two capitals, one capital and one small, or both small, in the shorthand of the Punnett square. Therefore, the child has a 25 percent chance of being a healthy noncarrier (AA), a 50 percent chance of being a healthy carriers (Aa), and a 25 percent chance of being affected with the disease (aa). So, statistically speaking, 75 percent of the time this couple will have a healthy child if the father *is* a carrier.

Scenario B: One partner is a healthy carrier; one is a healthy noncarrier.

	Noncarrier partner	
	A	A
Carrier A	AA	AA
Partner a	Aa	Aa

Now, still considering the same couple, let's imagine that the father is a healthy noncarrier. Here, 50 percent of the children will also be healthy noncarriers (AA) and 50 percent will be healthy carriers (Aa). No children can be affected by the disease.

Scenario C: One partner is a healthy carrier; one is an affected partner.

	Affected partner	
	a	a
Carrier A	aA	aA
Partner a	aa	aa

Finally, imagine that the male partner is affected with this autosomal recessive condition himself; that is, he is "aa." Here, 50 percent of the children are carriers (Aa), and 50 percent are affected (aa). None are healthy noncarriers.

If the father is affected, he will know it. So the question is, If he is not affected, what is the chance that he is a carrier? Remember, there are no physical clues that can tell us. If he does not undergo genetic testing, we can only estimate his risk based on what the disease is, its prevalence in the population, or in his particular ethnic group, and whether he has biological relatives known to carry the abnormal allele. For example, if the father is Caucasian, non-Mediterranean, his chance of being a sickle-cell carrier is very low, but if he is an African American, the risk is about 1 in 12. For cystic fibrosis, if the father is Caucasian, his risk is about 1 in 30 that he is a carrier. The risks are greater if he has a first- or second-degree relative with the condition or known to be a healthy carrier.

Now let us imagine another couple who want to know their risk of having a child with an autosomal recessive condition like CF or SCA. In this case, both are healthy and have no known risks in their families.

If they're both healthy, they are either AA or Aa; either may be a healthy noncarrier or a healthy carrier—we just don't which. If they are both carriers, their likelihood of having an affected child is 25 percent (see scenario A above). If one is a carrier and one is a noncarrier, none of their children will be affected by the disease, but, statistically, half will be carriers (see scenario B above). If both of these parents are noncarriers, none of their children will have the disease, nor will they be carriers.

But note this important fact: Even with no family history of the disease itself, family members can still be carriers. Let me explain with a personal example.

I recently attended the wedding of a second cousin, Bob, whom I had never met. And at the reception, a relative of my dad—let's call her Ruth—asked me how my parents were doing. My brother had died two years before, and my parents are still struggling emotionally, so I mentioned that. And Ruth said, "Well, you know that my daughter died." I asked her how and when she had died. When Ruth told me it was cystic fibrosis I said, "Wait a second. . . . How are you related to my father?" She said she was my father's first cousin. Since her daughter had died of cystic fibrosis, I thought, that means Ruth is a obligate carrier. I did a quick calculation and realized that my risk of being a CF carrier was much higher than the 1 in 30 that I had assumed. In fact, here is the calculation.

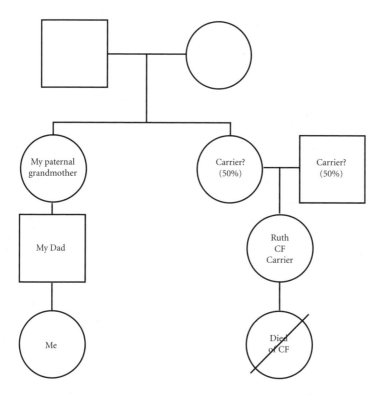

Figure 1: A Family Genogram
[Note: Circles represent females; squares represent males.]

So what is my own chance of being a carrier? Well, it depends on which of Ruth's parents was a carrier. If my paternal grandmother's sister *was* a carrier, and assuming that no one in the family had ever died of CF (a hard thing to know given our limited medical understanding of the disease in earlier decades), then my grandmother has at least a 50 percent chance of being a carrier, my father has at least a 25 percent chance, and I have at least a 12.5 percent chance–not 1 in 30 as I presumed based on my ethnicity. Of course, if my paternal grandmother's sister was *not* a carrier—that is, if it was Ruth's father who passed the gene to Ruth—then my grandmother's chance of being a carrier is much lower. It is not zero, as the chance of either of my grandmother's parents being carriers is at least 1 in 30, based on their ethnicity. But even if we know for certain that my grandmother was *not* a carrier, my dad *can* still be a carrier (if he inherited the allele from his father). So if my grandmother is a carrier, my risk is even higher than 12.5 percent because I also have the risk from my paternal grandfather's side And of course my mother's family may also carry this gene unknowingly. So, calculating my own odds is quite complicated, based on ethnicity data as well as personal data, if known.

That night, after the wedding, I went home and asked my parents, "So, what did Ruth's daughter die of?" And my mother answered, "Oh, some kind of lung problem, but she's so distant that it doesn't matter to you." So I drew the genogram above for my parents to show them that her death was relevant to me. I was really surprised that no one had thought to mention this to me, given how meticulous I had been with my own prepregnancy testing. Indeed, had you asked me about my family history, I would have told you there was no cystic fibrosis in my family.

So when a couple tells a doctor there is no instance of cystic fibrosis in their families, that could indicate several possibilities. First, it may be true. Second, it is possible that, like me, they don't know their extended families, and thus the medical implications, very well. Third, even when extended family is well acquainted, they may be ignorant of actual causes of death. Just a few generations ago, doctors may not have told families the real cause, even if they knew it themselves. Even today, when I ask college students what their grandparents died of, the most common answer is "old age." Similarly, in the case of a childhood death, the child may have simply been called "sickly," with no named disease or condition.

Now that I have a more accurate picture of my risk, what should I have told Bob, who was getting married that night, about his risk of being a CF carrier? Although Bob's father and my father are first cousins, Bob's father is adopted, so the information that I gleaned that night was not relevant for him except in the generic sense that we really do not know our family trees very well.

One of the lessons here is that a recessive gene can actually be passed for generations without being expressed. A blue-eyed child may appear after generations of brown-eyed parents. An Rh-negative trait can suddenly surface after many decades. So family medical histories, which tell only about expressed traits, are only somewhat useful.

Let us now consider a third case. A young man comes to your pre-natal clinic wanting to know what he should tell his future wife about his risk. The man has a brother affected with an autosomal recessive condition, but both of their parents are healthy. What is his risk?

If this man has an affected brother and this is an autosomal recessive condition, what we know is that both of his parents must be obligate carriers. We are back to scenario A. Both of his parents must carry a recessive gene—at least in the Mendelian world, which is our current focus. So he wants to know what risk he should disclose to his significant other.

Let's look again at scenario A, but now from the perspective of the adult offspring. We'll call it scenario D.

Scenario D: Risk of a healthy child being a carrier when both parents are obligate carriers.

		Carrier parent	
		A	a
Carrier	A	AA	aA
Parent	a	Aa	aa

At first glance, one might think that the young man has a 50 percent chance of being a carrier. But we already have some important information: He is not affected by the disease himself. He is not "aa"; he must be in one of the other three categories. Therefore, the odds are 2 in 3 that he is a carrier, 1 in 3 that he is a noncarrier.

Autosomal Dominant Conditions

Keeping our Mendelian perspective for now, let's look at autosomal dominant conditions, which require just *one* abnormal allele in order to result in the actual disease. There is no "carrier" state: if you have the gene you have the disease. And in general, you will have just one abnormal allele of this type; two are often lethal. A fetus with two abnormal alleles will likely be spontaneously aborted, or if it grows to term, it may be stillborn. In principle, the allele can be from either parent—indeed, in Mendel's world, this is always true, as it does not matter in pea plants. But in fact, in post-Mendelian genetics, we will learn that a gene's expression may depend on whether it comes from Mom or Dad. And we will learn that not all autosomal dominant genes are completely penetrant (meaning that some individuals will have the gene but the disease will never express).

Let's consider achondroplastic dwarfism, because the allele responsible for this condition acts most closely to what Mendel expected from autosomal dominant conditions. Imagine that a woman comes to your clinic who has achondroplastic dwarfism—a condition associated with physical abnormalities but normal mental abilities. She wants to assess her risk of having a child with the condition; her future partner is unknown. Let's designate this female partner with her one abnormal allele "Bb," where the capital B refers to the gene for achondroplasia.

Again the question is, What is her risk? The answer, of course, depends on the future father. Is he an adult of normal stature or does he also have achondroplasia? Let's consider the two scenarios.

Scenario E: Female partner is affected; Male partner is normal stature.

| | Affected partner | |
	B	b
Normal stature b	Bb	bb
Partner b	Bb	bb

Thus, if the father is of normal stature, the child will have a 50 percent chance of being an achondroplastic dwarf like its mother and a 50 percent chance of normal stature.

In contrast, if the father is also an achondroplastic dwarf, then he is also "Bb."

Scenario F: Both partners are affected.

	Affected partner	
	B	b
Affected B	BB* *usually fatal	bB
Partner b	Bb	bb

Here, if the child were to inherit two copies of the achondroplastic allele, it would most likely be incompatible with life. Assuming such a child would not survive, we can disregard the "BB" possibility from our calculations. So a surviving child has a two-in-three chance of being affected (Bb) and a one-in-three chance of being of normal stature (bb).

We see, therefore, that there are fewer "unknowns" with autosomal dominant conditions. First, as shown above, there are fewer scenarios because of fewer variables: if you have one allele, you have the disorder. One's chances of being affected are greater than with autosomal recessive conditions. Moreover, an adult with an autosomal dominant condition may have symptoms or have other family members who are affected, and so the adult will know that there is a risk of passing on this allele to an offspring. In contrast, a healthy carrier of an autosomal recessive condition such as CF might not even know that the abnormal allele runs in his or her family and that he or she is a healthy carrier.

X-Linked Conditions

Now let's look at X-linked disorders, which are carried by females but actually displayed by males—generally speaking. The gene for such a disease is located on the X sex chromosome. Recall that females have two X chromosomes: they may carry the abnormal gene on one of them, while the other carries a normal version of the gene. Therefore, females rarely have symptoms of X-linked disorders; they are healthy carriers. But males generally have just one X chromosome, paired with a Y, and are therefore very likely to be symptomatic. They have no "normal" allele to offset the "abnormal" one.

One common X-linked recessive condition is hemophilia, factor VIII deficiency in particular. This condition causes abnormal clotting and bleeding, particularly into the joints. Sometimes it is diagnosed in infancy when, for example, a male child bleeds profusely after a minor procedure such as a circumcision. Another common one is Duchenne muscular dystrophy (DMD), a progressive neurological disease. These boys are born healthy but start having muscle weakness within a few years. Typically a parent complains to the physician, "Don was walking just like his sisters, then around age four he became very, very clumsy." If he has DMD, this boy will wind up in a wheelchair and will probably die by the age of thirty of respiratory failure due to muscle weakness.

X-linked disorders are generally recessive. Imagine a girl inherits an X-linked recessive condition from one parent: we will notate it as X^r, showing a recessive trait on an X chromosome. So this girl is designated X^rX. A boy with the condition is designated X^rY; he will be symptomatic. When would a girl be symptomatic with an X-linked condition? She would need to carry the trait on *both* of her X chromosomes: X^rX^r, so she would need to have inherited one abnormal allele from each parent. But if her father has X^r chromosome, then he will be affected by the condition. Historically this was a rare event because affected individuals usually died before reaching reproductive age. Let's consider the five possible scenarios.

Scenario G: Healthy carrier mother; healthy father
Scenario H: Healthy carrier mother; affected father
Scenario I: Healthy mother; affected father
Scenario J: Affected mother; affected father
Scenario K: Affected mother, healthy father

Scenario G: Healthy carrier mother, healthy father.

		Carrier mother	
		X	X^r
Healthy	X	XX	X^rX
Father	Y	XY	X^rY

Statistically speaking, if this couple has a daughter (XX or X^{r}X), she will be healthy, although she will have a one-in-two chance of being a carrier. If they have a son (XY or X^{r}Y), he has a one-in-two chance of being healthy and a one-in-two chance of being affected.

Scenario H: Healthy carrier mother, affected father.

| | | Carrier mother | |
		X	X^r
Affected	X^r	XX^r	X^{r}X^r
Father	Y	XY	X^{r}Y

A daughter of this union has a 50 percent chance of being affected and a 50 percent chance of being a carrier. (Because this is a recessive condition, and she has two X chromosomes, *both* parents must give her an abnormal allele in order for her to be symptomatic.) Her brother, too, has a 50 percent chance of being affected; because he has only one X chromosome, he needs only *one* abnormal allele to be affected. But he also has a 50 percent chance of being healthy.

Scenario I: Healthy mother, affected father.

| | | Healthy mother | |
		X	X
Affected	X^r	XX^r	XX^r
Father	Y	XY	XY

Here, notably, sons are always healthy. Indeed, an affected father cannot pass an X-linked condition to his son because he gives his son the Y chromosome! However, all of his daughters will be carriers. The daughters can only be affected if both mother and father carry the abnormal allele (see scenarios H, above, and J, below).

Scenario J: Affected mother, affected father

	Affected mother X^r	X^r
Affected X^r	X^rX^r	X^rX^r
Father Y	X^rY	X^rY

Here, all children are affected. This is an unusual scenario; rarely do women suffer from X-linked recessive conditions, and historically, affected individuals usually die before they reach reproductive age.

Finally, here is the last scenario.

Scenario K: Affected mother, healthy father

	Affected mother X^r	X^r
Healthy X	X^rX	X^rX
Father Y	X^rY	X^rY

All sons of this union will be affected, and all daughters will be carriers. This drives in the point that X-linked conditions are passed from mothers to sons. Again, this is an almost unheard of scenario.

So imagine, again, that you're a counselor at a prenatal clinic. A couple comes in; the male partner has hemophilia, an X-linked condition. What is their likelihood of having an affected child?

In this case, we know only that the man has the disease; he is X^rY. His partner might be fully healthy, with no carrier status for hemophilia. Or she may be a carrier and not know it—and keep in mind that if a family has many generations of girls, their carrier status could go undetected. Thus, this family's prospects may be scenario H (healthy carrier mother, affected father), in which case they have a 50 percent chance of having an affected son *or* an affected daughter. So girls *can* have hemophilia—but it is rare: the parents must be a reproducing hemophiliac father and a carrier mother. Or, the family may be like scenario I (healthy mother, affected father); they will have healthy sons and carrier daughters. If the male partner is affected, all of his daughters are obligate carriers. So this couple's risk depends in part on whether they have boys or girls.

The typical case in X-linked recessive conditions, then, is a healthy carrier mom and a healthy male partner (as in scenario G). Historically, before we knew where the gene was, such a couple could only be told, "All your daughters will be healthy, although half will be carriers. Half of your sons will be healthy and half will have hemophilia." The medical recommendation (if you didn't want to have a child with hemophilia), then, was to abort all male children. Now that we can perform amniocentesis and examine the X chromosome directly for an abnormal allele, we can determine whether the boy will be affected or not, and even whether the girl will be a carrier or not. Of course, now that we have pre-implantation genetic diagnosis (PGD), we can examine the fertilized eggs and only implant healthy boys and girls. Actually, since PGD bypasses the abortion issue, parents may even choose to examine the X- -chromosomes of their daughters and only implant noncarrier daughters so that these girls, as women, will not have to struggle with the risk of passing on this condition. Decisions will continue to get a lot more complicated.

So let us imagine we are back at the prenatal clinic. A young woman comes in wanting to know what she should tell her future husband about her risk. She has a brother affected with hemophilia. Both of her parents are healthy, meaning that her father is not a carrier (if he were, he would be symptomatic). What are her chances of being a carrier, and what is the couple's risk of having an affected child?

Well, the woman's mother is an obligate carrier because she has an affected son. So we are back at scenario G. What is the young woman's risk of being a healthy carrier herself? Fifty percent. And that's the information she can give her future spouse. Then, as for their risk of having an affected child: it will look exactly like the young woman's parents' situation. They have a 75 percent chance of healthy children, although statistically one of three healthy children will be a carrier daughter. But they also have a 25 percent chance of having an affected male. Of course, if she is not a carrier, their risk is zero.

That's Mendelian genetics. Today we know that there is a lot more complexity to conditions inherited in this fashion than originally understood. We also know that much of modern genetics is inherited in a post-Mendelian fashion. In the next chapter, we will fast-forward one century and explore some of these different types of inheritances.

3

From Peapods to the Human Genome Project: Post-Mendelian Genetics

Lainie Friedman Ross

Now let's turn from the nineteenth century to the twentieth century, from Mendel's peapods to the Human Genome Project. Recall that after Mendel wrote his paper on inheritance in 1865, it was lost. It was rediscovered independently by several geneticists at the turn of the century—at which point everyone started studying Mendelian genetics. Now let's fast-forward nine decades to the start of the Human Genome Project in 1990, and to modern, post-Mendelian genetics.

What changed? First, Mendel assumed that paternal alleles and maternal alleles were equivalent, but we now realize that genes "know" whether they are maternally or paternally derived. That is, some conditions only express if the abnormal allele comes from the father, others only if it comes from the mother. Second, Mendel assumed that all traits were transmitted independently. By 1911, Alfred Sturtevant realized that genes located close to each other on a chromosome were more likely to transmit together, and those that were distant would separate more independently. Third, Mendel assumed that carriers of autosomal recessive conditions were healthy—that is, completely asymptomatic—but we now know that is not always the case.

But probably most important is the realization that genetics is not merely a matter of single gene disorders or single gene traits, such as flower color and pod shape in Mendel's pea plants. Mendelian genetics is about single gene disorders. In humans there are more than 3,600 single gene disorders, but they occur in only 3 percent of all individuals born alive. These disorders are even cataloged on a website called OMIM (Online Mendelian Inheritance of Man) at http://www.ncbi.nlm.nih.gov/omim/.

But we now know that human inheritance is much more complicated. Most conditions are polygenic (involve many genes), and their expression depends upon gene-gene and environment-gene interactions. In this chapter we will consider three types of post-Mendelian genetic scenarios: (1) chromosomal variations, (2) multifactorial disorders, and (3) novel mechanisms of inheritance.

Chromosomal Variations

Although the "normal" human—or at least the average human—has 46 chromosomes, the number can sometimes vary. Some humans are born with 47, for example, those with trisomy 21 or Down syndrome. Down syndrome is associated with mental retardation as well as with some classic physical stigmata (such as a large tongue, or a simian or single crease in the palm) and an increased risk of certain conditions such as heart disease or leukemia. Others are born with 45 chromosomes, such as those with Turner syndrome. Persons with Turner syndrome have one X chromosome and no other sex chromosome. They are physically female. A baby with Turner syndrome may have a "webbed" neck at birth; as a young woman she is often short in stature and her arms may fall down at a particular angle that distinguishes her from most other women. Most will have IQs in the normal range. She will be infertile.

Remember, all 46 chromosomes are coiled up in the nucleus of every cell (except in the gametes, which have only 23 chromosomes). They are very tiny. Figure 1 pictures a healthy karyotype: a normal set of chromosomes arranged from largest to smallest with the sex chromosomes at the end.[1] How is such an image made? When one wants to examine chromosomes, for example in amniocentesis, the geneticist takes a picture of the cell's nucleus when it is dividing, when the chromosomes separate from the coil and become visible. The geneticist then literally cuts and pastes the chromosomes to count them and to examine them for morphologic abnormalities. By convention, the chromosomes are numbered from largest to smallest, with the sex chromosomes placed at the end.

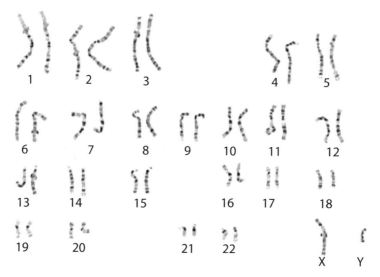

Figure 1. Normal Male Karyotype

We can tell this is the karyotype of a healthy male because it has one X and one Y. A healthy female would have two X chromosomes. Note the chromosomes numbered 21 If, instead of two chromosomes 21, there were three, that would be diagnostic of trisomy 21 or Down Syndrome (see Figure 2).[2]

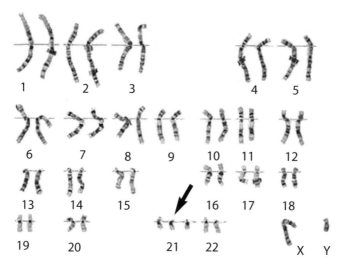

Figure 2. Karyotype of Male with Trisomy 21

Another type of abnormality is a chromosomal translocation. During meiosis, cells with 46 chromosomes divide into gamete cells with only 23 chromosomes. During the process of meiosis, each chromosome pair aligns. When they separate, they may break, and part of one chromosome may become part of a different chromosome. Figure 3 below pictures a balanced translocation. This individual has the appropriate amount of chromosomal material, and the individual will be clinically healthy.[3]

In this case, let's label the four chromosomes A, B, C, and D. (The notations "p" and "q" refer to the respective ends of a chromosome.) Remember that despite the translocation, A and B are a pair and C and D are a pair. So during meiosis—when a cell reduces from 46 to 23 chromosomes—an individual gets one chromosome from the first pair and one from the second. If the gamete gets B and D or A and C, it has the full complement of genetic material. However, if the gamete gets A and D, it has too much of chromosome 7 and too little of chromosome 21. Similarly, if the gamete gets B and C, it has too much of chromosome 21 and too little of chromosome 7. The offspring from such gametes have an unbalanced translocation.[4] If they survive in utero, they often have significant clinical problems and severe mental retardation.

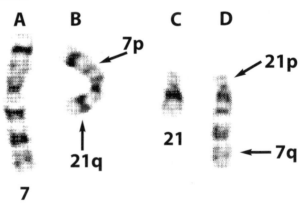

Figure 3: Balanced Translocation

Figure 3 reveals part of a karyotype in which the individual has the full complement of genetic material. The rearrangement of chromosomal material is balanced. Compare this with figure 4, which illustrates an individual who has inherited too much chromosome 7 and too little chromosome 21 from a parent whose karyotype looks like figure 3 above, and a normal chromosome 7 and 21 (E and F respectively) from another parent. The rearrangement in this individual is unbalanced.

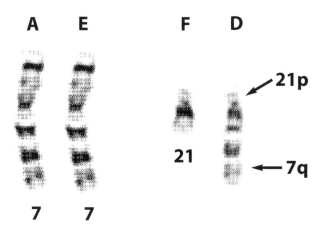

Figure 4: Unbalanced Translocation

Chromosomal abnormalities are post-Mendelian because Mendel did not know about chromosomes. Rather, he thought that all "factors," or what we now refer to as "genes," were independent. But we now know better. We have 23 sets of chromosomes and some 30,000 genes, and genes on the same chromosome often transmit dependently. (In fact, the closer that two genes are on a chromosome, the more likely it is they will transmit together.)

Multifactorial Disorders

Despite what Mendel thought, one gene does not always equal one disease. It is much more complicated than that. For example, if you want to understand your cardiovascular risk, you would probably have to look at more than 70 genes now known to be related to cardiovascular disease (CVD). Some may increase one's predisposition to heart disease, and some are protective. Some interact with each other favorably and some interact unfavorably. Some interact with the environment and then with other genes.

And yet, even if we knew all about your 70-plus relevant genes, we still couldn't tell you whether you were going to have CVD. We might be able to tell you your risk is 5 percent higher than the general population's. (And how we're going to use that information is another tricky question.) So there are many genes that can influence disease but may be neither prerequisites for the disease nor sufficient cause for it. There is no particular gene, for example, that everybody with hypertension is going to have. And in fact, someone may have hypertension despite having only genes that are thought to be protective. Environment plays a major role in the expression of many diseases. Thus, even if I know your complete genome, I will not be able to predict whether or not you will get CVD. Genes alone do not determine any diseases; rather, genes plus environment plus their interactions do.

Novel Mechanisms of Inheritance

Novel mechanisms of inheritance are rules of inheritance that are non-Mendelian. Let's look first at uniparental disomy, which occurs when an offspring receives both copies of a particular chromosome from only one of its parents. The disomy can be two copies of the *same* chromosome (isodisomy) or one copy of *each* of the given parent's chromosomes (heterodisomy). How does this happen? Imagine that when a gamete forms, one chromosome pair does not separate. Then one gamete gets two copies of chromosome 15, for example, and the other gets no copies. When one of these gametes joins with a partner's gamete (which generally has one copy of each chromosome), the zygote formed from the union of the two gametes will have three or one chromosome respectively. One of two different processes can then occur to lead to uniparental disomy: "trisomy rescue" where the loss of the extra chromosome—specifically the partner's chromosome 15—occurs after fusion of the two gametes into a zygote or early embryo; or by monosomy duplication in which the partner's single chromosome duplicates post-zygotically.

Let's consider monosomy duplication in more detail. Remember that the full instructions—all 46 chromosomes—are repeated in every cell in our body. With all that duplication, cells are going to make mistakes. Fortunately, we have repair genes: genes that notice an "A" where a "T" should be—and then correct the problem. Imagine an ovum or a sperm cell that is missing all of one chromosome (we will use chromosome 15 as our example). The repair gene notices and says, "Oops! Need another copy." And so even though the new zygote is missing a chromosome from Dad, Mom's chromosome can be replicated. This is called monosomy duplication. Now all of a sudden the zygote has 46 chromosomes, just as it needs, but with a difference: both copies of chromosome 15 are from Mom. Now, from a Mendelian perspective, that's fine: you have two copies of the factors, and all should be well. But we're not in Mendel's world—we're in a post-Mendelian world, and we know that our genes are imprinted; they know whether they come from Mom or Dad. And even if they're both healthy alleles, the body says, "Uh-oh! That's not a healthy combination."

The classic example of this is seen in the difference between Prader-Willi syndrome and Angelman syndrome. Both are due to an abnormality at the same location on chromosome 15, resulting in two very different problems. Children with Prader-Willi are born with very poor, floppy muscle tone, and they don't eat well. But as they get older, they have mental retardation as well as an uncontrollable urge to eat. On the other hand, children with Angelman syndrome are sometimes known as "happy puppets": they are mentally retarded, have no speech, but laugh a lot. They also have seizures and severe sleep disorders.

Both Prader-Willi syndrome and Angelman syndrome involve genetic defects located on the proximal arm of chromosome 15 (15p), and each can be the result of a micro-deletion (the loss of a small part of chromosome 15) or uniparental disomy. So imagine that a child is missing part (or all) of chromosome 15 inherited from Dad. Even if Mom's gene (or chromosome) replicates itself, and the zygote has two copies of the gene, they are both maternal. Imprinting means that the gene knows if it comes from Mom or Dad. And indeed, that will be an affected child. If the paternally inherited chromosome 15 is lacking, the child will have Prader-Willi syndrome; if the maternally inherited chromosome 15 is lacking, Angelman syndrome is the result.

These two diseases dramatize the fact that genes remember if they came from Mom or Dad. And even more amazing, if a female child with Prader-Willi—which is caused by lacking the paternal copy of the gene—were to reproduce and her children were to inherit this micro-deletion, the deletion would now be maternal—and her children would suffer from Angelman syndrome. That's the extent to which the genes remember their origins.

Our understanding of imprinting is relatively new. Consider the following case: Johnny is a three-year-old with cystic fibrosis (CF). Through genetic testing, we learn that Johnny has two copies of ∆F508, the most common genetic defect in CF. From classic Mendelian genetics, we know that Johnny must have two copies of the abnormal gene—one from each parent—since CF is an autosomal recessive disorder.

Now Johnny's parents get divorced. Johnny's father and his new partner go for genetic counseling regarding their risk for having a child with CF. But genetic testing reveals that Johnny's father is not a carrier. He wonders whether he's still obligated to pay child support. Johnny's mother is irate. She denies infidelity. So how can Johnny have CF if his father is not a carrier? Certainly, it *could* be misattributed paternity. It could be that Johnny's dad is not Johnny's biological dad. But there's another possibility: Johnny could have simply inherited both chromosomes 7 from his mother. Other chromosomal testing would prove or disprove that Johnny's dad is his biological father.

Unfortunately, this understanding is recent. In past decades, misattributed paternity may have been erroneously assumed in autosomal recessive conditions when dad was not a carrier simply because it was the only known explanation in a situation like Johnny's.

Triplet Repeat Expansions

Of the several diseases in this category, the best known is Huntington's disease. Some genes have a number of nucleotide base repeats. The gene responsible for Huntington's has repeats of the nucleotide sequence CAG. Normally the gene has only a few such sequences (3–5). If the gene has more than 40 CAG sequences (a triplet repeat), the individual will develop Huntington's disease. It also turns out that if the gene has many CAG repeats, it is prone to add even more repeats (triplet repeat expansion), and the more repeats, the more severe the disease in terms of onset and course of illness. Huntington's disease also demonstrates genetic imprinting—meaning that cells "know" if the gene comes from Mom or Dad (discussed above). If you get the Huntington gene from your father, there is a greater likelihood of an increased number of repeats and that your disease will present earlier and more severely. In contrast, if you get the gene from your mother, the genetic expression will probably be milder. (Thank God there's something we don't get to blame on moms.)

Another condition based on triplet repeat expansions is known as fragile X, which is found on the X chromosome. It consists of more than 200 repeats of the trinucleotide sequence CGG. If boys inherit the fragile X chromosome—and remember boys only have one X chromosome—they will be mentally retarded. But in this case there is a carrier state in which some female carriers of fragile X actually also have some degree of mental retardation. Why? One answer is the Lyon hypothesis, which states that in every cell in females, only one of her two X chromosomes is active. Imagine a woman who has one normal X chromosome and one abnormal. If all the abnormal X's happen to be activated in the brain, it means that in the brain, the fragile X is giving the instructions. Then she may have mental retardation. But if all the active fragile X genes are in the kidneys, they're going to have less impact.

Another noteworthy point: Not all genetic material is found in the nucleus; some DNA is found outside the nucleus in the mitochondria (the cell's power source). It comes from the mother in both boys and girls. There are a few rare mitochondrial disorders, which can be prevented by transferring the nucleus of the embryo into another oocyte (female gamete). This technique is called nuclear transfer and is necessary for cloning—another subject altogether. In this case, however, the embryo will have genetic material from three sources: nuclear genetic material from both original parents and mitochondrial DNA from the oocyte into which the nucleus is transferred. This suggests three biological parents—and a Brave New World.

Clinical Genetics

Let us move to a brief survey of clinical genetics: testing, therapies, and some preliminary ethical questions. First, how do we do genetic testing? We can perform genetic testing by looking at chromosomes—but the translation of one's genotype (genetic code) into phenotype (outward physical appearance) is not straightforward. For example, some phenotypic women are genetically male (XY). They have what is called androgen insensitivity syndrome or testicular feminization. These women tend to be tall and thin. They are also infertile. They are phenotypically female because they do not respond to testosterone. All fetuses begin as female, and exposure and responsiveness to testosterone is what makes boys become phenotypic boys (i.e., have a scrotum and penis). Women with androgen insensitivity are unresponsive to testosterone even as fetuses in utero. So these women make large amount of testosterone, but they cannot respond to it, so these fetuses remain female. For example, a women who is XY would fail a Barr body test (a genetic test for gender, explained below), although physically she would look female. The take-home message, then, is that genetics and the translation of genotype into phenotype is quite complex.

We can also perform genetic testing by looking at the genes within the chromosomes or by looking at metabolites, or the gene's product. For example, we can test for cystic fibrosis by measuring the saltiness of a person's sweat. People with CF have very salty sweat. So we don't necessarily have to look at your chromosomes or your genes; we can look at the metabolites they create—such as excess salt in sweat. Genetic testing, as you can see, is not physically risky at all. At most it requires a simple blood test, or maybe a swab from the inside of your cheek, or maybe a sample of your sweat. And so the risks of genetic testing are not physical; rather, the risks lie in how this information gets used—the psychosocial, ethical, and legal implications—and those questions are fascinatingly complex.

When do we do genetic testing? Sometimes we do it on healthy people to understand, for example, their risk of heart disease, or for developing Huntington's disease. We may do it for women or couples to determine their risk of having an affected child (reproductive risks). And finally, we test the symptomatic—for example, a clumsy child whose parents say he used to walk just fine. But we also do genetic testing for nonmedical purposes. Genetic testing can be performed to rule out a criminal suspect when the criminal has left genetic material at the scene (for example, fluids associated with a rape). It has also been used inaccurately to determine gender by the International Olympics Committee (IOC). Let me explain in more detail.

In the mid-1960s, the IOC began to test Olympic athletes for gender. The initial test was a physical exam, but this led to widespread criticism by the athletes and the public, so the IOC began genetic testing in 1968 using a Barr body test. Recall that in each cell of a typical woman there are two X chromosomes, one of which is inactive. The inactive X chromosome appears as a Barr body—a dense stainable structure that can be seen with light microscopy. The existence of a Barr body was used as proof of female gender for the Olympics. But it is inaccurate as some women (women with Turner syndrome or testicular feminization) do not have a second X-chromosome. And some individuals could be phenotypically (physically) male and have a Barr body (for example, men with 47 chromosomes, XXY).

What is also critical to remember is that our ability to test is much, much further advanced than our ability to treat. In fact, it is much, much further advanced than our ability even to know what it means. Consider, for example, a new technology called tandem mass spectrometry—a method by which we can examine hundreds of metabolites at a time for a small incremental increase in financial cost. The problem is that even if we determine that an individual has an abnormal metabolic profile, we may not know what it means. For example, imagine that we find a person has an increased histidine level (an amino acid that is necessary for making more complex protein). What does it mean? Well, the answer is ambiguous: some people with abnormal histidine levels are mentally retarded, but many are asymptomatic. And if we advised everyone with high histidine levels to go on a histidine-restricted diet, it would cause *more* mental retardation, as children cannot produce adequate histidine except through their diet. This illustrates that we do not necessarily know what to do with some of the information we are getting. In some cases, we don't even know if the abnormality is clinically relevant or simply a normal variant. Indeed, we have reasons to be wary of genetic testing at this time.

We also have reason to be wary about gene therapy. Hundreds of experimental trials on gene therapy have already been done on thousands of subjects. Jesse Gelsinger made headline news in 1999 because he died secondary to a gene transfer experiment. So have others. And the number of successes are very few. One major success was in April 2000, when doctors Alain Fischer and Marina Cavazzana-Calvo at the Necker Children's Hospital in Paris announced that they had used gene therapy to successfully insert corrective genes into the bone marrow stem cells of two babies with a form of X-linked severe combined immunodeficiency syndrome (SCID). Such children historically have lived in a bubble or died of infection in infancy.

Prior to this historic milestone, there was some treatment for children with a particular form of SCID called adenosine deaminase deficiency (ADA). ADA is one of the genetic causes of severe combined immune deficiency, and an enzyme replacement therapy called PEG-ADA has had some clinical efficacy. Alternatively, such children have been treated by bone marrow transplantation from a histocompatible sibling. The first gene transfer trial ever performed was done for two children with ADA deficiency at the National Institutes of Health in 1990. The approach was to target mature peripheral blood T-cells rather than bone marrow stem cells. A retroviral vector was used to transfer the ADA gene into the T-cells. The children continued to receive ADA; doctors were afraid to discontinue it and then see them die of a severe infection. But the experiments in France, later replicated in the United Kingdom and the United States, have been successful without additional therapy.[5]

Although gene therapy is in its infancy, that doesn't mean that if you have a genetic condition there is nothing medicine can offer. People with sickle-cell anemia live a lot longer than they used to because we're better at treating vaso-occlusive crises (VOC), which occur when the blood sickles and occludes the blood vessels, causing infarctions or obstructions. There are even some drugs that people can take to try to reduce their risk of having a VOC. Giving penicillin to children with sickle cell anemia has cut their mortality rate drastically; such children used to die from infections in the first years of life. And we're much better at treating lung problems in people with cystic fibrosis. We give them vitamins and other nutrients to overcome some of their gastrointestinal problems. So we have dietary solutions, we have medical solutions—many traditional medical treatments for genetic disorders.

Why do we do genetic testing? Again, we may do it to make a clinical diagnosis, to assess reproductive risks, or to provide people with personalized predictive risk assessments for particular conditions or diseases. Let's consider predictive genetic testing in depth; this is the most controversial because it is not inherently clinically relevant but has important psychosocial and reproductive implications. Predictive genetic testing may be *predispositional*—that is, it is meant to determine if an individual is at higher risk than the general population. For example, women with the BRCA1 gene—which is an autosomal dominant gene—have an 85 percent chance of developing breast cancer. If we were in the Mendelian world, we would believe that the gene confers the disease: if you have the breast cancer gene, you would get breast cancer. But in fact we do not live in a Mendelian world, and so we need a more nuanced point of view. We can calculate that although you have this autosomal dominant gene, your chance of developing breast cancer (by age 85) is 85 percent, compared to an 11 percent chance in the general population.

Presymptomatic testing is done to determine the presence of genes that do, almost 100 percent of the time, predict the disease. Huntington's disease is the perfect example, because over 99 percent of all people with the gene get the disease. But even then, it's not 100 percent—what we've learned is that nothing is 100 percent in genetics: genes are not deterministic. So even if you have this autosomal dominant gene, you do not necessarily get the disease.

Penetrance is the percentage of individuals with an abnormal or mutant gene who develop the disease. Whereas Mendel thought if you had the gene, you would have the disease; we now know that your chance may be as low as 30 percent and as high as almost 100 percent. Expressivity refers to the marked variation in clinical features by the same gene—even the same mutation, even within the same family. Let me explain. It turns out that sickle cell disease is a genetically simple disease because there is one change in one nucleotide in the whole gene. This change causes a single amino acid difference between a normal and abnormal allele. If you have one abnormal allele, then you're a sickle cell carrier; and if you have the change in both copies of your genes, you have sickle cell disease. But some people have a quite mild form of the disease, and others quite severe—even though they all have the same mutation.

In cystic fibrosis, by contrast, there are over 1,000 variations of abnormal alleles. And it turns out that some of those variations can cause severe disease. However, knowing which mutations an individual has does not necessarily tell us whether the individual will have a severe or mild form of the disease because two people with the same genetic mutation can have very different expressions. One person can be severely affected and, for example, present in the newborn period with an ileus—which is when your stools get really hard and block your intestines. This can lead to perforation of the intestines, even in utero, which can kill a fetus. The other person may not have any symptoms except for being a little small and having frequent colds as a child. Same mutation, same family—different expression of the disease. Some CF mutations are known to be much less severe than others and some, for example, only present as male infertility. These individuals may not even realize they have this CF variant unless unless they're trying to conceive. So, some genetic diseases have one mutation (SCA), some have a thousand mutations (CF), and the genotype does not accurately predict phenotype.

Now you understand why most doctors do not understand this stuff—it's complex. For almost every question you ask the doctor about a genetic disease, the answer is, correctly, "It depends." Any other answer is simply wrong. Well, that's not very satisfying to a patient. You want some certainty and all you hear is, "It depends, it depends, maybe. . . ." You feel like you're not getting very far.

But let's look at genetic testing in pediatrics, which certainly can be useful. For example, testing children at birth for sickle-cell disease lets us identify those who need penicillin prophylaxis. With cystic fibrosis, however, it is less obvious whether early treatment reduces mortality, and thus, whether CF screening should be part of newborn screening. This question was first raised in the 1980s when Wisconsin initiated a statewide newborn screening experiment to see if children who were treated early would do better. Newborn screening was done experimentally. Five years and millions of dollars later, the research did not show decreased mortality. But, as is typical of all good institutions, once the infrastructure is in place, it tends to stay there, and testing continued despite the inconclusive results. Today this testing is mandatory in some states, such as Wisconsin, despite the lack of definitive data to show that early testing reduces morbidity and mortality. Actually, recent data are encouraging. In 2001, it was shown that the kids who were diagnosed before they became symptomatic tend to be a little fatter and a little taller than their nonpresymptomatically diagnosed peers with CF.

So is it advantageous to diagnose children with CF presymptomatically? The jury is still out. There may be some slight clinical advantage in determining that these children have CF even before they become symptomatic. But we need to consider all of the risks *and* all of the benefits. Not only that, beyond the clinical ones, we need to consider the psychosocial and reproductive risks and benefits. Do you want to know that your newborn has been found to have CF? Or would you rather be happily ignorant until your child becomes symptomatic? How will this knowledge affect the way you treat this child? How will it influence your future reproductive decisions? Will you inform family members? And how will it affect the way they treat your child? It also turns out that the most effective way to screen for CF is to measure the amount of trypsinogen in the blood and to look for certain abnormal CF alleles. As such, CF screening identifies healthy carriers (children who have the trait). Such children screen positive, and they are only differentiated from children with CF disease by follow-up testing. This "false positive" testing has led to some significant psychological stress in some families. It also identifies carrier status in the child and at least one parent, which may or may not be information that the parents wanted.

If newborn screening for CF is controversial, consider that in Wales voluntary newborn screening of boys is done for Duchenne muscular dystrophy (DMD), an X-linked condition for which there is no treatment. These boys will become clumsy by the age of four to six, in wheelchairs in their teen years, and dead before they're thirty. The knowledge confers no medical advantage for the kids (at least currently), but much food for thought for these parents. Do they want to have further children? Or more specifically, do they want to risk having more male children? (Daughters will be healthy, although half will be carriers.) Or do they want to adopt, or try in vitro fertilization, or use a donated egg. . . . There are many possibilities.

The questions are, first, how will families use this information? Second, do the clinical, psychosocial, and reproductive benefits outweigh the clinical, psychosocial, and reproductive risks? And third, do families want this information? And will their attitude change if treatment becomes available?

As if these questions weren't complicated enough, when you introduce the question of health insurance, the situation is even more troubling. Will your insurance company say, "Since you agreed to get prenatal testing and you now know your child has cystic fibrosis, will this be considered a preexisting condition if your child is born?" I hope not. It would conflate eliminating the disease and eliminating the child. In Wales, where newborn DMD testing is offered, there is national health insurance, so insurance is less of an issue, although it is still relevant for life insurance.

Ethical and Policy Issues

When I present clinical cases, I often begin by providing an overview of seven ethical and policy questions raised by genetic testing and the resulting information.

1. Who are the appropriate decision makers?
2. When is the appropriate time for testing?
3. Which genetic tests should be required? Encouraged? Permitted? Discouraged?

4. Whose interests should be considered in the decision? (Remember, families share genes.)
5. Disclosure issues: Privacy for whom? Confidentiality from whom? Is there ever a duty to disclose? And if so, to whom?
6. Is genetic information different from other medical information? And if so, how?
7. Do we have obligations to be tested, or to refrain from being tested, because of the needs and interests of our family? Of our communities?

For me, the crux of these seven questions lies in a broader issue: whether, and to what extent, genetic relations create moral obligations. In other words, does the fact—or *should* the fact—that you are biologically or genetically related to someone morally entitle that person to some input into your own decision to undergo testing? What are the implications for your family and community if you decide to undergo genetic screening for the breast cancer gene? Clearly, if you are tested, this information will be relevant to your twin sister. It will also say something about one of your parents, and it could say something about the risks of your children. So should you consider these people's perspectives and opinions in your decision? And should they be a part of the decision-making process?

These questions depart sharply from the traditional bioethics model, which assumes a private interaction between physician and patient. In fact, the traditional bioethics model places the patient and physician in a soundproof room in which together they decide what is best for the patient—with no consideration of the people outside of that room. And I argue that this model doesn't work for many decisions, and that genetics is forcing us to realize that. But it's not unique to genetics. Elsewhere, I have argued that relationships create moral obligations that are not unique to genetic testing. Think about it with regard to living-donor organ transplantation. Are you obligated to give a kidney to your brother? And if so, is it just because he's your brother and his body will tolerate your kidney immunologically? And if the answer is yes, it can easily lead to an argument that we also have obligations to strangers.

The *New York Times* reported a story in 2000 that dramatizes this point.[6] An Orthodox rabbi from Brooklyn had preliminary testing to serve as a bone marrow donor because there were two people in the

Orthodox Jewish community in New Jersey who needed bone marrow. Although he was not a match, his name and work-up were placed on the international bone marrow registry. A year later he got a call from the bone marrow bank. The caller said, "We have a match—not anybody you know. Would you agree to be a donor?" The rabbi did, and the transplant was successful. And eight years later, the two finally met. The recipient was now fifteen, an Italian boy who had been treated in Seattle at the age of seven. The boy and his family are from a small town in Italy of about 800 people, and they decided to invite this rabbi to visit. And the story was beautiful. The family went out of their way to provide him with kosher food and so on.

So here we have an Orthodox rabbi who hoped he was going to be immunologically compatible with two sick Jewish individuals in New Jersey and found instead that he was compatible with a little Catholic boy from a small town in Italy. And so the question becomes, do we have obligations based purely on genetics? And if so, are we equally obligated to our brother and to an unknown person on another continent?

I would actually say there is some degree of moral obligation within families. But even within families, it is not a strict moral obligation; it's not a perfect duty. And yet I find it much harder to argue that we have even an imperfect moral obligation to donate to strangers. The story of the rabbi, however, shows that we can have surprising genetic relations—that is, we find ourselves histocompatible, immunologically compatible, with people we might not expect. What is the medical relevance of this? Organ transplantation works best when individuals share the major histocompatible antigens. Still, unless the donor and recipient are identical twins, they will not share all of the minor histocompatibility antigens, and the recipient will need to take anti-rejection medication. The closer we are immunologically or genetically to each other the less anti-rejection medicine is needed and the more likely the organ is to survive.

Remarkably, two people who are remote geographically can be very close genetically. Does that imply, perhaps, that the rabbi and the little boy share an ancestor? It could. The rabbi was Sephardic, so their ancestors could indeed have come from a similar region. But it could also be pure chance.

Just to complicate further the moral picture, potential donors must also consider their own risk in donating. Donating bone marrow is safer than donating a kidney, which is safer than donating part of your liver. Some donors die from the procedure. As such, potential organ donors must ask what are their larger spheres of accountability. For example, should a person agree to donate to one of her children if she is a single mother with several children? And how do you reassure her that she's still a good mom if she doesn't donate because, in fact, she wants to protect herself for the sake of her other children?

We should also note that genetic information is not symmetrical: it gives us information about ourselves, our parents, and our offspring— real or potential—with varying degrees of accuracy. For example, if I am tested and learn that I have an autosomal dominant allele, that means I inherited it from one of my parents. If I have the disease and I know which one of my parents has the disease, it is clear. But what if my parent and I are currently asymptomatic? What if I have undergone predictive genetic testing to determine whether I carry the abnormal allele for an autosomal dominant disorder such as Huntington's disease because of an affected grandparent? If I am negative, we still do not know whether or not my parent carries the allele. But if I am positive, we have just diagnosed one of my parents. (Unless, of course, I got it from a random mutation—possible but highly unlikely.) In contrast, we have only learned something tentative about my children: that they have a 50 percent chance of having the gene. Thus, genetic relationships are not symmetrical: in this case, if I am positive, I know something with 100 percent confidence about a parent, but I can only calculate odds about a child—50 percent in this case. If I am negative, there is ambiguity about my parent but 100 percent certainty that my children will be unaffected.

So one of the questions arising from the clinical cases is this: With whom does one have an obligation to share genetic information? Imagine, for example, a boy is diagnosed with Duchenne muscular dystrophy (DMD). Since it is X-linked, Mom is an obligate carrier. That means that *her* mother was a carrier and therefore that her sisters have a 50 percent chance of being carriers. Does she have an obligation to inform her mother? How about her sisters?

Let's consider her mother first. What factors are relevant? Is her mother past childbearing age? Will she feel devastated by something that she couldn't control? Guilty? What about her mother's other relatives? She could have a sister with daughters of childbearing age. And if Mom has it, that means Grandma has it, and this could have implications for our patient's maternal first cousins. And it might be that one of *her* Grandmother's sisters has it, and this could have implications for her maternal second cousins, people she may not know. Genetics makes us realize that we are connected even if we are not socially connected. This information may be useful to cousins whom she has never met. Since the woman is an obligate carrier, it means that her mother is an obligate carrier, which means that her mother's sister has a 50 percent chance of carrying it, which means her female first cousins have a 25 percent chance of carrying it. That's a pretty high likelihood. So it's not just about Mom. That's why genetics is all about families and communities: you can't just think nuclear.

Nor are genetic relationships themselves symmetrical. What does this mean? Consider siblings. Because you and your siblings both get one set of chromosomes from Mom and one set from Dad, you can either get the same chromosomes and be 100 percent histocompatible, or you can be 50 percent, or 0 percent. But you share 50 percent of your genetic material with each of your parents, no more, no less. So, the fact is genetically you may be more similar to your siblings than you are to your parents. Or you may be totally dissimilar. But the fact is the closest genetic matches are between siblings, and this is why transplant surgeons prefer kidney donations from qualified siblings rather than from parents.

And while parents often feel they have a moral obligation to serve as donors to their children—and I would argue that morally they do have an imperfect obligation to the children they bring into this world—the question remains, do we have moral obligations to our siblings? Remember, we were never consulted about their existence. So with my brothers, I didn't ask for them to be born into the same family in which I live—and yet here we are, united because our parents decided to share genes with us. If I'm 100 percent histocompatible with my brother, the transplant surgeon wants *me,* and not my parents, to donate. So do I owe my brother a kidney?

Let's also consider some of the issues that are raised when genetic relationships do not entail social relationships. We'll look again at Duchenne muscular dystrophy (DMD). This time, however, rather than asking whether parents should be allowed to get predictive information about their child, let's examine the more extended family. Imagine adult half sisters—they have the same mother and different fathers, born years apart in different cities. The children from the first marriage live with their father and because of distance do not really know their mother. Then the first daughter has a son who is diagnosed with DMD. Now recall that DMD is X-linked, which means that Mom is an obligate carrier, albeit unknowingly, and her daughters from her second marriage are also at risk of being healthy carriers. What obligation does this daughter have to her estranged mother? To her half sisters whom she has never met?

In philosophy (and in the law), we speak of a concept called "the duty to warn." This duty states that I have a duty to warn you when I create an imminent direct risk of harm to you. But the fact is—is it a harm if one of her half sisters gives birth to a child with a disability? The child otherwise would not have been born. Is it a harm or not? And have I done the potential mother a harm by not giving her the option of choosing whether or not to give birth to a child with a disability? And from the child's perspective, is it a harm? Could not the child think that it is better to have a short good life than no life at all? We must also consider the harm that such knowledge may cause. The potential mother may prefer not to know the health problems her future children could have. She may believe that it would be better to enjoy the first four years of this child's life than to receive a call from an unknown or estranged relative and be told about this risk. Imagine that she is pregnant and how the information may take away from her enjoyment of her pregnancy. Or imagine that the relative locates her when she is nursing her one-week-old son. When she shares this family history information with her pediatrician at the next well-child visit, the pediatrician may offer testing. If she consents to testing and her son is found to have the gene, what impact will this have on their relationship? Clearly, this information will color her experiences although he will be asymptomatic for the next four years. And even if she decides against testing, the knowledge can have an impact on their relationship: How will she interpret his falling at the playground? Will she worry if this is normal toddler clumsiness versus the onset of muscular dystrophy?

Some would argue that if the woman does not disclose the genetic information to her estranged family that she has made decisions for them that are not hers to make. But has she really made decisions for them? On one level, yes, but on another level, no. First, the woman did not cause her mother or sisters to have this abnormal gene. Second, any woman can ask to be tested for a myriad of conditions and therefore know whether her future children are at risk for a particular condition. Currently, however, it would be unlikely for an obstetrician to suggest testing for Duchenne muscular dystrophy to a woman who comes in without a family history.

Even if one decides that she does have a moral obligation, it is not clear that we would want to impose a legal obligation. It gets complicated and tricky, in part because legal families unbind (for example, divorce and death) and in part because families, even intimate families, do not do a great job of communicating. It would require significant intrusion by the state to enforce intrafamilial communication. And the question remains, How far do these obligations to warn extend? It is one thing to suggest that I have a duty to warn a sibling who lives in the next community, but do I have a duty to warn relatives I have never met? And if so, how do we ensure that I have accounted for all of my relatives? And at what level of risk does the obligation no longer hold? How do we draw this line, and why?

The questions raised by the Human Genome Project are complicated because they must take into account individuals and their families and communities of varying degree of intimacy and genetic relatedness. Nevertheless, the Human Genome Project has made it clear that a medical ethics paradigm that places exclusive focus on the doctor-patient relationship is inadequate, and that we must consider the doctor-patient relationship within the wider communities in which this relationship occurs.

PART TWO

BEING HUMAN

4

Theological Anthropology and the Human Genome Project

Theodore W. Jennings Jr.

The task of gaining some preliminary clarity about the relevance of the Human Genome Project to theological anthropology—and vice versa—is a daunting but important one. It is important because of the extraordinary scientific breakthroughs of the last few years, some of which have captured headlines and media attention with their promise of unraveling a number of mysteries about human beings, posing a number of ethical dilemmas that seem to require urgent attention.

On the other hand, it is daunting because these developments are so recent, the areas to be explored so vast, and the level of current knowledge still so schematic and even sketchy, that we may expect significant revisions in what we now think is known. These revisions, too, may occur quickly, in the course of the next few years and even months.[1] Thus a theological interpretation of the scientific community's own interpretation of this new data and perspective can at best be tentative and exploratory.

This chapter will not comment on the specific ethical dilemmas that most often grab the headlines: those that bear upon screening for particular genes for medical, insurance, or employment prospects; the possibility of cloning; or even, save indirectly, on the questions of ownership of information on human genetic makeup. In theological ethics, it is generally unwise to approach specific ethical dilemmas in the absence of a wider perspective that will help reveal what may be at stake or even how a particular issue may be helpfully framed. Moreover, theological ethics is productively conceived not as problem solving but as forming a worldview and a set of dispositions that enable believers to respond to their world in ways that embody basic faith values.

Theology and Science

In the face of both the importance and the difficulty of this challenge, it may be helpful to recall some basic principles that generally guide the relation of theology to science. In the first place, we may insist upon the relevance of scientific exploration and interpretation for theological reflection.

Since the earliest beginnings of Christian theological reflection (with relatively few but glaring exceptions), theologians have supposed that it was an essential aspect of their work to positively relate the exposition and explication of Christian doctrine to the insights and perspectives of what until quite recently was called "natural philosophy."

The reason for this is quite simply that Christian theology is concerned with a truthful, reliable, and plausible interpretation of the world and of the human being's place in it. For Christian doctrine or teaching to be intelligible, it must be articulated within the languages people use to make sense of their world, their surroundings, their existence.

Moreover, the "confidence ingredient" in faith is that it applies to the heart or center of reality, not to a private esoteric sphere hidden from view. Indeed, Christian theology has, for the most part, affirmed the natural world as the sphere of divine care and affirmation, in creation, incarnation, and redemption.

It is salutary to recall this, since one all-too-common feature of modern theology has been a gnostic retreat from the world—the natural world especially, but very often the historical and social world as well. Certain forms of pietism retreat from the world, leaving politics, economics, history, and science to their own devices. In some early twentieth-century theologies, we again see an essentially gnostic withdrawal from any interpretation of the natural (or even historical) world; I think for example of Tillich or Bultmann. Indeed, there is a marked tendency to suppose that science and religion are distinct and mutually impermeable spheres of interpretation and understanding. [2] This is conditioned by an understandable if regrettable reaction to modern fundamentalism, which seemed to offer a revealed pseudo-science as an antidote to emergent modern science. Often this was seen, at least among the university educated, as a losing proposition. Fundamentalism made faith implausible to those who were convinced by paradigms of knowledge, understanding, and interpretation developed under the aegis of modern science. At one level, of course, one may suppose that religious fundamentalism was no more than a reaction to an equally ignorant scientistic fundamentalism, one that regarded itself as the bearer of irreversible and immutable truth—as the mechanism of a literal "revelation" of the truth understood as univocal and immutable. That is a science in denial about its own nature.[3]

The relation between theology and natural science is not one of identity (nor is it of opposed identities in which theology is compelled simply to accept the dictates of scientific revelation). Nor is it one of mutual irrelevance ("You deal with facts, we deal with meanings"). Rather, I think, it is best understood in terms of what, in a somewhat different context, Karl Barth called the analogy of faith. That is, as the interpretation or even the construction of Christian doctrine, theology may be attentive to new perspectives on the world, perhaps finding analogies that illumine faith or that provoke its clarification.

Most of the difficulties between science and theology in the modern period have arisen not because theology was opposed to science as such, but because it sought to defend one science against another; because it had adapted too literally to one scientific worldview, which it then sought to defend against another. Think, for example, of the attempt to defend Ptolemaic science against Copernican science (or Galileo's argument for it); or the attempt to buttress a Babylonian worldview against an evolutionary one. The same may be true of those theologians who defended Aristotelian natural philosophy against later scientific perspectives. Often, I am suggesting, the difficulties are caused by a too-close identification with science (at a particular stage), not by a refusal of science altogether.

Where does the answer lie? Not in the abandonment of the theological task of interpreting the natural world in conversation with the then current knowledge—the gnostic or even existentialist approach. Nor is it in a literal appropriation of the latest science or conformity thereto. It lies in the ongoing willingness to seek analogies for understanding and interpretation in the work of scientists, people who also are concerned to understand the world in which we live: the same world that is for the theologian, as Calvin said, the "theater of the glory of God."

The Insight of Gregory of Nyssa

A selection from Gregory of Nyssa is, to my mind, an exemplary illustration of this approach. In Nyssa's text "On the Making of Man," there is a remarkable coherence with some of the themes suggested by the Human Genome Project.

Gregory of Nyssa was one of the most important of the early theologians of the church. Together with Gregory Nazianzan and Basil "the Great," he was one of the Cappadocian Fathers responsible for the formulations of Trinitarian and christological doctrine during the fourth century. The text "On the Making of Man" is one I have used for thirty years in teaching theological anthropology. It represents the best thinking on the subject at the most creative period of Christian theology in the first millennium of theology.

The text also represents one of the most curious and perhaps fatal accidents of theological reflection. Basil had begun a wonderful reflection on the Hexammeron, the six days of creation from Genesis, thereby valorizing one particular text, the first chapter of Genesis, as a starting point for theology's reflection on the world and on humanity. This was not by any means so obvious a choice as it perhaps now seems. It was a brilliant piece of theological construction. However, it was unfinished.

Fatefully, Basil only completed his reflection on the first five and a half days of creation before he died. Hence Gregory undertook, as a work of love for his elder colleague, to complete the work by a reflection on the second half of the sixth day of creation: on the making of man. This had the rather unintended but fateful consequence of separating reflection on theological anthropology from reflection on the natural world. Since Gregory's text was the very first attempt at such a theological anthropology, and since his reputation as one of the greatest of all theologians would guarantee the study of this text, it was made to seem possible to reflect on theological anthropology without adequate attention to the world of nature within which the human being lived (or vice versa).

Nevertheless, Gregory's interpretation of human origin, nature, and so on is exemplary in that he consistently seeks to relate his view of the human being to whatever was then known about the human being as a part of the natural world.

Gregory does not do this slavishly, in the sense of trying to maintain that whatever was then known about human beings was already clearly specified in the Bible. But nor does he suppose that the explication of the biblical text was irrelevant to then current knowledge. He is not a literalist in either direction but one who interprets across fields of knowledge back and forth, seeking a way of articulating Christian faith within the language of the best knowledge then available. Thus he reminds the reader, "We, imagining the truth, as far as we can, by means of conjectures and similitudes, do not set forth that which occurs to our mind authoritatively but will place it in the form of a theoretical speculation before our kindly readers."[4]

It is in this spirit that Gregory explores the specific features of the human organism. Examining the links between human physiology and the faculty of reason, he engages in some interesting reflections on hands and vocal cords, for example. A few brief citations may help to recall the character of his reflections. After noting the human animal's upright posture, which allows the "foremost limbs" to develop as hands, Gregory notes: "Especially do these ministering hands adapt themselves to the requirements of reason; indeed if one were to say that the ministration of hands is a special property of the rational nature, he would not be entirely wrong."[5] This he then relates to the human facial structure, noting that unlike other animals humans need not use their heads to graze or to kill prey: "Nature added [hands] to our body preeminently for the sake of reason. For if man were desti- tute of hands the various parts of his face would have been arranged like those of the quadrupeds, to suit the purpose of his feeding."[6] The difference in the shape of the head then makes it possible to develop finely tuned "vocal organs" in order to communicate thought: "The human mind being a discoverer of all sorts of conceptions, seeing that it is unable, by the mere presence of soul, to reveal to those who hear by bodily senses the motions of its understanding, touches, like some skillful composer, these animated instruments, and makes known its hidden thoughts by means of the sound produced upon them."[7]

One can see in this selection Gregory's remarkable discussion of the way in which the whole of the human body is adapted for reason, which he took to be the distinguishing mark of the human being. Of course he has not forgotten to insist that the human being is also con- stituted to partake of plant and animal nature as well. In the develop- ment of his ideas, he explicitly refers to the "skilled physicians" who contribute to such knowledge.[8] He even reflects on what can be known or surmised about sleep, yawning, and dreams.[9]

Bringing Theology to the Human Genome Project

Gregory looked for analogies in the "science" of his day in order to articulate, even to create, Christian teaching. I suggest we do the same in our own time with respect to emerging genetic science generally and the Human Genome Project in particular.

Three analogies are perhaps the most fruitful and important in this investigation. These three initial areas that are crucial for theological anthropology are:

1. Solidarity: The cohesiveness of human life with all other forms of life; the oneness of human creatures with all other creatures.

2. Speciation: The unity of human beings as a species against all attempts to divide humanity, that is, the species-specific identity of human beings without which neither fall nor redemption can be adequately conceived.

3. Individuation: The astonishing variability of the human being, or what might be called, for lack of a better term, individuation within the species identity.

Let us examine these three points more closely.

Solidarity

I have already indicated that the separation of theological anthropology from a theological reflection on the natural world could have and often has had gravely damaging consequences for theology generally. Gregory guards against such separation, however, seeking at every stage to see the human creature as a part of the natural order and especially as part of what we today might term the biosphere.

Too often theological anthropology has given short shrift to what may be called human creatureliness, in favor of moving rapidly to an ill-conceived doctrine of the imago Dei, which is then understood as separating the human being from other creatures. In consequence the specificity of human being is understood as opposed to, and as separating human being from, creaturely existence. Hence the attempt to locate the image of God in what cannot be found in creatures generally: the faculty of reason in particular.

One of the most telling aspects of genetic research is that humans hold so much of their genetic profile in common with even the lowliest forms of life—by all accounts well over half. Human being is deeply embedded within the world of all creatures. Less than 2 percent of our genes separate us from our nearest animal relatives, and (if genes are but a tiny fraction of DNA, then) an incredibly tiny amount of our actual DNA may be regarded as species specific.

Whatever else we are, we are quite simply an integral piece of the whole biosphere. The haste with which theologians have emphasized what divides us from creation, as opposed to what we share with creation, has deeply distorted theological anthropology. Creatureliness has too seldom been a theme in its own right. We all recognize the way in which modern consciousness has used this distortion to justify the separation of humanity from the ecology of its earthly life. Indeed, this distortion may permit our techno-domination of the planet in ways that are quite likely to make it uninhabitable for us; it has already resulted in the extermination of untold myriads of life forms.

Gregory recognizes that human creatures are still creatures and, moreover, that our specialness does not separate us from other creatures. He emphasizes our dependence upon them as a call to mutual benefit and care.[10] By contrast, let us note the gnostic tendencies apparent in Tillich's and Niebuhr's casting of creatureliness as an adjunct to fallenness—reflecting their own modernist and existentialist presuppositions. Tillich sees creatureliness as a fall from essence while Niebuhr regards it as the inherently unstable paradox of finite freedom. Both tend to see creatureliness as a problem rather than as the supreme gift: a place within a larger and miraculous web of life.[11]

Speciation

A related perspective that may be gleaned from contemporary genetic research is that human beings are recognizable as human beings not only in distinction from other species but, even more importantly, in relation to one another. At the level of genes, what distinguishes human population groups from one another is almost negligible. As a European American, I am hardly at all less different from my sibling than I am from a Navajo, a Zulu, a Han Chinese, a Palestinian, or an Australian aborigine. We are more than 99.9 percent the same.

At the immediate practical level, this means that race, as a category invented by early modern Europeans, is a complete fiction, a fabrication of the will to domination. One of the most interesting, alarming, and instructive inventions of modernity and of modern science has been the theory of white supremacy. From a theological perspective, this has always been unspeakable heresy that makes utter nonsense of the most basic affirmations of Christian faith. The very intelligibility of Christian doctrine rests upon the unbroken unity of human beings.

Without this unity of humanity, it would be impossible to account for the significance, for example, of incarnation as something that affects all human beings, that is at least potentially good news for all human beings.

This is well illustrated in Anselm's *Cur Deus Homo*. At the end of his reflections on "Why God Became Human," Anselm indicates why the incarnation and death of Christ could not save the angels. The reason he proposes is that each angel is a species.[12] Thus what affected one could not affect all. But human beings are a single species; thus what affects one does affect all. Without this principle, the universality of sin or the effect of incarnation and redemption could not even be intelligible.

In this connection, recall a suggestion of Gregory of Nyssa in another text: "Just as the principle of death had its origin in a single person and passed to the whole of human nature, similarly the principle of the resurrection originated in one man and extends to all humanity."[13] Thus he is also able to affirm: "There is no reason for those who do not take too narrow a view of things to find anything strange in the fact that God assumed our nature. . . . In the other case [Incarnation] he united himself with our nature, in order that by its union with the divine it might become divine. . . . With his return from death, our mortal race begins its return to immortal life."[14] This principle of species unity does not negate the first principle of interspecies solidarity; in fact, it depends upon it.

This is true for arguments about the intelligibility of incarnation; for example, the argument that God as creator of nature is not alien to the body as a part of nature. Thus Athanasius writes in chapter 1 of *On the Incarnation*: "It will in no way be contradictory if the Father worked its [the universe's] salvation by the same one through whom he created it." He later picks up this theme again: "But if, although creation is created, it is not unfitting for the Word to be in it, neither is it unfitting that he should be in a man . . . man is a part of the whole. . . .

So it is not unseemly that the Word should be in a man. . . ."[15] More-over, the redemption of humanity is deeply connected to the redemption of the whole of nature.

Individuation

As a European American, I am no different than my faculty colleague who is African American or another who is Korean. There is no discernible basis for racialization, and still less for the supremacy of one human group over another.

But we are different. Each one of us is quite peculiar, distinctive. This distinctiveness occurs against the massive backdrop of what we share in common with all other life forms and the still more impressive uniformity of what we share with other humans. But distinctiveness is nevertheless quite apparent.

At the moment this distinctiveness has primarily criminological applications, whether at the level of fingerprints or more recently of DNA testing. These testing techniques are probably still in their infancy, so far relying, intriguingly enough, on the utter distinctiveness not of gene sequences but of a particular stretch of mere "junk DNA."

What does this distinctiveness suggest to us? First, it suggests the irreplaceability of any human being. No one of us is replaceable by any other. The loss of one of us is therefore an immeasurable loss—a perspective that makes the crime of murder even more appalling. It also suggests that any one of us can be identified as a distinct variation upon our common humanity. This individual variability is of serious consequence for ethics. That individuation is not just a "spiritual" or mental reality but a biological one also of great consequence, for it suggests that bodies matter. Moreover, the variability of individuals within a species suggests that nature (and nature's God) loves variability, loves profligate variation. But from its inception, the Human Genome Project has been in danger of violating this principle, an insight that belongs to it as much as to theology—a point to which we will return. But for now let us contemplate the importance of profligate variability and its message for us, given our tendency to relegate all discernible difference to deviation or degeneracy.

Let us also remind ourselves of what Matt Ridley repeatedly emphasizes in his work *Genome: The Autobiography of a Species in 23 Chapters.* Genes aren't there to cause disease, Ridley points out, and moreover (the point's corollary), almost all variability is benign; that is, blue eyes aren't a deformation of brown eyes, nor vice versa. Paying too close attention to what are loosely called genetic causes of disease can be a complete distortion of science.[16]

Redemption and Resurrection

Another essay by Gregory of Nyssa has a strong connection with themes suggested by the new genetics: his remarkable treatise on the "The Soul and the Resurrection of the Body."[17] Indeed, one of the most common topics of the theology of the early church was the treatment of the resurrection of the body. But this theme has fallen on hard times in the modern period. Theology has largely been overtaken, as has the culture of modernity, with a gnostic worldview, which, among other things, conceives of future hope largely in terms of something like the immortality of the soul. This is but one indication of modernity's penchant for an anti-body, anti-nature gnosticism.

Of undeniable import for theological anthropology is the way in which advances in biology generally, and molecular biology and genetic research particularly, recalls the essential bodiliness of the human being. We are inescapably reminded by genetics that we are our bodies. Or as Ernst Käsemann said in interpreting Paul: "My body is that part of the earth that I am."[18]

What may be termed the psychosomatic unity of the human person has been largely ignored in modernity, so much so that it has even been imagined that theologians might be alarmed by a reminder that human beings *are* bodies—not just their bodies' possessors or inhabitors. Gregory struggles with this, at least to the point of affirming the co-creation of soul and body, with neither preceding the other,[19] and also their interrelation: both are affected by sin, both by redemption, and so on. The same point is made by Irenaeus: "Man, and not just a part of man, was made in the likeness of God. Now the soul and the spirit are certainly a part of man but certainly not *the* man...."[20]

The Human Genome Project reminds us of this indispensable fact even at the level of our most prized individuality. We are individual precisely as bodies and we are bodies precisely as the expression of DNA. It is as bodies that we are in solidarity with our species and in solidarity with all of life. Without our bodies we are not and cannot be ourselves.

It was this perception of human being that made late Jewish and early Christian intuition of the resurrection of the body so essential to the expression of faith and hope. (This is no less true for Islam as well).[21]

This absolutely basic feature of Christian teaching has, in recent centuries, largely been met with incomprehension as we have sought to find our identity in an alleged part of ourselves untouched by physicality or what Descartes termed *res extensa*. Descartes supposed, as was noted in chapter 1, that what is important about us is associated with *res cogitans*, things of the mind, rather than *res extensa*, other things such as the body. The Cartesian view takes sides with mind (or spirit or soul) rather than with body, which suffers the vicissitudes of birth and death, of pleasure and suffering, of aging and decay. For early theologians, too, that is precisely what made ancient gnosticism so attractive. It is what made topics such as incarnation, crucifixion, and resurrection so important for early theologians to clarify and to defend against a general suspicion of the body and nature.

Modern genetics does not prove or establish the resurrection of the body any more than the incarnation does, or indeed creation. (In relation to the science of his own day, Gregory may have been somewhat hyperbolic when he supposed "that the preaching of the resurrection contains nothing beyond those facts which are known to us experimentally.")[22] But modern genetics does offer us fertile fields within which we may begin again to think what has so often in modern times seemed unthinkable. That is, it may provide us with certain analogies that faith can use to rethink itself.

Individuality in a Genome

What does it mean to know or to suppose that the whole genome of any individual is contained entire within any of its cells whatever? That the entire structure and specificity of any individual is inscribed in the most minuscule fragment, imperceptible to the eye of any of us? Any cell whatever, however humble, contains all the information required to assemble an entire individual human being: nail filings, drops of blood or semen, hair follicles, anything at all. Imagining such a scenario for other creatures formed the plot of Michael Crichton's novel *Jurassic Park*, later a film and pop-culture artifact.

What our ancestors in the faith could have done with such a delicious bit of information! For them a very difficult conundrum for the affirmation of the resurrection of the body was that Christian bodies, at least, were rather susceptible to gruesome fates: being burned at the stake, eaten by lions, or lost at sea and consumed by voracious fish.[23] How could God find all the scattered pieces to remake a whole human being again? (Note that for these fathers such a human being was necessarily the body of that human being.)

But one of the fruits of genetic research is the realization that you don't have to have all the bits. Any bit, from any stage of that body's life, would do perfectly well to reassemble the entire particular, living, breathing, flesh-and-blood human being. Modern genetics would have provided an especially telling way to clarify one of ancient faith's most basic intuitions about human being and the destiny of human being. Of course it all still depends upon the absolute grace of God. But at least it does not entail a God other than the one who creates us and loves us as the bodies that we are.

At the risk of seeming positively bizarre to our gnostic sensibilities, let me also point to a practice of Christianity in late antiquity and the early medieval period, a practice that seems quite bizarre to us now but which actually may be understood by recourse to modern genetics. I mean what Carolyn Walker Bynum has identified as the religious trade in holy body parts. Peter Brown in his *Cult of the Saints* brilliantly laid out the historical origin of this expression of popular piety. And Bynum wonderfully substantiates it in her *Resurrection of the Body*.[24]

The practice grew, quite simply, from the fascination with acquiring bits of cadavers that were identified with or as the bodies of particular personages from the faith's origins. Kneecaps and shin bones, fingers and skull bits, fingernails and even foreskins were in great demand as the basis of cultic adoration; these relics in turn were used to establish churches, cathedrals, etc. There was the perception, you see, that Saint Frank or Sally somehow was actually or even fully present in scraps of the flesh and blood that somehow remained after their death, that Peter's kneecap was somehow Peter himself and so a concrete bodily link to Peter's experience and reality as the follower and subsequently vicar of Christ.

Seen now from the angle of the genetic revolution taking place in our time, this no longer seems as quaint, or indeed barbaric, as it did to modernist Protestant sensibilities. For of course Peter *is* wholly present in his kneecap, or shin bone, or fingernail filing or what have you—the very same Peter who followed Jesus around Galilee. Some enterprising and theologically astute types even wondered about the possibility of a bit of Jesus lying about that had not been "ascended": for example, his foreskin from his childhood circumcision (a very powerful representation, by the way, of the Jewishness of Jesus).[25] Still, I am not suggesting a return to the cult of body parts, even if it does seem to me in some respects preferable to a spiritualizing of faith that leaves it unconnected not only to Peter's body but to our own or that of our neighbor.

None of this establishes the resurrection of the body. But it does provide us with ways of thinking about the body, and any possible future for the body, that may well give us pause. Contemporary genetic research does indeed suggest what might be termed the material or biological basis for a thinking or rethinking of the resurrection of the body. For if you or I or those whose lives are crushed out by vicious systems of destruction in our world are to be conceived of as having a future, it will be as the bodies that we, or they, are. Apart from the individuality inscribed in our DNA, we are not individuals at all. There is no redemption worth mentioning that is not also, as Paul said, a redemption of our mortal bodies (Rom. 8:11).

Humanity in the Genome

The second aspect of genetic research findings that is relevant for reflection on resurrection and redemption is the suggestion that the DNA of any person contains, as well, the DNA history of not only humanity as a whole but of life in general. This perspective is relevant, first, as applied to the views of Irenaeus regarding the basis of redemption. Namely, Jesus "recapitulates" the whole of humanity in himself and so restarts human history at the bodily level as "one Christ Jesus who came by means of the whole dispensational arrangements, and gathering together all things in himself. But in every respect, too, he is Man, the formation of God; and thus he took up man [the human] into himself . . . the Word becoming human, thus summing up all things in Himself."[26]

Now Irenaeus is obviously not asserting that Jesus is the progenitor of subsequent humanity in the same way that it was imagined that Adam and Eve were. But he does offer a way of grasping how any one person includes all humanity, even in the specific particularity of that human being.

It should also be clear that at the chromosomal level we have provided a way of thinking about a response to the feminist theological question: How can a male savior save women?[27] For to be a male is to have half of one's genetic makeup derived from female (X) and half from male (Y). That is, males are dual gendered at the biological level; maleness is only a slight variation on femaleness, which is the base and default gender for the human.

Just as important as these reflections, however, may be the way in which the whole of life on this planet is represented in a human genome, any human genome. The early church was persuaded that the prospect for a future for humanity, a future figured as the resurrection of the body, entailed a future for the entire natural world as well—precisely because it was the body that was to be raised. That is, if the body as a part of nature had a future, then the rest of nature (of which the body was only a part) had a future as well.[28] Thus, from the Cappadocians to John Wesley, an essential part of Christian "eschatology" has been the "restoration of all things"; that is, something like the resurrection of the body and the bodies of nature.

An important part of what has gone wrong in modern theology is the loss of this sense of connectedness to the rest of the life world. Lacking this, some suppose it possible to imagine a future for human beings (or selected ones) apart from a future for the earth and its creatures. This has encouraged a number of anomalies at the faith level, including a cavalier disregard of nature's good and the supposition among certain kinds of Christians that the utter destruction of the planet (whether by nuclear holocaust or global warming) is a matter of indifference to faith: We'll get raptured or something like that; who cares if the earth is left a burning husk? That is gnosticism abetting global biocide.[29]

Thus it is of some importance, I think, that genetic research actually makes it possible to grasp again the connectedness of human life to the biosphere and so, in the key of hope, to think of the resurrection of the earth as well as of the body.

The Pervasiveness of "Sin"

It is also critical to examine the theme of original or universal "sin." This may seem out of place here, since it is customary to think of sin as something prior to redemption. But the present order actually conforms better to the logic of faith, since faith only conceives of universal sin as the shadow side of the universal scope of redemption. Sin does not stand on its own; it is the question to which redemption is an answer. So it is only when thinking of the universal and indeed cosmic efficacy of redemption that Paul is driven to think also of the universality of sin as the universal need for redemption.

Now some may want to find cognates for the doctrine of universal sin in particular features of genetic research findings. Thus some may suppose that the equivalent of a universal equivalent of the mythic gene for criminal behavior should be awaited or hypothesized. (See chapter 7, on violence and the genome.) Others may find in the overwhelming evidence of "selfish DNA"[30] an adequate starting point for reflection. Others may see "sin" in the apparently conflictual character of chromosomal and genetic competition especially as focused in the image of an arms race used by Ridley to designate among other things the male versus female character of genetic competition.[31]

Certainly Augustine's attempt to explain the transmission of original sin through the inordinate desire that fuels sexual pleasure in procreation, although a misguided attempt, has the virtue for our purposes of being at least a biological explanation in accord with the best available science of his time.[32] Better science might provide the basis for a better interpretation.

But while a number of avenues here might be explored, I think our knowledge is thus far too inadequate and the analogies too limited and even misleading to be of much use. For example, a genetic feature common to human beings and other life forms would be of only limited help here, since the notion of original sin really only applies to human beings.

But there is a way in which genetic research at its current state of development provides a much clearer reflection of the notion of the universality of sin. Here we have a project that embodies seemingly the best things about our species, an infinite curiosity about its world, a commitment to understand the world of which it is a part, together with the disciplined attention and care that that project entails.

At the same time there are legitimate concerns that the Human Genome Project may have reinscribed a human evil in its very first results, due to the biased sample under study. As we know, the first human genetic profile ever mapped was based on the DNA of employees of the National Institutes of Health. It may thus reiterate, through this particular "sample," the normativity of European domination. To the extent to which this is true, the project can be seen as carelessly Eurocentric from its very inception and, to that extent, white suprema-cist. It is to be hoped that the Human Genome Diversity Project will significantly improve this situation.[33]

Moreover, the Human Genome Project is almost entirely subservient to systems of inordinate self-interest of society's dominant institutions. It is a willing tool of the economic lust for profit and consequent dis-dain for the poor characteristic of the entire medical-industrial com-plex. (We will return to this point in a moment.)

Now these characterizations may seem extreme, but I think such for-mulations are necessary to jar us awake from complacency. It should come as no surprise that scientists are as prone as anyone else to sub-servience to the machinery of division, domination, and death. Indeed, their own presumption of objectivity and innocence—a presumption shared by the culture—may make them even more vulnerable.

If we were under any illusions here, we would only need to remind ourselves of the horrifying history of eugenics, in which some scien-tists were eager accomplices, or of biologists' justification of morally repugnant notions of race, or of draconian social policy drafted under the heading of Darwinian natural selection. It would be naïve to sup-pose that these are simply aberrations.

Such scientific blindness can occur, among other ways, through the pretension to objectivity and universality that so pervades the work of scientists who are often astonishingly naïve about their own and other people's engagement in sin. Thus scientists may be even more blind than others to the way in which their work is based on and biased by cultural assumptions and structures that are often evil.

I don't think it is an accident that science (like theology) has often been the willing handmaid of the slave system, of colonial exploitation, of racism, and now of rapacious capitalism.

A couple of quick concrete examples may be helpful. Ridley's *Genome* lets us in on a dirty secret to which I have already alluded: that the enterprise that advertises itself as "the Human Genome Project" is nothing of the kind. It begins with a Eurocentrically biased sample of and so inevitably sets itself up to describe European traits as "normal" and all others as diverging from the norm. We have the reflections also from the Tuskegee volume to consult as well.[34] For of course the Human Genome Project is, as Ridley points out briskly and as some of the Tuskegee writers point out with appropriate alarm, is an entire misnomer. It uses a desperately restricted sample to come up with *"the"* human genome, thereby consigning a considerable range of human diversity to deviation from this initial profile of *the* human.

This is abetted by a tendency to link genes with disease and deformity. That is, the genes we speak of are typically the ones that, by varying from some norm, produce horrifying consequences. Now this kind of self-advertising is precisely what gets genetic research funded. And it gets funded because it holds out the prospect of enormous profit for some. There is a lot of money to be made in combating disease—or rather in combating some diseases, those that people may be induced to pay for "curing."[35]

What I am pointing to here is the way in which science often perverts itself in the quest for funding, for popular and media attention, and so on. Even the best of what we are and do is infected with subservience to evil. And this has a name: original sin.

Imago Dei

We should not end on this grim note, however urgently I believe that this corruption must be considered. Instead, let us turn to the main remaining element of theological anthropology: the idea that human beings are created in the image and likeness of God.

This doctrine has wonderful expressions, including Irenaeus's "The glory of God is a living human being," and Gregory of Nyssa's "For not as yet had that great and precious thing, man, come into the world of being; it was not to be looked for that the ruler should appear before the subjects of his rule."[36] But it has also sparked considerable debate among theologians, a debate that may also be replicated unknowingly in the arena of biology.

Thus, for example, some may seek in the genome the basis for rationality or linguistic ability or consciousness or free will or what have you, all qualities that have at some point been offered as candidates for the content of the image of God.

A common mistake, as I see it, of theological anthropology in this sphere has been to identify the image of God with that which separates human beings from other life forms. Gregory of Nyssa does not make that mistake. He realizes that it is precisely as creature that the human is called to be the image of God. Thus he points to that which relates us to other species as that in which the divine image is to be discerned:

"He would have neglected his rule over the other creatures if he had no need of the co-operation of his subjects."[37] In common with all theologians of his time, he rejects the notion that the divine is to be identified with unilateral power or domination and so sees in cooperative responsibility the concrete sign of this image.

In more recent theology Karl Barth has seen in such relational ideas as co-humanity the locus for reflection on the divine image.[38] This clue would suggest that it is in the mutually interdependent or community orientation of human beings, in their responsibility to and for one another, that the divine image is to be discerned. Gregory misses but comes close to this idea when he remarks that the divine, and so the divine image, is not only reason but also love.[39] And, as Ridley's reflections early in his book indicate, this is not too far from what may also be discerned in the Human Genome Project.

In any case, there are aspects of the genome project, the brighter side of the shadow I referred to earlier, that may illustrate the way in which human beings respond to a call that may be inscribed also in their bodies. Our DNA may contain the call to be the way life becomes conscious of itself in such a way as to care for all of life, to take responsibility for the benefit of all of life.

It is in this vocation of attentive care for others and for the planet that we may see the traces of what theologians have called the image and likeness of God. In Gregory's words, "The Deity beholds and hears all things . . . you too have the power of the apprehension of things . . . and the understanding that inquires into things and searches them out."[40]

Reflections on Romans

In conclusion let us turn to the most basic text of Christian theological anthropology. The remarkable perspectives of Paul in his letter to the Romans suggestively hint at the connections between elements of Paul's argument and some of the perspectives being generated by the Human Genome Project.

First, it should be evident that the cogency of Paul's argument depends to a significant degree on the species solidarity of the human being. The possibility of summing up humanity as "Adam" and perceiving Christ as the new or second Adam requires a very strong sense of the unity of human being. So strong is this solidarity that the name of something like an individual (Adam) can also be the name (and reality) of humanity as such (the earthling). As Romans 5 makes clear, sin and redemption apply not in the first place to individuals in isolation from one another, but to the species as a whole.

Second, Paul supposes that the fundamental reorientation or transformation of the human being also entails the transformation of the whole of creation as manifested in the natural world (Romans 8). That the whole of creation has been implicated, has been damaged by human disorder, can be verified by reflection upon our ecological disasters. Thus "all of creation groans" with yearning for the manifestation of a humanity delivered from distortion. Even more graphically Paul's metaphor suggests the groaning of the mother giving birth, suggests that the whole of nature is struggling to give birth to a liberated humanity. What we now know about the relation of human genetics to the gene pool of all living beings gives us new tools for thinking about Paul's metaphor in a post-mythological age.

Moreover, Paul's supposition that the transformation of the cosmos entails the transformation of "our mortal bodies" reasserts the biological connectedness of all of life, a connectedness not abrogated but affirmed in the hope for the resurrection of the dead.

Paul's recognition of human diversity whether in cultural, gendered, or class positions is robust, yet he also affirms the overarching unity in ways that genetic science may help us to think about. The world disclosed to us by molecular biology and genetic research may seem quite strange with its technical jargon and its sometimes dizzying array of challenges to modern humans' assumptions about themselves. But however daunting its language, procedures, and perspectives may initially seem, it also offers to theologians a rich field of inquiry and reflection. As often as not it sends us back to the sources of theological reflection, finding new salience for lost or neglected themes of our own intellectual heritage.

In this chapter, I have been able only to identify schematically some of the analogies that may link the disparate thought worlds of theology and molecular and genetic biology. Our work is cut out for us, as we need to build bridges with the new science and new technologies— bridges that will enable us all to become clearer about ourselves, the world of which we are a tiny if wonderfully interesting part, and the common hope we may share for the future of life so deeply menaced by the powers of death yet so deeply oriented toward diversity, solidarity, and abundance.

5

Adam, Eve, and the Genome

Ken Stone

The Genome as "Text"

When I was asked to contribute to this book and, earlier, to the course that inspired it, I was actually rather reluctant to do so. As a scholar of the Bible I do teach a seminar on Genesis, the biblical book that is home to the Adam and Eve referred to in this volume's title. However, I'm not a scientist; I'm not really even a theologian, technically. Given those limitations, I wondered whether I could contribute meaningfully to this conversation between theological anthropology and the Human Genome Project.

However, as I looked over the course materials, I began to think that the perspectives of those of us who are trained in textual studies might indeed help further the conversation between religion and science, or at least cast that conversation in a new light. Specifically I found myself asking: How does this conversation relate to my own training in interdisciplinary biblical studies, with particular interests in anthropological interpretations of the Bible and in lesbian and gay studies? There do seem to be possibilities for dialogue here, several of which I want to explore briefly.

In order to do so, though, I need to say a few words about my own interdisciplinary approach to biblical interpretation, because that approach will shape the questions I'm going to ask about the Genome Project. First, the scope of my training and interest in "anthropological" interpretations of the Bible is primarily social and cultural anthropology rather than theological anthropology. In my opinion and in the opinion of some other biblical scholars, a number of the questions raised by social and cultural anthropologists in the course of their analysis of other cultures can usefully be deployed in the analysis of biblical texts.[1] Thus I tend to interpret biblical texts—and, by extension, other texts as well—especially in terms of their social and cultural dimensions rather than, for example, in relation to psychology or psychoanalysis. Psychological or psychoanalytic readings of the Bible and of other texts are, of course, entirely legitimate.[2] However, my own tendency is to focus on biblical texts as cultural products, which emerge out of specific social contexts, presuppose certain cultural assumptions and values, and attempt to intervene in social conflicts in particular ways. Naturally this focus does not rule out careful attention to the literary and linguistic structures of a text. Close reading is always important. But when reading any given biblical text, I do not focus only on its literary form. I also ask: How does the text both assume and respond to larger frameworks of collective meaning that exist within its concrete setting? How does the text take up, contest, or advocate for specific positions within its culture's own web of collective agreement and disagreement?[3] Many cultural anthropologists would argue today that we should use anthropological questions and methods to analyze not only supposedly "distant and exotic" cultures (as anthropologists have traditionally claimed to do), but also, in a sort of "shift to the here and now," that we should use very similar questions and methods to interpret our own cultures.[4] By extension, I would suggest to both theologians and scientists that we can apply such anthropological questions not only to biblical and other ancient texts but also to other kinds of texts from our own culture—including, for example, scientific and theological texts. That is to say, scientific and theological texts are also products of specific cultures and can be analyzed as such.

Another element of my interdisciplinary approach concerns questions of gender and sexuality. Along with a few other biblical scholars, I have become convinced that it is productive to read biblical texts in the light of contemporary approaches to sexuality, including (but not restricted to) those approaches that have recently emerged from lesbian and gay studies and "queer theory."[5] This means, among many other things, that whenever I read texts, I am likely to be asking myself how its argument relies upon or challenges certain assumptions about sex, gender, and sexuality. Moreover, I am interested not only in individual assumptions but also, and more often, in social and cultural assumptions about sex, gender, and sexuality. Thus my interest in the study of sexuality and my interest in cultural anthropology tend to converge; indeed, I am very sympathetic to those who argue for considering sexual matters as subjects for social and cultural analysis.[6] At any rate, we know that sexual questions have already made an explicit appearance in discussions about science and genetics by way of arguments about the possible existence of a "gay gene."

So these influences shape the questions I ask, as a researcher and scholar, whenever I read a text. And as a sort of "professional reader of texts," I find it particularly interesting that a number of writers do speak about the genome itself as a text. Matt Ridley offers a very explicit and thoroughgoing example. "Imagine that the genome is a book," he tells us; and then he goes on to compare the component parts of the genome (chromosomes, genes, and so on) to the component parts of a book (chapters, stories, paragraphs, words, and so on). Indeed, according to Ridley this comparison "is not, strictly speaking, even a metaphor. It is literally true."[7] After all, he points out, the genome, like a book, can be "read." Ridley even discusses the genome as a particular type of text, the "autobiography," raising thereby the very important question of "genre"—to which I will return in a moment.

Ridley, of course, is a science writer, not a theologian. However, the tendency to speak about genetics in relation to things that need to be read or interpreted can also be found among theologians. So, for example, the theologian Ted Peters discusses the impact of genetic research in terms of what he calls "the gene myth." When Peters uses the language of "myth," he seems to refer to sets of cultural presuppositions that filter our perception of the various phenomena we encounter, including new scientific research. Peters apparently thinks—and I believe he is right—that whenever we encounter such research, we do so through the lens of specific cultural assumptions that affect the significance we give it. Peters uses the phrase "gene myth" to refer in particular to "a cultural thought form that says, 'It's all in the genes!'"[8] A clear example can be seen in the "gay gene" controversy, to which Peters devotes a chapter in his book *Playing God.* Peters points out that, in the popular reception of research into the possibility that same-sex desires are partially caused by genetic or other biological factors, it often seems to be assumed that the discovery of a biological cause for sexual orientation will lead to a more positive evaluation of lesbian and gay rights. I'll come back to this assumption in a few minutes. But Peters points out, against this assumption, that genetic science does not in itself necessarily answer the theological and ethical questions about homosexuality. In Peters' words, even "if eventually we accept as fact that male homosexuality is genetically inherited," nevertheless *"[t]he scientific fact does not itself determine the direction of the ethical interpretation of that fact.*"⁹ The theological and ethical analysis still has to be done. Peters relates the frequent absence of this distinction to the widespread cultural influence of the "gene myth." According to this myth, genetics determines our behavior and thus even our own guilt or innocence. The "gene myth" leads people to believe, first, that there must be a yes-or-no answer to the question of whether genetics determines sexual preference and, second, that the answer to this question will determine the theological and ethical evaluation of homosexuality.

In any case, Peters, like Ridley, does find it useful to talk about genetics in relation to the language of "myth." It appears that when the genome is being discussed, whether by science writers or by theologians, language about "books," "reading," "myth," and so forth find their way into the discussion. Inasmuch as the reading of books and the interpretation of myths are inherent to biblical scholarship, it seems productive to ask whether some of the issues we negotiate when reading a biblical text or other ancient myth can help us to reframe, or cast in a new light, issues we encounter in the dialogue between science and theology.

The Quest for a "Gay Gene" as "Etiological Text"

In order to explore this possibility in more detail, let us return to this matter of the so-called "gay gene." When people ask questions about the "gay gene," those questions are frequently formulated in a particular way. Often what is really being asked is, "How did gay or lesbian people *get to be* gay or lesbian?" We are noting something about our own world—the fact that there are people whose sexual desires lead them to self-identify as gay or lesbians—and we are asking how that situation came into existence.

Now biblical scholars might recognize in the structure of these questions a particular form or genre of discourse, which we call "etiology" or "etiological discourse." Such discourse tries to answer the question, "How did situation X come to be the way it is?" An etiology is produced when someone, encountering a phenomenon that is true or is accepted to be true in his or her world, wants to know or to explain how that phenomenon got to be the way it is. Very often, especially in the Bible, that explanation takes the form of a story. In the opinion of biblical scholars, etiologies are stories that give "explanations of origins" and so can be described as "origin accounts."[10]

Of course, the asking of such questions, and the production of such stories and myths, are common across history and most cultures. Certainly we know that etiological questions and answers flourished not only in the lands that produced the Bible but also elsewhere in the ancient world. Indeed, a very interesting and well-known example of a story that might be considered an etiology, and that is perhaps not completely unrelated to the issues at stake in the "gay gene" debates, appears in Plato's *Symposium*. Here a character named Aristophanes tells a particular story about how human beings came to assume their current form and, at the same time, how it is that certain males are sexually attracted to other males, that certain females are sexually attracted to other females, and that other persons, male and female, are attracted to individuals of the opposite sex.[11] To be sure, scholars disagree on the story's precise implications for our understanding of ancient attitudes toward sexual matters.[12] But for our purposes, the important point is that Aristophanes' tale could be considered an example of etiological discourse. Aristophanes attempts to account for patterns—sexual patterns—that he understands to be true in his own place and time, by recounting a story that claims to tell us how those patterns came to be.

Perhaps this bears some resemblance to what some discussions of genetic research are attempting to do. Genetic researchers are asking etiological questions when they ask, for example, "Where do gays come from—why is it that there are gay people? How did they get that way?" Is same-sex sexual desire "all in the genes," or does it perhaps result from a combination of genetic and other factors? When Simon LeVay and Dean Hamer—both scientists who study sexual orientation—present their research to general audiences, I believe we might characterize those presentations as modern examples of etiological discourse.[13] In making this comparison, I am not claiming that the modern scientists in fact understand same-sex desires in the same way that Aristophanes (or Plato through Aristophanes) did. But both Aristophanes and the modern scientists are, through discourse, trying to explain the origins of sexual phenomena known, or assumed to be known, to its audience.

However, when researchers or readers of scientific research ask and attempt to answer these sorts of questions, they may confuse etiological questions with ethical ones. If we look carefully at the debates about "gay genes," Peters is at least partially right to suggest that some debaters do believe that the answer to the etiological questions will have a particular kind of impact on the ethical evaluation of homosexuality. If we could decide whether homosexuality was a question of biology, the reasoning goes, then that would necessarily influence how we interpret homosexuality ethically and react to it socially and politically.[14] And while this might indeed make a difference to a lot of people, I'm not as convinced about this as many folks seem to be.

But as a biblical scholar, I suggest that the attempt to answer ethical questions by producing etiological discourse can produce very problematic results and may be a risky strategy. Scholars from other disciplinary backgrounds, too, have raised cautionary questions about the potential assumptions behind, and consequences of, debates over the etiology of sexual orientation.[15] But to make my own point, I'd like to consider a couple of examples found in my own primary object of research, the Hebrew Bible. Etiological discourse is very common in the Hebrew Bible, and especially in the book of Genesis—which, of course, also happens to be a book of great interest to people concerned with the dialogue between science and theology. Over a century ago, the great biblical scholar Hermann Gunkel pointed out the frequent appearance in Genesis of stories with an etiological interest. Significantly for our purposes, Gunkel went on to suggest that the questions motivating biblical etiologies "are usually the same that we ourselves are asking and trying to answer in our scientific researches."[16] Gunkel, of course, being very much a man of his time and place, probably took it for granted that our modern "scientific" answers to etiological questions are more adequate than those supplied by what he called "primitive people." In the present context, though, I am interested primarily in exploiting Gunkel's suggested parallel between biblical etiology and modern science, to generate some questions about contemporary genetic research and reframe the ways in which we approach such research from a theological point of view.

The Story of Adam and Eve as "Etiological Text"

A well-known example of a biblical narrative that incorporates etiological discourse is the story of Adam and Eve, found in Genesis 2–3.[17] In the course of recounting this tale, the narrator offers narrative explanations for a number of phenomena known to the story's author and audience. The narrative attempts to explain, for example, why women suffer severe pain in childbirth. The fact of such pain could easily be seen or experienced by members of the story's audience, but the tale attempts to account for the severity of that pain by telling how it came to be. So, too, it tries to explain why agricultural labor, though necessary for survival, was so difficult. Again, the fact that food could only be obtained with great toil in the harsh environment of ancient Palestine was obvious to the story's audience, but the tale attempts to account for that difficulty by telling how it came about. The story claims that both of these burdens, as experienced at the time of the story's composition, came into existence when God punished the first humans for disobedience:

> To the woman [God] said, "I will greatly increase your pangs in childbearing; in pain you shall bring forth children, yet your desire shall be for your husband, and he shall rule over you." And to the man he said, "Because you have listened to the voice of your wife, and have eaten of the tree about which I commanded you, 'You shall not eat of it,' cursed is the ground because of you; in toil you shall eat of it all the days of your life; thorns and thistles it shall bring forth for you; and you shall eat the plants of the field. By the sweat of your face you shall eat bread until you return to the ground, for out of it you were taken; you are dust, and to dust you shall return." (Gen. 3:16-19)[18]

This passage, and the story that leads up to it, were clearly written in part to answer etiological questions about the conditions under which ancient Palestinian women and men lived.

But there are several dimensions of this story's etiological interest that might cause us to raise critical questions about such discourse. First, we have to notice that pain in childbirth and the severity of agricultural labor are here problems to be explained, not realities to be celebrated. Etiologies in the story of Adam and Eve are, for the most part, attempts to account for unpleasant realities of life in the society that produced the story. The story emerges out of a culture that is wrestling with the question: Why must we put up with pain in childbirth and backbreaking agricultural work? It is precisely the negative evaluations that lead to the etiological questions.[19] This is worth remembering, I think, when we consider the significance of etiological questions about homosexuality. Some etiological explanations may indeed correlate with a positive evaluation, but in the Bible, etiology seems to correspond more frequently with a negative evaluation. By extension, perhaps we need to ask ourselves whether the urge to understand *why* homosexuality exists is itself rooted in a negative social assumption that ideally it *should not* exist.

Moreover, this same story shows us that etiologies can, on occasion, justify social inequality and subordination. The story appears to acknowledge, as one of the realities of the social world of its author and audience, that women are subordinate to men. Why is it, the story asks, that men "rule" over women? Here again, the passage quoted above offers an explanation: like the pain of childbirth, the subordination of women to men is understood as a punishment of Eve and a consequence of her disobedience (Gen. 3:16). Of course, this explanation may also imply that this subordination is an unpleasant reality of female life, as is the pain of childbirth. Nevertheless, this unpleasant reality seems also to be an accepted reality; and we have good reason to worry about the ways in which this etiological account can be used to "naturalize" the subordination of women (by comparing it to the pain of childbirth, for example) or even to "sacralize" such subordination (by understanding it as something that, however unpleasant, was instituted by God).[20] Indeed, at a later time, the author of the New Testament book of 1 Timothy reread the story of Adam and Eve in order to argue that God ordained female submission to men:

> Let a woman learn in silence with full submission. I permit no woman to teach or to have authority over a man; she is to keep silent. For Adam was formed first, then Eve; and Adam was not deceived, but the woman was deceived and became a transgressor. Yet she will be saved through childbearing, provided they continue in faith and love and holiness, with modesty. (1 Tim. 2:11-15)

Here the author of 1 Timothy argues for the subordination of women by appealing to the older etiological account. Of course, this argument rested upon a particular interpretation of the story of Adam and Eve; and ideally it would be worth our while to contest this reading of Genesis.[21] But notice in this case that etiological questions are not only being asked by the person who authored the story of Adam and Eve, but also by another person reading that story later on, whose interests and cultural assumptions may partly overlap with and partly diverge from the earlier author's. Perhaps we nonscientists find ourselves in a parallel situation today when we interpret the findings of genetic researchers. We are not doing this research ourselves—that is, we are not generating the initial scientific "etiological" narratives. Rather, we have to read and interpret the etiological narratives appropriated from science, in much the same way that the author of 1 Timothy had to read the story of the Garden of Eden appropriated from a different context. When the author of 1 Timothy reads the Garden of Eden story, that author attempts to reach conclusions for the current era—ethical and theological conclusions, social and political conclusions—out of a text that was etiological in its origins. The result, as we can see with the advantage of historical and cultural distance, was rather problematic, at least for anyone who might wish to analyze the subordination of women critically rather than simply accepting and explaining it.

In any case, the appeal to etiological discourse has, in 1 Timothy, taken the place of careful ethical and social analysis, and it seems to me that something like this frequently happens when the issue of gay genes is raised. Etiological discourse becomes confused with ethical and social analysis, as Peters points out. To ask about the impact of genetics and biology on one's sexual desires is an etiological question, and that type of question is quite different from the ethical and social questions that perhaps actually should be asked.

One reason we should hesitate to use etiological discourse to answer ethical questions is the fact that etiological questions generally tend to justify cultural assumptions that should themselves be subject to critical analysis. The very asking of an etiological question tends to make certain assumptions about the nature of the phenomenon being investigated. Those questions could themselves be subject to critical analysis, but framing the matter etiologically can prevent critical analysis, since etiological questions are formulated precisely to explain the origins of something whose existence and nature are simply assumed.

Let us think again about the "gay gene" example. Scholars who criticize the research on possible genetic determinants of sexual orientation do so on several grounds. They note that such research tends simply to presuppose that we can clearly classify persons based on their own biological sex and the sex of that person's primary objects of sexual desire. Yet as the feminist biologist Anne Fausto-Sterling has pointed out in a very interesting book, the actual complexities of sex and gender are obscured rather than clarified by exactly such presuppositions.[22] Fausto-Sterling tends to agree with those anthropologists and historians who question our tendency to think about sex and gender matters in strictly binary terms: male versus female, heterosexual versus homosexual, and so on. Such divisions cannot account for all of the cross-cultural and historical evidence, they say.[23] Indeed, Fausto-Sterling goes on to suggest that biological research has itself sometimes been formulated and interpreted on the basis of such cultural prejudices. In addition, Fausto-Sterling argues that other dualisms frequently distort sex and gender research, including the dualisms between nature and nurture, or between biology and society. Such dualisms limit the types of answers thought to be possible for questions about the origins of sexual orientation; indeed, they frequently *structure* our etiological questions about sex and gender and so are not themselves interrogated. Fausto-Sterling forces us to recognize that our etiological questions are structured by our social assumptions and concerns just as biblical etiological questions were structured by ancient assumptions and concerns. They tend actually to justify and solidify those assumptions and concerns and to restrict the range of possible answers to our questions by ruling out answers that are too complex to cohere neatly with our presuppositions. For example, once binary categories are assumed, a researcher may ask etiologically about the ways in which individuals manifest the characteristic of this or that category—oblivious of the fact that the experiences and even the bodies of many persons do not actually fit the categories very well. The focus on etiological questions makes critical analysis of the assumptions behind the questions difficult to carry out.

Who Asks Etiological Questions?

So that's one question I want us always to be ready to ask: What sorts of assumptions are obscured or left out of account by etiological questions? Another is: Who asks etiological questions and why? Because you can argue, as biblical scholars sometimes do, that etiological questions and the attempt to answer them are difficult to separate from political assumptions and political agendas.

Yet another example from the book of Genesis may illustrate this point: a passage found in Genesis 19, at the end of the Sodom and Gomorrah story.

Now Lot went up out of Zoar and settled in the hills with his two daughters, for he was afraid to stay in Zoar; so he lived in a cave with his two daughters. And the firstborn said to the younger, "Our father is old and there is not a man on earth to come in to us after the manner of all the world. Come, let us make our father drink wine, and we will lie with him, so that we may preserve offspring through our father." So they made their father drink wine that night; and the firstborn went in, and lay with her father; he did not know when she lay down or when she rose. On the next day, the firstborn said to the younger, "Look, I lay last night with my father; let us make him drink wine tonight also; then you go in and lie with him, so that we may preserve offspring through our father." So they made their father drink wine that night also; and the younger rose, and lay with him; and he did not know when she lay down or when she rose. Thus both the daughters of Lot became pregnant by their father. The firstborn bore a son, and named him Moab; he is the ancestor of the Moabites to this day. The younger also bore a son and named him Ben-ammi; he is the ancestor of the Ammonites to this day. (Gen. 19:30-38)

Now here, too, we have a kind of etiological scenario. The text as formulated is, in part, an attempt to answer the question, where did the Ammonites and the Moabites come from? How did they get to be here? The Israelites were looking at these two peoples who were in some ways similar to the Israelites and in other ways different, but who in any case were considered distinct groups of people. And in that context, they told a story about the ancestors of these Moabites and the Ammonites, ancestors who are understood by the Israelites to be descended from supposed ancestors of the Israelites themselves but also to constitute a different line of that "family."

Notice, by the way, that these questions are not being asked or answered here by the Ammonites and the Moabites themselves. Perhaps the Ammonites and Moabites did discuss such questions, but what we have in front of us is an *Israelite* attempt to answer the etiological questions. Now it appears, from both biblical and nonbiblical evidence, that the Israelites did not always get along with these other groups of people. And our evaluation of this particular etiological myth may depend a little bit on our knowledge that the questions about Moabites and Ammonites are being raised and answered by *ene-*

mies of these peoples. Are the questioners sympathetic or hostile? I do not mean to imply that the etiological myth would be any less "interested" in the Marxian sense—that is, motivated by its own interest and concerns—if, in fact, the etiological questions were being raised and answered by Ammonites and Moabites. The Moabites and Ammonites would still have had their own reasons for asking the etiological question and for answering it in the particular ways that they might have chosen (unfortunately, we do not have their version for the sake of comparison). The point is that different interests, agendas, and biases would have been at work.

In any case, we have here an attempt to explain the origin and nature of a kind of symbolic boundary between different groups of people. Different groups of Semitic peoples are living on both sides of the Jordan River, and people on one side of that river—the Israelites—are telling a story that attempts to answer specific questions about the origin of this situation. How did the Ammonites and Moabites come into existence? But this did not happen in a vacuum. The story was told in a particular context to a particular audience, and that audience had specific cultural assumptions about the nature of the ethnic boundary between themselves and their neighbors.

Now by reading the story carefully, we may even be able to uncover, and analyze critically, some of those assumptions. If we do so, and if we are familiar with other historical evidence, we may notice that the biblical text draws this boundary between the Israelites and their neighbors more definitively than one might expect. Other historical sources point to less pronounced distinctions between these peoples, especially in the case of the Moabites, about whom somewhat more is known. The longest extant example of a Moabite text, the famous Mesha inscription or "Moabite stone," is not only "strikingly similar in language and even style to classical Hebrew prose," in the words of one scholar, but also shares important assumptions about political and religious structures and institutions with the biblical texts.[24] Thus biblical references to the Moabites, arguably, solidify a distinction between Moabites and Israelites that can seem rather more ambiguous when all of the ancient sociocultural evidence is taken into account. However, because the etiological discourse of Genesis 19 simply assumes this distinction and then tries to account for its origins, the fact that the Israelites may not actually have been all that different from the Moabites is obscured.

Other cultural assumptions structure the etiological narrative as well. For example, some biblical scholars have suggested that this story, by characterizing the Moabites and Ammonites as descendants of incestuous unions, both assumes and contributes to a stereotype of sexual misconduct. According to one interpretation, if they can be "dehumanized through sexual innuendo," they more easily become "fair game for Israelite exploitation and oppression."[25] Certainly throughout the biblical accounts of Israel's past, conflicts are noted between the Israelites on the one hand and the Ammonites and Moabites on the other; moreover, the question of sexual contact between Israelites and Moabites seems to be a recurring issue of concern in biblical literature. Thus one can quite plausibly argue, at the very least, that in Genesis 19 an etiological account of the origins of non-Israelite peoples plays upon motifs of illicit sexual couplings, which reappear in other references to these same peoples elsewhere in the Hebrew Bible as well (in Num. 25: 1-9, for example). And once again, when reading such texts, we must always remember that it is the Israelites who are telling and hearing these stories. We should read these narratives critically, recognizing the ways in which they both presuppose and extend problematic social assumptions about differences between the Israelites and their enemies. So when we think about that other etiological question, "How did some people get to be gay?" we have to recognize that the interests and assumptions of contemporary audiences may be at work in both the articulation of the question and the shape of the answers. We need to analyze contemporary etiological questions with the same critical eye that we would use for ancient ones.

One of the ways we use that critical faculty is by asking who has the cultural authority and resources to articulate the answers that come to be persuasive. In biblical studies it is now acknowledged that the texts of the Hebrew Bible—including the etiological texts I have been discussing—were written by, and reflect the interests and biases of, a very particular segment of society: a largely male, largely urban, largely priestly or scribal elite whose literacy alone distinguished them from most of the ancient Palestinian populace.[26] Recognition of this fact does not, of course, rule out the possibility that other segments of society might have given similar answers. Nevertheless, we have to remember that the cultural and economic resources to disseminate widely accepted answers to etiological questions were only available to some people. If we were able to ask other ancient Israelites, we might find that they would give different answers to etiological questions, or even ask different questions altogether. Indeed, even if their questions or answers were similar, we might have reason to suspect the influence of that small but culturally authoritative segment of society to whom we owe so much of the biblical literature.

So also in the modern dialogue between religion and science, I think it is necessary to reflect critically on the ways in which modern culture has given so much authority to science. A story from science trumps most other stories in our society. And from scientific stories we move almost without pause to make ethical, theological, and political judgments. In pointing this out, I do not wish to be understood as opposing science or taking an excessively negative view of it. Nevertheless, with respect to the matter of the "gay gene," it is important to remember that the history of scientific research into sexual matters has not always been a happy or benign one.[27] Thus, people whose sexual desires and practices differ from the mainstream may have some reason for being reserved in their praise or quick acceptance of "authoritative" statements from science. Those of us who are gay or lesbian, and who consequently "for too long have been the objects rather than the subjects of expert discourses on sexuality," in the words of one scholar,[28] must not cede entirely to scientists or to other privileged segments of society the authority to make ethical and political judgments about homosexuality.

In fact, within the gay community opinion is divided about the research that might uncover a genetic basis for homosexuality or lesbianism. Some might say we need such a discovery because then the mainstream will stop persecuting us. Others point out that the discovery of a "gay gene" could lead to aborting fetuses with that genetic marker. You will find a real split down the line on that very issue even among gay folks, who certainly have an interest in how this information ultimately matters.

In any case, we need always to inquire about the context in which scientific research is taking place, just as most biblical scholars find it important to inquire about the contexts in which biblical texts were written. Some knowledge of that context helps us understand which questions are thought to be worth asking. And very often, it turns out that conflict and controversy are a significant element of the context. We know that there were conflicts between the Israelites and their Moabite and Ammonite neighbors. This knowledge gives us some insight into the etiological questions asked by the Israelites and the shape of those answers that finally became persuasive. So both research into the etiology of homosexuality and religious appeals to that research are taking place today in a context where conflicts over homosexuality are frequent and often severe. I don't think it's an accident that research into the possible genetic components of same-sex desire emerged in that context. Of course, scientists don't always state explicitly why they pursue the research that they do. It may be difficult to read Dean Hamer's work, for example, and state a clear individual motivation for his research, that is, to know *why* he chose to study this and not that. Indeed, many current approaches to science would make you believe that prior motivations are not all that relevant to the results of scientific research. Nevertheless, if homosexuality were not already a loaded ethical and political issue, I have to wonder whether it would matter so much *why* some individuals are sexually attracted to members of the same sex and others are not. Ultimately, I can't help but wonder whether the shape of the research questions and perhaps, on occasion, even the shape of the answers has been profoundly influenced by that context.

I don't understand myself to have resolved any scientific or theological questions here. The textual comparison of biblical and genetic materials is meant, rather, to be evocative of new kinds of questions. It is certainly not meant to exhaust the religion-and-science discussion. But as I pursued this line of investigation, unexpected convergences and illuminations convinced me that this is a fruitful avenue to pursue as we continue to ask, "Who is the human being and why should you be mindful of us?"

PART THREE

CRITICAL ISSUES

6

Dreaming the Soul: African American Skepticism Encounters the Human Genome Project

Lee H. Butler Jr.

> For God does speak—now one way, now another—though people may not perceive it. In a dream, in a vision of the night, when deep sleep falls on people as they slumber in their beds, God may speak in their ears and terrify them with warnings, to turn humanity from wrongdoing and keep them from pride, to preserve their souls from the pit, their life from perishing by the sword. (Job 33:14-18 NIV)

The history of genetic research in the twentieth century has aspects of nightmare. These images terrify and warn us of what we must guard against in any powerful human endeavor. And modern genetics is an endeavor of tremendous human power.

From the beginning of the last century until just after World War II, theories of genetics were employed over and over as a way to "scientifically" document supposed theories of racial inferiority. Daniel Kevles, in his edited volume, "Scientific and Social Issues in the Human Genome Project," shows how not only German but also British and American scientists engaged in the most blatant attempts to scientifically justify stereotypes of ethnicity, race, and class. This came to a head, as is well known, in the Nazi brutality that so shocked many scientists that they avoided the field of genetics as tainted for almost a quarter of a century thereafter.[1]

Clearly, even today, while the Human Genome Project is an extraordinary adventure in science, there is no reason to be sanguine that racial prejudice has magically disappeared. We are still living in an era of scientific racism. As with any momentous human discovery, there is potential both for great good and for great destruction.

It is interesting to note that some of the scientific findings of the Human Genome Project are actually congruent with African and African American spirituality and narrative. After all, science has discovered that there really was an Eve, and she lived in Africa.[2] But the points of congruence are not enough reason for African Americans to be totally invested in the methods or outcomes of the Human Genome Project. I believe there are also radical divergences based upon basic human understandings that are informed by both dualistic and nondualistic views of the human being.

To the extent to which science can become a religion for some, there is a danger of overspiritualizing the benefits of the Human Genome Project. Religion, as a quality of human functioning, provides organizational meaning to the cosmos and identifies the dynamics of our reason for being. From this perspective, religion is a system that promotes human survival. Religion also defines the dynamic roles and functions of everyone and everything within the cosmos, including our relationships. Although there are many different definitions for spirituality, I hold spirituality to be an integrative process that makes the many parts of our being one. The hope that the Genome Project will aid in bringing about human unity is one of the spiritual dangers of the project.

To deeply appropriate the benefits of the Human Genome Project, we must perceive the ways in which it might contribute to a religious understanding of humanity and its impact upon African American history and spirituality. But we must not only see the dream of the project, we must also listen to the terrifying nightmare implicit in the project. If we are not attentive to the full revelation and experience of this dream, we will not be able to preserve our "souls from the pit." Without some of the critical questions raised by the African and African American encounter with scientific racism, how can we make sure that the good of this research will be appreciated, and how will we build effective safeguards against exploitation?

In order to begin to discern the religious and spiritual significance of the message of the Human Genome Project, we must acknowledge there is a theological as well as a genetic structure that constitutes humanity. This acknowledgment, however, must also include the very problematic and painful history of scientific racism. It is in light of the history of genetics and racism in the twentieth century that science dare not presume its innocence or "objectivity" where race is concerned. Only after we have deeply encountered the structural dynamics of race in the United States, a country whose consciousness so relies on the scientific fields, can we begin to appropriately and adequately critique the project.

I have chosen "dream" as the metaphor to reflect upon the prominent understanding of the human being within our American social and cultural context. And as a primary hermeneutic for guiding the usage of this metaphor, my social location is the African American historical and religious experience.

Dreaming, as an expression of spirituality, is one of the mediums of our religious activities. Historically, dreaming has been a spiritual resource for navigating life. It is a form of divine revelation about the activities of human beings, who are, according to most creation myths, spiritual beings. Dreams help us to navigate the cruelty and brutality of the world, and they give us hope for overcoming despair. For African Americans, dreaming has been a matter of survival, as well as a resource for maintaining our conversations with God.

My introduction to a theory of dream interpretation came in 1993, when I was initiated into analytical psychology. As a young seminarian preparing for Christian ministry, I was taught that Jung was the most Christian among psychologists. This statement was followed by the famous quote from his 1959 BBC interview, in which John Freeman asked if he believed in God. Jung's answer, which turned on many a seminarian, was, "I don't need to believe; I know." This was the foundation for the period of my life when I self-identified as a Jungian. I was introduced to his model of the psyche and the most significant concepts and processes of analytical psychology. I was persuaded by his concern for the human spirit, for his positive regard of religiosity, and his psycho-anthropological exploration of humanity. I was so awestruck with him that I participated in organizing a Jungian dream-work group. I was on my way to becoming a Baptist pastor and an analyst; I conscientiously began to see the world analytically, through a psychologist's eyes. Yet, as much as I appreciated the interpretive frame I was acquiring, I started to see a discriminatory attitude against persons of African decent. The analysis that follows flows from my investigation of African and African American epistemology and descriptions of humanity. I now use that research to critically engage dominant models and offer alternatives.

Racism in American History as a Feature of the American Dream

One of the founding intellectuals of the United States was Thomas Jefferson. Scientist and statesman, Jefferson typified the ideals and, as we shall see, the flaws of his age: the Age of Enlightenment. The definition of who the human being is, and who he *(sic)* is not, is the central question of the Enlightenment.

Indeed, Thomas Jefferson was the leading American intellectual of the Enlightenment. Erik Erikson notes that a study of Jefferson is the study of "a life history synonymous with the creation of the new nation."[3] Erikson identifies this one man's personality, beliefs, and life story to be the same as the ethos of the nation. Identity, as a formative process, is a relational process. Typically, within this process one personality either shares with or leads another into a particular understanding of the self. In that way, one personality may identify with the other and express the same outlook on life. This is what Erikson has suggested occurred between Jefferson and the young United States of America.

Those things Jefferson believed about life were embodied as the characteristics of the nation. To review Jefferson's life is not just to look at an individual who represented the masses of the nation; Jefferson's life and works were instrumental to the construction of American consciousness. In his writings and by his living, Jefferson defined and embodied the nation's position on entitlement and privilege. He offered a groundswell of hope by stating all to be entitled as human beings. From his influence arose a popular culture of equality, opportunity, and prosperity disseminated through the language of "life, liberty, and the pursuit of happiness." He declared all these things from his entitled, high-culture social position—but still, his declarations became American mass culture. Since Jefferson's life history, according to Erikson, is synonymous with the life of the new nation, then the same cognitive dissonance present within Jefferson will be present within the nation.

Some of the most formative historical statements of American consciousness—"Give me liberty or give me death"; "We hold these truths to be self-evident: that all *men* are created equal"—were made by the European aristocracy that had settled in America. Adopting the Dream meant adopting the style and values of the first high-culture American dreamers and discarding one's own. But many aspects of the Dream are projections; and as with projections, the Dream contains elements that are distorted, larger-than-life denials of reality. The American Dream was raised to consciousness and interpreted within the context of the struggle for freedom.

The American struggle for freedom was directly influenced by the Enlightenment. The Enlightenment brought a shift in our understanding of human agency; now the struggle for freedom was understood as a human responsibility. But the underside of the experience was the simultaneous creation of a group, or of groups, considered less than human, and therefore unfree, based on the establishment of race, class, and gender lines. The American Dream degrades otherness. From our separate encampments of particularity, the unfree have been battling one another to claim our piece of a projected Dream. Through an acquisition of the Dream, people blame one another for what they perceive to be the reasons why they have been unable to achieve the promises of the Dream. One unfree group blames other unfree groups for their individual and collective lack of liberty and prosperity. The nation's history is clear. Multiple groups have had more privileges than others to participate in the American Dream. Those dividing lines, which continue to be sustained institutionally, are also maintained through domestic terrorism. Every unfree group has experienced terrorism. Night Riders, police brutality, trees with "strange fruit," trucks with bodies in tow, firebombing of churches and federal buildings, rape, spousal and child abuse—all are the terrorist activities of America in the name of freedom and the Dream.

Because we all desire freedom from the various oppressions in our lives, we continue to cling to the American Dream in our struggle to be free. Desiring to live unfettered by the constraints of the underprivileged, we cling to the Dream of a better tomorrow as we face the challenges of the day. Today, we dream deliverance from the instability of our social systems, hoping to reclaim our families, traditions, neighborhoods, and nations. We dream deliverance from the insecurities that have produced our growing intolerance. And we dream deliverance from diminishing economic opportunities, which create the perception of fewer privileges. As we Americans dream, we wrestle with our issues of privilege and entitlement while fighting to overcome our national and international esteem problem. Whenever these issues have combined in the past, they have been negotiated through nationalism, elitism, carpetbagging, scapegoating—or they have been covered by theatrical comedy.

Participation in the American Dream stresses the denial of many valued cultural identifications, language, for example. "Speak English— you're in America now" is frequently heard. There is constant pressure for people to conform to a declared norm of society. In addition, to identify promoting a consistent sense of self, it also reveals "a persistent sharing of some kind of essential character with others—the maintenance of an inner solidarity with a group."[4] The Dream promotes a consistent sense of the American self. Hence, the American Dream is an organizing component of the American identity. Through the process of shunning what is different and encouraging sameness, the Dream promotes cultural assimilation and individualism. This shunning, which is sometimes a shaming, has been perpetuated by the preexisting paternalism. Perhaps more basic is the ethnocentrism that considers other groups less mature and significant. The Dream is an institution of a culture that supports a number of idolatrous belief systems that flourish by oppression. To that extent, the Dream has become bankrupt of hope. The Dream may be another way to articulate notions of dominance and of justification for the mass destruction of others. Shunning groups largely relies on stereotypical characterizations. The groups most often shunned are those who either refuse to participate in the Dream or are denied the opportunity to do so.

This is, perhaps, the primary reason why a "New Dream" had to emerge during the 1960s civil rights/human rights struggle. The American Dream had a visible defect, whereby it offered freedom and justice to a few. Most of the American resistance cultures have been relegated to an inferior position, so the "New Dream" extends equality to all people. Since its emergence, many of the stereotypical characterizations seem to no longer be expressed in overt ways. Although many assume that the greater struggle has been completed—that the errors of the stereotyping have been corrected—the typing continues in covert movements and unconscious processes. Furthermore, the stereotypes are not new images, but the same images that have always been ascribed. Ethnic stereotypes have incredible longevity.

One of the jokes about domestic life, although in poor taste, has to do with having a bad day at work and "going home to kick the dog." There is, unfortunately, something instructive about this joke. Whenever the United States is in crisis, or experiences a bad day in the world, someone here at home is labeled a dog to be kicked. As we continue to negotiate with difference and indifference, will we progress as a nation to new ways of relating or regress to previous atrocities? While a crisis is a time of extreme vulnerability, it also presents heightened possibilities. Unfortunately, a state of crisis tends to reactivate former defense mechanisms, due to the strong desire for security and stability. It is just easier for folks to go home and kick the dog than it is to find new ways to cope with life's discomforts. The activities of racism are one of those former defense mechanisms.

We can pull this broad range of ideas together by looking at Jefferson once again and observing the American Dream as Jefferson actually lived it out. Historically the Dream projected America as the New Israel, the land where God's covenant is fulfilled. And like the Hebrews subduing the inhabitants of the land of Canaan, the new Americans believed themselves to be participating in the work of the Divine. This belief persisted through the colonial and antebellum periods into the frontier expansion era and beyond.[5]

To better understand the metaphor of the American Dream as a vision of hope and despair, consider the illusive nature of dreams from a psychological perspective. Carl Jung wrote that a "dream is a fragment of involuntary psychic activity, just conscious enough to be reproducible in the waking state."[6] And "even though dreams refer to a definite attitude of consciousness and a definite psychic situation, their roots lie deep in the unfathomable recesses of the unconscious."[7] Because dreams originate in the unconscious, the "manifest dream" has a hidden meaning. The manifest dream has to do with the specific content and sequence of the dream. Sigmund Freud calls the manifest dream "the text of the dream." This means that the specific details of the dream may be a long way from its actual point.

Another way of looking at dreams is from the perspective of a "guiding myth." Like a guiding light, this is a story that provides meaning to one's life circumstances and direction for moving into the future. It states some truth about the nature of human existence and provides the confidence for endurance. But more to the point, dreams are the guidance system of the psyche; and the American Dream is the guidance system of the collective American consciousness. Yet, like the manifest dream, the American Dream originated in the unconscious and is filled with hidden meaning. Furthermore, if our unconscious dream life, which is heavily influenced by our conscious realities, perceives a sense of meaninglessness, then our existence becomes a tumultuous and frantic push to acquire meaning and stability. That push might begin to express negativity out of a sense of fear of the future. Another possibility is to misinterpret the dream content in a wishful way. If these two points are combined, that is, the frantic push and a misinterpretation, then great suffering can occur for the dreamer, no matter whether free or unfree.

Consider popular culture's representations of Jefferson, one of the originators of the American Dream. There have been several popular recent media depictions of his life and contributions. As a result, one might choose to argue that these recent portrayals, powered by popular culture, are the nation's efforts to live its best intentionally. But let's think about other possible interpretations and intentions.

Ask Sister Sally Hemings how she was able to participate in the American Dream beneath Jefferson's roof. Ask her what she was entitled to, according to *Master* Jefferson. According to his Declaration, she was entitled to liberty. But she never saw her freedom. On what grounds could he declare independence and enslavement at the same time? How could the inequitable ground upon which he stood be considered sacred and moral ground? Even today, what is Sally Hemings entitled to? Are the contemporary questions of paternity raised by her descendants about economic inheritance, or are they about the importance of family history and human dignity? A legal brief prepared in April 2000 by an attorney in Virginia concludes that the "Tom and Sally myth . . . is a tale which should return to its status as no more than a footnote to the Jefferson legacy."[8] A footnote to the Jefferson legacy . . . What about the Hemings's legacy? What truths do we really hold to be self-evident? The Tom and Sally story, with all its race and gender implications, suggests the popular culture influence to be an extension of high-culture concerns.

A Way out of the Nightmare:
A Different Dream of Being Human

African American Christianity is grounded in our human struggle for freedom and justice. Implicit within this religious tradition and history is another definition of what it means to be human. The Jeffersonian ideal of the property-owning male is static and fundamentally alienated from the material conditions of existence. Those who have been denied the right to even basic material necessities know that to be human is to struggle to make the world a better place. Through the influences of African American Christianity, the United States has another source for developing a theological anthropology, an intellectual tradition different from Jefferson's—one in which what counts is the content of one's character, and the color of one's skin is not perceived as a deficiency.

Although the majority of black believers have identified with the Protestant denominations, those of us who are Baptist, Methodist, Presbyterian, and so on, are Protestant only to the extent that we have faithfully resisted the oppression we have known in America. We did not participate in the Protestant Reformation, and we owe no debt to the culture or comments of the Reformers. The founders of the mainstream denominational traditions did not fight to improve our standing in the world. Their message did not contribute to our efforts to maintain our full humanity. Nor did the message of the Reformers positively influence the standard of life that we were forced to endure on these shores.

The Protestant slavers of North America considered Africans to be soulless servants. For generations, we were thought to bear the mark of Cain or the curse of Ham. "Faithful" Protestant believers regarded Africans as chattel to be used for their personal pleasure and economic gain. A legacy such as this is hardly the foundation for the African American faith tradition that has nurtured generations of believers, nor is it the most valuable resource for interpreting African American dreams.

The Christian church in America has rarely acted on behalf of Africans in our quest for freedom and justice. Racism and economic enterprises have frequently existed by a "hand-in-glove" relationship. At the beginning of the Atlantic slave trade, when there was an opportunity for the church to speak the words of peace and love on our behalf, the "missionary to the Indians," Bartolomé de Las Casas, made Africans the sacrificial lambs for the slaughter in order to end the Amerindian genocide.[9] Consequently, the foundations of African American Christianity are not found in missionary evangelization. Its foundations are African religions, African spirituality, and our struggle to maintain our human dignity in the face of evil. The force of

African American Christianity as a resistant culture is located in its maintenance of a heritage of unity and rituals of sacrifice for the greater good.

African American Christianity as a resistance culture refused to be nominated by the basic American religious value system. That system valued individual survival and "white-only" privileges. Yet our survival system was based on communal and familial wholeness, with privileges emanating from our human compassion and regard for one another. Our conversion experiences were so powerful and persuasive that turning away from the truths derived from those experiences would have meant death. We endured many brutalities in order to show the convictions of our beliefs. Guided by our spiritual heritage, we resisted becoming what the American religious context told us we were. Through resistance, we sustained our identity as the children of God and maintained the community relationships that supported our being. Dreaming has been a very powerful resource for resistance and survival in America. One might assume dreaming to be a fanciful means of escape. However, dreaming offers the place where living into change begins. In a world filled with hatred that traumatized every fiber of the being, dreaming restored the body to the soul and inspired hope for living through the pain.

Dreaming has helped African Americans to maintain a connection between the sacred and the secular, the individual and the collective, through an assurance that we have not been abandoned by God and that relationships still matter. Dreaming has always let us know that freedom is just a day away. America's desires to separate and compartmentalize has influenced, but has not reformed, the ways Africans in America use dreams as a resource for daily living. During the antebellum period, dreaming was a way to resist conforming to imposed identities. Understood as God's language, it was a continual source of revelation. For the enslaved, it did not simply reveal something about the life of the dreamer. The dream also prophesied and pointed to some future event or condition.

Because of the spiritual principle of communality, dreams were not just for the benefit of the individual. They were for the benefit of the family and community. For a people living with the constant demolition of family, to dream of family members, both living and the living dead, was salvific for the dreamer as well as for those who listened to the retelling. Consequently, dreaming helped enslaved Africans to resist a chattel identity by maintaining family connections that a system of bondage sought to destroy.

African Americans have always regarded dreaming as a gift from God. In more contemporary times, dreaming has helped us to survive in spite of harsh economic realities. It has been believed, for example, that God, the giver of all good gifts, provides us with the means for daily living by giving us the "daily number." Dreaming numbers to play has kept many a family going through the years; this has been true even in my own lifetime. Often children, those considered the pure in heart, were asked to share their dreams with numeric significance. Churchgoer and gin-jointer alike put their nickels and dimes down on whatever number was given them in a dream.

Another contemporary function of dreaming has been to inform us of the condition of family members. It has been believed that God has kept us informed of the impregnating gift of life. This information regarding future generations is communicated through the symbol of the fish. When grandmother has a dream about fish, she begins to look around and inquire of a pregnancy among her children (or grandchildren). The fish represents a new life being added to extend the family relationship. The importance of this all-pervasive symbol is that life continues to be valued and family relationships remain paramount in spite of the negative popular opinions about African American family values.

Dreaming of Freedom

Our African heritage, with its own mythological history, requires that an interpreter of African American dreaming have some familiarity with African mythology, cosmology, and African American history. For example, one might easily conclude that Harriet Tubman and Martin Luther King Jr. were mystics and did not represent the African American population as it relates to dreaming. But the visionary experience of dreaming has not been understood to be limited to mystics among African Americans. Revelatory and prophetic dreams are considered commonplace throughout the culture. Dreaming has been one of the ways the community has maintained itself. Tubman's and King's dreams, both regarded as visions from God, were given interpretive shape and meaning by the African American thematic emphasis upon freedom.

Our bondage in America, joined with the blatant disregard for our inalienable rights as human beings, have etched the theme of freedom permanently upon the souls of African Americans. Although the two figures are generations apart, both are considered saviors of the people, and they stand together as an example of the legacy of resistance that is African American culture. Both moved against social and political injustice with religious zeal and fervor. Both dreamed dreams of the people and for the people, directed by a God who loves the people. Their dreams were neither mystical nor highly symbolic. To the contrary, their dreams were based in the tangible reality of the everyday; these dreams could be implemented for living into the future.

Harriet Tubman, identified as the Moses of African American people, was in constant communication with God as she led captives to freedom on the Underground Railroad. The tracks of the various routes to freedom were surveyed and laid by Tubman's dreams. Her dreams were motivation for her constant resistance of the evils of slavery and participated in her survival as she led groups of enslaved Africans out of captivity. The African heritage of dreams, which pointed to social direction and communal salvation, undoubtedly inspired her passengers on the Railroad to believe God was with them. She dreamed small dreams of escape routes to freedom and big dreams of freedom for all people.

Martin Luther King Jr.'s dreams, in their shape and character, were not very different from Tubman's dreams. Perhaps best known for his "I Have a Dream" speech, King was guided by more dreams than the one he communicated on the steps of the Lincoln Memorial in Washington, D.C. His continual retellings of his dreams were also more than just metaphorical or allegorical presentations of images and ideas. In his dreams, King saw the future. African Americans understood that he was not simply speaking poetically and rallied behind these visions from God. The retelling of these dreams inspired the African American community and transformed a nation.

King's dreams can be interpreted from within both the resistance and survival traditions of African American culture. In the tradition of the spirituals, the language he used to share his dreams was biblical, but the Bible was the language of the people. Participating in the resistance culture, his dreams presented an alternate vision of what the world would become. Resisting the tenets of white supremacy, his vision peered through the brutality and suffering of racial segregation and viewed a world where he could exclaim,

Free at last, free at last. Thank God Almighty, we're free at last!"
Seeing the end of his own life, yet understanding that he would live
on within the community, King declared: "Like anybody, I would like
to live a long life; longevity has its place. But I'm not concerned
about that now. I just want to do God's will. And He's allowed me
to go up the mountain. And I've looked over. And I've seen the
Promised Land. I may not get there with you. But I want to you
to know tonight that we as a people will get to the promised land.
And I'm happy tonight, I'm not worried about anything. I'm not
fearing any man. Mine eyes have seen the glory of the coming of the
Lord.[10]

This dream communicated the central theme of African and African
American identity as shaped by communality, that being, "I am because
we are, and because we are, I am." His dream participated in the survival
tradition through embracing the belief that the community's well-
being supersedes an individual's life.

The New Dream

The task of a racial identity is to probe the question of human origins.
Dreaming, as a revelational process, directs one to that very end.
Because the American dream identifies who is capable of participation
in American life and who is qualified to be a citizen, the Dream, in
effect, defines humanity. The American Dream is the dream of the
nation under God with liberty and justice for its citizens, which continues to largely mean white, European, and Christian. The Human
Genome Project is, in many ways, a dream, which dynamically resembles the American Dream. Just as the American Dream influences our
consciousness and encourages conscious and unconscious destructive
behaviors, the Genome Project has the same destructive potential.
Whereas racism redefines God, and the American Dream declares our
relationships and the need for God, the Genome Project may have the
unconscious effect of fueling the genocidal impulse that runs so deep
within America.

African and African American spirituality and dream interpretation
may be an aid for helping to declare and maintain the spiritual
integrity of the Genome Project and preserve the sanctity of all life.
One of the fundamental guiding principles of African life is the idea of

communality. Most Africans think first and foremost in terms of the good of the group, that is, the community. Second, they think of themselves, but only as individuals related to the group. Communality holds everyone, the living and the ancestors, in close proximity. African communality acknowledges the interrelatedness of all things and people. Communality is the understanding that all life is interconnected. It sets the tone for seeing and being in the world. The highest community value is cooperation. Although African life has a hierarchical structure, there is a clear interdependence of relationality that extends from the spirit world through the natural world. A communal relationship exists among the Supreme Being, divinities, and ancestors, who are all a part of the spirit world. This world extends to and includes the communal relationships of human beings, who also have a relationship with all of nature. And we cannot overlook the fact that nature is inhabited by the divine spirits.

Life, in the African worldview, is an intimate and integrated web. This web of connection, which is life, views all of life as spiritual. One result of this understanding is a special sense of responsibility for the well-being of everyone and everything. There is a recognition that human actions or inactivity have an impact upon all of life, making us responsible for the maintenance of the connections. To emphasize this perspective, one view of the world holds that human beings are the priests who mediate between the spirit world and nature.

The key features that guide communality are spirituality and responsibility. African spirituality is more than an engagement of spiritual matters, such as prayer. It is also more than an engagement of the spirit world, such as talking to ancestors. African spirituality is the acknowledgment that life is in everything. Moreover, it is not just the acknowledgment but the engagement with *all* aspects of life. African spirituality is a process that integrates all parts of the human self with other selves. It integrates individual and collective lives with all other realms of existence, including nature, humanity, spirit world, and God's world. Spirituality makes all of one's parts a unified whole, all of one's relationships harmonious and whole, all of one's ritual practices purposefully relational.

This sense of self, which is a collective sense, makes understandable the statement, "I am because we are; and because we are, I am." An individual life is given meaning only within the context of the life of the whole community. This also means that one's responsibility extends beyond one's self. The individual "me, myself, and I" is substituted with "we and us." According to this view, we are as responsible for the well-being of others as we are for ourselves.

Communality is the context for understanding dreams within Africa. Dreams are a spiritual phenomenon for maintaining relationships and continuity in life. Because Africans have a causal relationship with the physical world, the spirit world reveals causality. To this extent, dreams are less symbolic and more direct and literal communications. When an African dreams of a dead relative, there is a tendency to understand the dream sequence as a visitation from that ancestor, who is still very much alive in the spirit world. The dream communicates something about the person's relationship to family and community. Its meaning is intended to keep them from harm by revealing what was previously hidden, or by revealing the person's responsibility or irresponsibility.

Because the dominant experience of the African in America has been a struggle against life-denying forces, dreams are resources for resistance and survival. The dream of the Human Genome Project is one that could be complimentary of the communality that is implicit in African American spirituality. The "litmus test" of the project will, perhaps, be reflected in its capacity to resist the life-denying impulses that are so much a part of the history of the United States. The project holds great potential for conveying the message "I am because we are; and because we are, I am" *human*.

On Being Human

The danger and tragedy of the Human Genome Project is the racist appetite. The unconscious dimensions of the Dream of nobility that was constructed with the founding of America could very easily be blended with the Genome Project to aggressively move against African Americans and other racial-ethnic peoples on matters of humanity and citizenship. It is of no real benefit to know that the racists who turn to science frequently misinterpret data. The voracious racist appetite for self-aggrandizement in the name of survival requires only the faintest scent of perceived powerlessness to declare "open season."

Jefferson understood the human being to be disembodied reason. Those who were not "rational" (that is, enslaved Africans and women), those who did not own property (the poor), those who were not

English, became "the other" and were considered less than human. Jefferson's America was organized around cognitive dissonance: two opposing ideas could exist side-by-side without any ostensible conflict. He could promote freedom for some, while at the same time denying others the freedom he advocated, and trample on dignity without seeing the contradiction. The Genome Project has the potential to embody this Jeffersonian legacy.

As Jennings so clearly states in chapter 4 of this book, humanity is decisively one. We are all woven from the same DNA strands. Scientific racism is the cruel fiction promoted by those who wish to control others. As the African American dream makes clear through its spiritual principles, humanity is one; I hope the Human Genome Project continues to mirror that truth.

7

A Gene for Violence?
Genetic Determinism and Sin

Susan Brooks Thistlethwaite

The only Christian doctrine that we can prove empirically is the doctrine of sin.[1] It is obvious from everyday observation that human beings do harm to one another and to the rest of creation in an astonishing variety of ways. Human beings constantly fall short of doing what they know is right and perversely often seem unable to do anything about it. "I do not understand my own actions. For I do not do what I want, but I do the very thing I hate" (Rom. 7:15). Paul speaks for all of us; "[A]ll have sinned and fall short of the glory of God" (Rom. 3:21). In Saint Augustine's famous reflection on stealing pears from a neighbor's orchard, he asks the question we all ultimately ask ourselves, and surely more than once, "Why did I do that?"[2]

As Ken Stone pointed out in his chapter, the etiology of a biblical, theological, or scientific story is critical to understanding its meaning. Today both science and theology are offering stories, as they have in the past, to answer the question, "Why did I do that?" Actually, for science this is a relatively new story. And it seems, from the perspective of genetic determinism, that the answer is clearly, "My genes made me do it."

A Short History of the Doctrine of Sin

Before we turn to genetic determinist explanations of human sin, however, let us examine the development of the doctrine of sin and the field of theological anthropology. If we turn to systematic theology texts written prior to the twentieth century, we won't find the topic "theological anthropology" as a major heading. Instead, we will find "human being," or rather "man," as a subheading under the topic "sin."

But starting in the late nineteenth century, liberals challenged the classical theological assertion—heretofore almost universal, with notable exceptions such as Peter Abelard and Pelagius—that the human being was hopelessly mired in sin.

This startling development in theology was the direct result of the influence of science. Charles Darwin's work on evolution hit nineteenth-century theology like an explosion. Human nature is not separate from the rest of nature, Darwin implied; indeed, neither human nature, nor the rest of creation is fixed, and creation did not take place in seven days. Several seemingly critical and constant features of theology were no longer tenable. But theologians are made of sterner stuff. Protestant theologians in particular did not crumble in the face of the Darwinian onslaught on fixed ideas in classical theology. (Neither did Catholic theologians, who roundly rejected the theory of evolution, only accepting it in the mid-twentieth century). Instead, evolution was captured, mixed with German romantic idealism, and baptized. *God* is the author of evolution, these Protestant theologians held, and human beings and the rest of creation are changing according to a divine plan.[3]

Thus the human being is no longer the depraved sinner who is destined, without an extrahistorical infusion of grace, to everlasting damnation. No, the human being can now be pictured, as nineteenth-century Romantic artists did constantly, in a benign and beautiful nature. Innocent at birth, raised with good education, aided by a socially reformed society and a dash of psychology to untangle any remaining kinks, the human being could only grow in the divine light.

The late nineteenth and early twentieth century saw the beginning of fields such as psychology, sociology, and developmental education. Optimism reigned. Human sins would perish in the face of social planning; human intellectual powers would be unleashed by education that stimulated children rather than punishing them, and the unconscious mind would expand under the influence of psychological theory. George Albert Coe, American theologian, educator, and social activist, perhaps summed up this attitude best when he announced at the beginning of the twentieth century that what lay before humanity—and he meant the United States—was the prospect of a "divine-human industrial democracy."[4] Religious leaders thought they knew how to educate people for democracy. They were working on society's urban problems—as in the famous settlement houses, such as Hull House in Chicago—and by the application of reason they would be able to make human beings not only wiser, but improve their character.

And then the twentieth century spiraled into a series of horrors: World War I, the Depression, World War II, and the Holocaust. Trenches in France seemed predug graves for millions. Ovens and gas chambers changed the scale of slaughter; any distinction between soldier and civilian seemed to be lost. The nuclear age ushered in the prospect of planetary annihilation and even the concept of the "death of death." For if everyone is killed and no one is left to mourn, how could we even speak of death? There is only a return of the planet to a lifeless rock, or a rock ruled by cockroaches. In the face of such violence, how could humanity be evolving away from sin?

So sin came back into theology in a big way in the twentieth century. Surely the human being is perverse and hopelessly fallen, many concluded. Only absolute evil can conceive of gas chambers as a "solution" to social planning.[5] Theology by mid-century had foregone a rosy view of human nature, and sin was back in force.

But perhaps not. There is no such thing in intellectual history as a complete reversal. While theologians may recapture the doctrine of sin, they cannot undo previous intellectual developments. Darwin is still Darwin. Sociology, psychology, anthropology, and now economics are social sciences that force theologians to reckon with new understandings of human nature, even as the sciences of physics and chemistry give human beings ever-new ways to sin against each other.

Perhaps the most interesting and challenging direction in theology in the latter half of the twentieth century was through these social sciences. From Latin America, theologians like Gustavo Gutiérrez questioned the assumed sinful laziness of the poor and began their theological works with an examination of developmental economics.[6] During the Civil Rights movement, black theologians used the fields of law and sociology to demonstrate how the social and legal conditions under which African Americans have to live distort and thwart their lives. And a new definition of social sin started to emerge.[7] Feminist theologians turned to psychology to demonstrate that women's nature is different from men's, and that therefore theological reflection on what constitutes sin for men is strikingly insufficient for women's existential condition.[8] African American women began to use both sociology and anthropology to further define sin and the distorting effects of racist theologies on African American women's lives.[9] Gay and lesbian theologians led the way in introducing postmodernist philosophy, as well as anthropology and psychology, in looking at the role of the body and sexuality in the construction of the doctrine of sin.[10] Over the course of the twentieth century, theological anthropology had so changed as to be almost unrecognizable. Human beings come in different races, genders, and gender preferences. They are embodied, economic actors whose intellectual powers are vast, but they are not objectively rational. Human beings are community-builders, myth-makers, and violent gangs that often achieve their identity by vilifying and persecuting others. Human beings are Martin Luther King Jr., Mohandas K. Gandhi, Mother Teresa, Joseph Stalin, Adolf Hitler, and Pol Pot—and many in between who have the capacity for tremendous violence as well as tremendous good. And the theological question continues to be "Why do I do that?" The answers, however, have become astonishingly more complex.

Genetic Determinism

Darwin, as noted above, has not departed from the intellectual scene. In fact, he has returned rather spectacularly as a sociobiologist. Sociobiology, now renamed even more explicitly "evolutionary psychology," is a comprehensive, interpretive response to the newer genetics. The sociobiologist argues that human genetic material largely determines human behavior, up to and definitely including our religious rituals as well as our sinful, violent behavior. Human culture is a by-product, or a container, if you will, for maintaining the conditions under which DNA thrives. This new field was launched in 1975 by Edward O. Wilson's *Sociobiology: The New Synthesis*[11] and given currency with the publication of Richard Dawkins's *The Selfish Gene*.[12]

Genes, not organisms, are the motors of evolution, in this view. Strikingly anthropomorphized, genes have a purposeful role that changes our view of the body's relationship with its genetic material. Genes drive humanity. In Dawkins's oft-quoted phrase, "The organism is only DNA's way of making more DNA."[13]

Human bodies are survival vehicles, rather like lunar landing modules, that function to maximize the reproduction of DNA. And genes are at the wheel. "The genes too control the behaviour of their survival machines, not directly with their fingers on puppet strings, but indirectly like the computer programmer," in Richard Dawkins's words.[14] This does not augur well for human freedom and character. "Much as we might wish to believe otherwise, universal love and the welfare of the species as a whole are concepts which simply do not make evolutionary sense."[15]

The human capacity to reason, to build culture, and to leap imaginatively beyond the material world and posit a transcendent being—these too are ground under the wheels of ruthless DNA. As genes struggle to survive, they find it enormously helpful to produce brains. Brains, particularly human brains, greatly enhance the survival potential of genes. And the product of brains, namely culture, replicates in a way that parallels sexual reproduction. Concepts evolve by transmission brain to brain. Dawkins calls these concepts "memes." The idea of God is judged an ancient meme that sustains itself because it serves an evolutionary purpose: it solves existential angst as a "superficially plausible answer to deep and troubling questions about existence."[16] One thinks of the erudite graffiti "'God is dead—Nietzsche'; 'Nietzsche is dead—God.'" But while Friedrich Nietzsche is certainly dead, according to Dawkins the remnant idea of God is not, because it still serves a practical, and we should note, wholly materialist purpose. And when it no longer does? Then Nietzsche will finally be right. God will be dead. Or so Dawkins would conclude.

It is no leap at all to see that genetic determinism proposes simply to replace the doctrine of sin with the doctrine of genetic compulsion.

Flies Who Rape?

One of the temptations in the new biology is to attribute far too much causality to genes. From the small study of the inmates in a mental/penal institution in Scotland that found an extra Y chromosome in 3.5 percent of the inmates, far more than the population at large, came the myth of the "violent chromosome."[17] It is also clear, from the discrediting of this research, that sensitivity to determinist explanations of human criminality exists. The failure to detect such determinist fallacies in a research context, however, continues.

An example is a work by Randy Thornhill and Craig T. Palmer, *A Natural History of Rape: Biological Bases of Sexual Coercion*.[18] The introduction notes, "The evolution-minded scientific approach that the authors espouse has resulted in many novel and nonintuitive insights about why rape occurs. . . ."[19]

The question the authors address is, exactly as Ken Stone has pointed out in chapter 5, an etiological one: "Why do men rape?" An entire chapter is devoted to this question. Social-science explanations are deemed inadequate to answer this question because they have neglected evolutionary science. The judgment by many, particularly feminist, social-science researchers, that "rape is not sex" but "a political act that indicate[s] nothing about male sexuality" is the focus of Thornhill and Palmer's concern. They posit that these theorists' neglect of evolutionary biology distorts their perspective.[20] The evolutionary message is: rape is about sexual procreation, pure and simple. "The widespread occurrence of rape in non-human species is completely incompatible with the social science explanation."[21]

Thornhill and Palmer draw an unfavorable comparison between social science explanations of rape as stemming from political ideology and their biologically based explanations. "Debates about what causes rape have been evaluated not on the basis of logic and evidence but on the basis of how the different positions might influence people to behave."[22] Yet these scientists themselves dedicate the volume to "the women and girls in our lives" and describe themselves as "scientists who would like to see rape eradicated from human life."[23] They too have a vested viewpoint.

The critique offered here is not to defend social scientists by arguing that they are free of "political ideology" and therefore more insightful about rape. The social science analysis of rape is, indeed, rooted in a politics. The critique, rather, is that these genetic scientists are blind to their own political ideology and have an astonishing ability to jump between species and apply the term *rape,* which means "illicit sexual intercourse" accomplished by "force, duress, intimidation, or deception as to the nature of the act,"[24] to animals from orangutans to scorpion flies. The term *illicit* itself means "illegal." Outside a legal context, and in the absence of any way to establish "consensuality" other than human observation of animal behavior—a problematic judgment call not only in the case of flies, but other animals as well—there is no meaning to the term *rape.*

Another disturbing aspect of Thornhill and Palmer's volume is its decidedly heterosexist cast. It presumes that males rape females. An introductory question, "Why are males the rapists and females (usually) the victims?" leads these researchers to neglect completely the great numbers of men who have been raped by other men and the occurrence of rape among women. The driving idea is that there "must" be an evolutionary logic to rape, and that logic is rooted in procreation. Positing human beings as slaves to the genetic success of their genes means that sexual procreation is a causal given in this research. "*Any* gene that *happens* to arise by random mutation, and *happens* to have the effect of increasing an organism's reproductive success, will become more frequent in future generations."[25] But other genetic mutations, by this premise, do arise, and do get procreated along with all the other genetic material.

Ironically, a less genetically determinist approach to the investigation of sexual procreation would be helpful to social science. This approach would take into account the ways in which human behavior departs from animal behavior, would use feminist and queer critical theory to expose the inevitable sexist and heterosexist interpretative pitfalls in both human and animal observation, and would recognize and analyze the convoluted power relations that underlie investigations of sexual coercion.

Flawed Science

Genetic determinism as the "myth of the all-powerful gene" is "based on flawed science," according to feminist scientists. Ruth Hubbard examines a *Boston Globe* article that "reports a survey by Lincoln Eaves, a behavioral geneticist, of research by various investigators on twelve hundred pairs of female twins whom the investigators considered to be prone to depression. Eaves said he found evidence of genetic causes for this depression, though the evidence is not provided in the article." In addition to the summary, "Eaves also administered a questionnaire 'asking whether the volunteers had suffered traumatic events, such as rape, assault, being fired from a job, and so forth.' He found that the women who were chronically depressed had suffered more traumatic events than those who weren't." Does this spur Eaves to examine trauma such as rape as a possible cause of depression? No, it does not. Because of his myopic focus on genetic causes, "Eaves 'suggested that [the women's] depressive outlook and manner may have made such random troubles more likely to happen.'" As Hubbard rightly exclaims,

"What kind of reasoning is that? The women had been raped, assaulted, or fired from their jobs, and they were depressed. The more traumatic events they had experienced, the more chronic the depression. This suggests that depression brings on problems?"[26]

From a feminist perspective, of course, violence against women is not "random," nor is it caused by the behavior of the women themselves. This is a classic example of the way in which apparent science is used to support the stereotype that women who are violently treated actually bring the violence on themselves and are therefore "appropriate victims." As Hubbard shows, the basic flaw is "genetic myopia," an ideological commitment to *some* genetic cause. Such a myopia led Lincoln Eaves to discount his own findings—that depression in women is caused by traumatic events—and to continue postulating genetic causes even in the absence of data.

Human Freedom and Genetics

In a curious way, some interpretations of the Human Genome Project risk becoming a scientific version of the gnostic heresy[27] that the fall is equatable with physical existence. Gnostics such as Mani posited a good God, a God of the spirit and the nonmaterial world, a God they held was described in the New Testament. They also described a God of the material world, the Creator, who is the God of the Hebrew Bible. In gnostic terms, body and spirit are split into a consummate dualism of sin and grace.

Interpretations of the role of genes in human life can bolster either side of this formulation: either the sin or the grace side. To overestimate the determinist role of genes in human life is to fall into a reductive physicalism, wherein everything is explained by genes, as discussed above. Human beings are no more than their biology, in this view. But to *under*estimate the role of genes—of our physical existence itself in the totality of the human person as created—is to fall into a radical dualism. In this view the soul (sometimes equated with the mind) is completely separate from physical existence and the essence of the human person consists in the soul/mind. Human beings are not their bodies.

The challenge theologians face is to construct a doctrine of the human person that takes newer genetic research seriously and also makes a case for human freedom and accountability. Our evolutionary history of continuity with other creatures, now substantially documented in the Human Genome Project, is regarded in Evangelical and Reformed Christianity as evidence for the fall.[28]

What has been helpfully described as "non-reductive physicalism" in the volume *Whatever Happened to the Soul? Scientific and Theological Portraits of Human Nature,* edited by Warren S. Brown, Nancey Murphy, and H. Newton Malony, is the concept that "the person is a physical organism whose complex functioning, both in society and in relation to God, gives rise to 'higher' human capacities such as morality and spirituality."[29]

Brain development, from this nondualistic perspective, can begin to account for the biological distinctiveness of human beings. Human morality, as a product of the expanded frontal lobe, gives human beings the capacity to anticipate the "consequences of one's actions, make value judgments and choose many alternative courses of action."[30] This is a strong case for a biological basis for free will. When this capacity was coupled with the development of language and writing, these authors claim, then law and recorded history become possible. These achievements of human culture have a biological basis, but the authors argue that this biological capacity also gives rise to the ability to have a relationship with God. "Human beings," as Thomas Torrance has said, "can be viewed as the 'focal point in the interrelations between God and the universe.' The self's existence as a personal, social, and spiritual being constitutes what the Bible calls the 'image and likeness of God.'"[31]

Human Dignity/In the Image of God

Since the 1980s eight Protestant denominations, the Church of Scotland, and the Roman Catholic Church have all issued statements on the new genetics. Several have completed or are completing revised statements in light of the achievements of the Human Genome Project.[32] Other statements have been produced, strikingly, by government-sponsored groups as well.

Considering the ethical ramifications of practices such as gene therapy, cloning, or genetic engineering, such documents often state, as a final argument for or against a proposed practice, that it will (or will not) "violate human dignity" or "impugn the image of God." These statements are often vague on the exact content of "human dignity" or the "image of God," but such is clearly the theological doctrine that is at stake in the world of the new genetics, in the view of many religious bodies.

In 1980, religious leaders from Protestant, Catholic, and Jewish communities took the almost unprecedented step[33] of writing a letter to Jimmy Carter, then president of the United States, to express their concerns about what genetic engineering might risk for humanity. In this statement an implicit theology of the human being is the operative concern. But the excerpt below also suggests some ways in which newer theological perspectives on sin, as outlined above, can perhaps further the conversation about how we are to assess the Human Genome Project from the perspective of theology.

> We are rapidly moving into a new era of fundamental danger triggered by the rapid growth of genetic engineering. Albeit, there may be opportunity for doing good; the very term suggests the danger. Who shall determine how human good is best served when new life forms are being engineered? Who shall control genetic experimentation and its results which could have untold implications for human survival? Who will benefit and who will bear any adverse consequences, directly or indirectly? . . . These are moral, ethical and religious questions. They deal with the fundamental nature of human life and the dignity and worth of the individual human being.[34]

Strikingly, the documents issued by the eight Protestant communions and the Roman Catholic Church have tended toward a more positive assessment both of human nature and of genetic science than is suggested in the letter above. They all assert that human beings are created in the image of God, from which they derive power and responsibility over creation. Technology is viewed as part of this power derived from the sovereign creator and as such can be harnessed, with discretion, to achieve goods for individuals and society. In effect, these church documents have a relatively traditional interpretation of the "image of God" or "human dignity" as residing in human rationality and capacity for moral judgment.[35] In many respects, these documents parallel the efforts collected in *Whatever Happened to the Soul?* to see the biological basis of human dignity and freedom in the development of the frontal lobe.

By contrast, the letter to President Carter contains some strongly cautionary language. The words "danger," "control," "survival," and "adverse" all hint at a lack of faith in the capacity of human beings, despite their creation in the image of God, to use restraint in their exercise of enormous power over others.

Social Sin and Human Violence

The social construction of sin needs to be considered not only in the context of the new genetics, but also in light of the theological responses to it—such as the creative arguments in *Whatever Happened to the Soul?* In eschewing both a mind/body dualism (conservative Christian) and scientifically reductionist (sociobiological) approach to the human being, these authors have called for theologians to deeply consider the biological basis of human life and culture, including religion. But these authors have as yet failed to appropriate newer theological approaches to the human being from liberation perspectives.

Let us look again at the sociobiological explanation for violence and its critics. "Rape is especially common in the orangutan,"[36] say Thornhill and Palmer, noting the high incidence of forced sexual intercourse in a species, which, as we know from the Human Genome Project, is very genetically similar to human beings. The social-science critics of Thornhill and Palmer, as well as of other sociobiologist arguments for the reproductive origins of forced sexuality, argue that the use of the word *rape* to describe such behavior in animals provides an evolutionary excuse for human rape.

> Sociobiologists offer what amounts to an evolutionary justification of rape. According to this perspective, rape is simply one way for males cut off from socially acceptable access to female sexual partners to ensure that their genetic endowment is passed on to another generation. To suggest, however, that rapists are driven by some genetic force beyond their control is untenable. . . . That relatively few men rape (though certainly more than are ever reported and caught), and that these men rape only under conditions where they are likely to get away with it, indicates that this behavior is very much learned, not genetically inherited.[37]

The opposition between "genetic origin" and "human free will" is especially clear in this quotation above. Of course, Thornhill and Palmer leave themselves open to such a dualistic response as they argue for a genetically determinist position on rape throughout the animal and human world. If a behavior has a genetic origin, then it becomes "a force beyond their control." How then can rape be subject to legal sanction, the critics of sociobiology ask? If genetic origin equals "force beyond our control," then arresting men for rape would be analogous to arresting men merely for becoming sexually aroused. Ironically, however, a different understanding of human nature could allow both to appreciate the genetic component in rape. Thornhill and Palmer, while arguing for a reproductive basis for rape-type behaviors in animals, actually describe behaviors that coerce. It is clear from their description of orangutan behavior that the chasing and subduing of females has several goals. One is sexual partnering, but another is to establish power and dominance, not only with females but also *over other males.*

The relationship of human rape to the establishment of power and dominance not only over women, but also in relationship to other men, especially in war, has been extensively documented.[38] A less dualistic interpretation of the human being would allow social scientists and geneticists to explore what in the human genome predisposes us to exercise dominance and to exploit power over others.

The social construction of sin, as described above in the theologies of Cone, Ruether, Gutiérrez, et al., was a breakthrough in the history of Christian theology because they considered human beings as social entities. Social sin suddenly could be understood in the complex interrelationships of human beings to one another, and their relationship to the history of flawed social relationships as the social inheritance of sin. This is exquisitely described by Mary Potter Engel.

> Evil and sin together may be called "wickedness," the complex condition of the lack of right relations in the world in which we live naturally, socially and individually. Though they are inseparable, it is important to distinguish the two. Evil, as Latin American liberation theology has taught us, is systemic. It is not superpersonal forces but structures of oppression, patterns larger than individuals and groups, that tempt us toward injustice and impiety. It is social, political, and economic arrangements that distort our perceptions or restrain our abilities to such an extent that we find it difficult to

choose or do good. By contrast, sin refers to those free, discrete acts of responsible individuals that create or reinforce these structures of oppression. Neither causes the other; evil and sin are mutually reinforcing.[39]

Human beings are violent toward one another and even toward themselves. But even more characteristically, human beings are violent toward one another in the name of good. And this, strikingly, is where we leave the orangutan, with his desire to assert dominance over females and other males, behind on the evolutionary ladder. The social construction of sin allows us to see human reason's infinite capacity to delude itself. For example, we may convince ourselves of the goodness not only of covert violence such as unemployment or substandard housing, but even overt violence, such as the wholesale slaughter of others in war. It is not until we see the infinite capacity for human beings to lie to themselves about the nature of their coercive acts that we will begin to actually plumb what is truly distinct about human nature. Moreover, we cannot offer a complex theological response to the Human Genome Project's capacity for social goods and ills without an understanding of the way in which human reason is not free, but bound to human self-interest in terms of class, race, gender, and a host of other social conditions.

If the human being is created in the image of God, does that signify solely the rational capacity to act responsibly? Such an assertion is a legacy of a patriarchal culture in which rational brain function alone served to define the human being—and indeed only the socially elite, upper-class white male Europeans. Platonic and Cartesian dualism facilitated this definition of the image of God as rational capacity, denigrating the body to the drag of physicality, often a synonym for sin. This dualism has had two very pernicious effects. Human beings in the West have been hard pressed to see how they sin with their rationality, and they have not appropriated the spiritual content of their physicality.

To Sin Rationally

The World Council of Churches, perhaps because of its wide representation of persons from outside the first world, has issued reports that show the influence of the theologies of liberation and particularly the hermeneutic of suspicion.[40] The premise of the World Council of Churches 1989 document "Biotechnology: Its Challenges to the Churches and the World" illustrates this sharply different theological approach. "Technology is not neutral or value free: it is as much an ideology as it is a tool of science. It has in fact become an instrument of power and is itself trapped in vast networks of power which are complex, systemic, often multinational, and exist primarily to maximize profit."[41] This document builds on work done in the early 1980s that resulted in a two-volume report, *Faith and Science in an Unjust World*. There the theme is much the same:

> Science and technology cannot be discussed as isolated entities; they must be seen within the economic, social and political contexts of particular societies. Whereas science and technology have definite positive aspects, for they can enhance the welfare of the people, this section concentrates on their negative aspects, especially in relation to power. All too often science and technology have been used as formidable tools of oppression in the hands of states, military groups and large private or public corporations.[42]

The World Council had selected two areas for sustained study in the area of "Church and Society": energy and the "Biological Revolution." The two papers presented at the conference on the "New Biology" both emphasized the economic-political-cultural context of this revolution. Dr. Jonathan King, associate professor of microbiology at the Massachusetts Institute of Technology, discussed this interface. "Though the scientific community generally views recombinant DNA technology as a feature of research, private corporations have moved rapidly to exploit it commercially, to produce for sale strains of economically or agriculturally valuable organisms." Dr. King noted with concern that "the attempt to protect capital investment and profit margins distorts certain features of scientific progress." Moreover, commenting on the future of human genetic engineering, he noted that the ethical problems attendant upon this technology can vary with the social mores of given societies. "Historically the values of many human genetically determined features, such as skin colour and hair character, were socially determined. What is a defect in one society is a desirable characteristic in another."[43]

Moreover, said King—echoing Ruth Hubbard's concerns as noted above—there is scientists' problematic tendency to place a distorted emphasis on genetic causality, even for disease. Indeed, he observed "a strong tendency to lose sight of the agents that caused the damage in the first place: mutagens, carcinogens, radiation, et cetera. Our problems are not in our genes, they are in recreating a society in which the genes of individuals are protected from unnecessary damage."[44]

Karen Lebacqz, associate professor of Christian ethics at the Pacific School of Religion in Berkeley, gave an explicitly liberation oriented presentation entitled "Bio-ethics: Some Challenges from a Liberation Perspective." Lebacqz noted the "individualistic orientation" of contemporary bioethics, with its focus on the individual patient and the individual physician. She also observed in contemporary bioethics an "ahistorical" approach that is abstractionist and consequently rigid, a tendency to take "scientific evidence as normative," and an approach that hides the "value-laden nature of 'facts' or data."

By contrast, Lebacqz argued, "liberation theologians and feminists are primarily concerned not with choosing the right action, but with structures and patterns of meaning." Her summary covered a range of liberation approaches.

> For example, Roy Sano argues that Asian American liberation theologians and people turn to apocalyptic rather than prophetic literature because apocalyptic literature gives a better base from which to observe the interweavings of the various powerful institutions. Dussell argues that what is at stake is recognizing the shape of evil in any and all institutions. Feminist theologians analyze the myths that undergird particular institutions by defining the "masculine" and "feminine" in society.[45]

In the liberation perspective, the "structure and pattern of meaning" of human sinfulness must be given a social context in order to helpfully engage not only with the Human Genome Project, but also all of modern science.

Liberation perspectives provide a helpful theological check on the tendency in religion/science dialogue to equate "human dignity" or "the image of God" with human rationality. This equation has many serious consequences. First, it tends to valorize the intellectual achievements of modern science without a deep interrogation of its value-laden assumptions and social embeddedness. Modern science is driven by values that are not necessarily only those of human betterment. Individuals pursue their own career advancement; profit-motivated private corporations step in; institutions may make decisions with reference only to the experience of elites. It should be noted that the religion is not free of any of these same temptations and dubious influences.

Another negative consequence of equating "human dignity" or "the image of God" with human rationality is that it ignores the physical basis of life, which is absolutely essential for any human being to live with dignity and in relationship to the Creator—indeed, to even live at all. The content of "image of God" must also include, as part of living with "dignity," the physical means to sustain life. This leads us to consider not only the social content of sin, but the social content of grace as we explore genetics and theological anthropology.

8

The Chemistry of Community

Susan Brooks Thistlethwaite

> Inherited factors can have an impact on our health, but their effects
> are embedded in a network of biological and ecological relation-
> ships. Genes are part of the metabolic apparatus of organisms that
> have multiple, mutual relationships with their environments. We
> breathe our "environment," eat it, sweat and excrete into it, move
> through it and with it.
>
> This is one reason that even "simple" Mendelian conditions
> exhibit varying degrees of severity. Concepts like "the organism,"
> "the gene," or "the environment" are useful as ways to organize our
> understanding of the world, but we must keep in mind that they do
> not describe the world as it is. They merely serve to separate out the
> specific aspects on which we want to focus our attention.
>
> As we have seen, genes affect our development because they
> specify the composition of proteins, but it is more realistic to think of
> genes as participating in various reactions than as controlling them.
>
> —Ruth Hubbard and Elijah Wald
> *Exploding the Gene Myth*[1]

Genetic science focuses on "the organism" or "the gene." But as we have
seen throughout this book, starting in Lainie Friedman Ross's first
chapter, people live their genes. Even when they are sick, they live their
genes embedded in a web of relationships, challenging the medical
model that places the patient alone in a room with a doctor. Nobody
lives like that, nobody gets sick like that, and nobody heals like that.

Further, it is becoming clearer that even a narrow focus on the gene
itself can yield a distorted picture. As one scholar puts it, cited by

Hubbard and Wald, "Although ... patterns of inheritance [dominant, X-linked, and chromosomal] have been linked to several thousand disorders, many other illnesses result from a complex interaction of genes and environment. These multifactorial conditions share a genetic component, but expression of those genes is also influenced by interactions with other genes and with the individual's entire environment."[2] That is, in order to actually understand how genetic material is expressed—or fails to be expressed, or is expressed in complex patterns, or is impeded or facilitated in its expression by other expressions—the nature/nurture divide must be collapsed. Human biology operates within the stew of environment, breathing it, eating it, excreting in it; in effect, you're soaking in it. The concept of either/or does not apply.

It is also interesting that of those in the sciences who are sounding the alarm against highly deterministic and mechanistic understandings of the workings of genes, many, though of course not all, are women. This is not the place for an exhaustive discussion of whether women "naturally" prioritize relationality; there is a large body of epistemological work that argues this both pro and con.[3] Suffice it here to note that the alarm is being sounded, and often by women.

As a laboratory scientist, Ruth Hubbard, whose words begin this chapter, is best known for her research on the molecular basis of light reception in vision. Since the mid-1970s, however, she has also focused her attention on the sociology and history of biology with special emphasis on genetics and on women's biology and health. In addition to *Exploding the Gene Myth,* cited here and in previous chapters, she is also the author of *The Politics of Women's Biology.*

Feminist and liberation theologies have much in common with feminist science, perhaps unsurprisingly. The world in its complex relationships, one being to another, and this world in its complex relationship to God, are the purview of these theologies. They begin by assuming one world in which humanity plays an important role, but far from the only role. The commitment of what are broadly called contextual theologies is to overturning dualistic understandings of body/spirit or nature/grace and the social dualisms dependent on such divisions as men/women, white/black, first world/third world.

What is of particular interest in this chapter, and indeed in this volume, is that this nondualistic understanding of the world helps to better explain how genes actually work. This, in turn, bridges the traditional gulf between religion and science and helps us understand human beings, creation, and the way this whole functions for biological flourishing or biological destruction.

It is becoming clearer that the quality of our human life together—in families and society, and the whole human community in relationship to the environment—heals or harms us. Far from being deterministic ("It's all in the genes"), the chemistry of gene expression has been shown to be enormously complex and, as is cited above, deeply connected with the stressors of an individual's whole environment. Adult-onset diseases are a good example. Genes turn off and turn on in response to the individual's environment. Our communities, our lives together, really do make us "one body"; if our society is sick, then so are we. Healthy communities, communities that put human well-being at the center, directly affect the health of the individuals within them.

The "Case" of Hypertension in African Americans

In September 1996, Tuskegee University held a conference on the Human Genome Project. It was not by accident that this venerable institution took up questions associated with the genome. Macon County, Alabama (Tuskegee is the county seat) was the location of the infamous Tuskegee Syphilis Study, conducted from 1932 to 1972. Rural males, mostly African American, were part of a study by the U.S. Public Health Service investigating syphilis. What makes this study so notorious, and such a flag for any genetics research, is that "the subjects were denied an effective treatment for syphilis that was discovered during the course of the study."[4] The "Tuskegee Studies" have become a synonym for racism in scientific research.

A participant at the 1996 conference, Richard S. Cooper, M.D., professor and chair of the Department of Preventive Medicine and Epidemiology at the Loyola University Stritch School of Medicine in Chicago, gave a paper on "Hypertension in the African Diaspora: Genes and the Environment." Notable for its relevance to our subject here, Cooper claimed that the farther from Africa persons of African descent reside, the more they suffer from hypertension. Comparing data from Nigeria, Barbados, and the United States, Cooper first marked an increase in the incidence of hypertension as one moved west from Africa. If "it's all in the genes," then those with African genetic heritages should not be so dissimilar.

It has been scientifically demonstrated that African Americans have higher incidences of hypertension than do European Americans.[5] This black/white comparison has constantly "obscured the larger differences among black populations" while "these populations have a high degree of genetic resemblance."[6] Cooper notes, "It is a public health truism that at the population level it is most often the social environment in which people live that accounts for the mean levels of a risk factor while among individuals genetic predisposition may play a larger role."[7]

The role of race in science is as the barometer of either "norm" or "other." Race is often what is not being examined. When a higher incidence of hypertension is found in African Americans, this is deemed to be off the norm. A subtle valorization of "white" genetic material lurks in the background. At the symposium, many argued along the lines "that genes are only expressed in a specific environment and do not mean anything in isolation."[8] The factor of race seems to influence a more genetically determinist explanation of higher levels of hypertension in African Americans.

This bias is obscuring the forthright investigation of the "social experience" and its relationship to differences in rates of hypertension. To conduct this study, Cooper and his researchers "chose population samples in West Africa—Nigeria and the Cameroons, both urban and rural, and three islands in the Caribbean—Jamaica, St. Lucia and Barbados—and the working class community of Maywood to the west of Chicago. . . . For the 'source population' we went to the Yoruba-speaking region of southwest Nigeria."[9]

While these researchers parsed their study for many factors including body weight, sodium intake, and exercise as examples, the pattern of increase in hypertension as African peoples migrate west was striking. What cannot be accurately measured, Cooper argues in his paper, is the social experience of being black in the United States. Adjusting for income, geographic location, years of education, diet, and exercise just does not get at the root cause of the stress of "living while black," to borrow from a subset of this experience, the traffic violation of DWB, "driving while black." The incongruence of white experience and black experience is well evoked by Cooper:

If I may use the analogy, black-white comparisons are like adjusting the number of pregnancies to account for hypertension risk between men and women. In epidemiology we call this the problem of zero exposure. If racism is a causal exposure, we cannot adjust for it. It cannot be measured in both groups and used as the basis for statistical adjustment.[10]

Genetic markers that have been found in these populations, and their relationship to hypertension is being scientifically explored. But as the work on breast cancer discussed below shows, a genetic link is just that, a link. It is one more factor in the complicated interaction of genes and environment.

Racism is part of the environment with which African Americans live in the United States. The only way to tease out the health effect of the stress of racism on these persons of African descent is *to compare different populations of African descent both within and outside Africa and the United States,* as this research shows. Racism, in these researchers' view, is not the only causal factor in hypertension, but it is a largely unexamined, and as this study suggests, a hugely important aspect of hypertension. It is also markedly instructive for looking at the work of genes in the environmental stew of real human lives.

The "Case" of Breast Cancer

The University of Bristol in England reported recently that those conducting a breast cancer study had concluded that women who exercised thirty minutes per day three times per week had 30 percent less incidence of breast cancer, particularly postmenopausally.[11]

There is little doubt that breast cancer, qua cancer, is genetic. This means that changes occur in the DNA. "But most cancer is genetic only in the sense that the DNA changes at the cellular level in the local tissue, not in the sense that affected DNA is transmitted by sperm or egg. Consequently, most cancer is not inherited in families. However, it has recently become clear that susceptibility to breast cancer is inherited in 5–10 percent of cases," wrote one team of scholars in 1993.[12]

Such a statement seems to contradict what is now the conventional wisdom—however erroneous—that breast cancer runs in families and that "breast cancer genes" have been found. This is a combination of the poor reporting on medical research found in the mainstream media and the fact that a small percentage of breast cancer *is* inherited.[13] Indeed, in studies of large families with high incidence of breast cancer through generations, BRCA1 and BRCA2 have been identified as genetic sites for mutations that lead to breast cancer.

Not everyone who carries these genes gets breast cancer, and many people who get breast cancer do not have these genetic mutations. So how does breast cancer, or other cancers, originate?

Many changes must occur, and they occur over time. As one scholar summarizes it:

> A normal somatic cell may have inherited [sic. BRCA1 or 2] or acquired (e.g., from a virus) a mutation that disposes it genetically toward less-regulated cell division. The mutation is passed to cellular progeny of the dividing cell. Eventually, one of these cells mutates at a second site, one of its cellular offspring mutates at a third site, and so on. Eventually, some descendant cell happens to accumulate a sufficient number of particular mutations (perhaps 5–10) to cross the threshold into a full-blown malignant cancerous form.[14]

As each of us undergoes this normal process by which cells are mended, sometimes this replication is impaired. "This mutational progression may be facilitated when one of the initial genetic lesions impairs a cell's capacity to mend environmentally induced damages to DNA, or when an individual has been exposed to environmental carcinogens during his or her lifetime."[15]

The causal relationship between lung cancer and inhaling pollutants such as cigarette smoke is now well established. But breast cancer? What kinds of environmental factors could be operative there?

It is uncertain, but a strong immune system seems to help. As Ruth Hubbard points out, "cancers develop slowly, probably over decades . . . and tiny cancers probably are initiated and quickly stopped repeatedly during every one's life history."[16] Keeping one's immune system in tip-top shape through exercise, as the University of Bristol study points out, seems to be effective in stopping these minute mutations before they can become cancers, as well as preventing the changes from occurring in the first place.

And yet, what other factors compromise our immune systems or strengthen our overall ability to fight disease, including cancer? The focus on the individual and her exercise, as in the Bristol study, is typical of the way a good deal of medical research is done. There is often a narrow focus on personal behaviors as defined by the middle class (women who go to gyms versus women who do not). Less effort is made to research the biologically stressful effects of living in substandard housing, living in areas with air pollution and other environmental toxins, having inadequate public transportation, and living with poor nutrition and high rates of unemployment—all factors of poverty and very high stressors of our systems.[17]

The rates of breast cancer in women of color are much higher than those of white women.[18] Not exercising three times a week is unlikely to be the whole explanation. A complex web of deleterious factors are at work, including racism in the health care system, lack of insurance, distrust of the white medical establishment, and high levels of daily stress. "It is well documented that race and class differences affect the type of care patients receive. . . . 'the darker a woman's skin and/or the lower her place on the economic scale, the poorer the care and efforts at explanation she got,'" notes scholar Dorothy Roberts, quoting Alexandra Dundas. "These women were more likely to be considered 'difficult' and 'to be talked down to, scolded, and patronized.'"[19] The stressors in the lives of all women, and particularly women of color, might help us see that when someone gets breast cancer, the factors that operate in the complicated DNA mechanisms must be seen in a much larger framework of healthy or unhealthy communities.

Grace

One aspect of research on the genome that is only beginning to be understood is the role of relationships (environmental, personal, societal) in "turning on and turning off" the genes. The health care establishment itself, as well as the economic factors that support or deny health care, are a part of this relational matrix.

Dominant American culture contains several factors that make it particularly difficult, if not impossible, to see the role of community in the workings of our genes. In the words of Gary Gunderson, "In our popular culture we tend to think of health as something that happens to individuals, not to communities. We have difficulty speaking about communities in anything other than the language of mechanical functions and services. The language of health initially seems odd because we have removed the word from its roots in relationship—wholeness—and quite literally privatized it, even *monetized* it."[20]

Theologians too have begun relatively recently to examine the way in which the quality of our relational life is a key factor in how we become human together, or how we fail to contribute to one another's growth in grace. Beverly Harrison has said that "by our acts of love or lovelessness we bring one another into being."[21]

In the language of classical theology, *grace* is the term Christian theologians use to describe how God works with the world to move it toward wholeness *(shalom)*. Especially since the Protestant Reformation, however, the work of grace has been held to be an individual transaction between God and the believer. Martin Luther's "justification by grace through faith" has meant that grace is the way the individual sinner becomes righteous.

Feminist and liberation theologians have opposed this narrow and individualistic view of faith, arguing instead that it is indeed the whole creation and especially our relationships to one another that are broken, familial as well as societal, and in need of restoration to relationship, not only to God but to one another. Leonardo Boff, in his work *Liberating Grace,* writes, "Grace signifies the presence of God in the world and in human beings. When God chooses to be present, the sick are made well, the fallen are raised up, the sinners are made just, the dead come back to life, the oppressed experience freedom, and the despairing feel consolation and warm intimacy."[22]

It is interesting that Boff explicitly describes the work of grace as including physical healing, even healing from death. The human body is not excluded from the work of grace, but included in the work God does with the world in restoration and new life.

But Boff does not explore the human dimension of restoration in the same way that several feminist theologians have done. This line of theological work has been exquisitely developed by Rita Nakashima Brock in her work *Journeys by Heart: A Christology of Erotic Power.* Brock uses the metaphor of the heart to mean "the structure of human life itself." She argues that humanity is not born "fallen," but into an original righteousness—a righteousness that is enormously vulnerable, however, because only other human beings can mediate our human nature to us and with us.

Heart is our original grace. In exploring the depths of heart we find incarnate in ourselves the divine reality of connection, of love. The grace we find through heart reveals the incarnate graciousness, generosity, and love necessary to human life. *But the heart's strength lies in its fragility.* To be born so open to the presence of others in the world gives us the enormous, creative capacity to make life whole. Yet such openness means that the terrifying and destructive factors of life are also taken into the self, a self that then requires loving presence to be restored to grace.[23]

It is strikingly clear that particularly in the case of hypertension for African Americans, the "broken heart"—as Brock would describe the way human beings fail to provide the graciousness, generosity, and love necessary to human life—is not a metaphor. Racism literally breaks the heart in increased levels of hypertension.

Carter Heyward is another theologian who has worked for decades to help Christians and others see that what she calls "right-relation" is at the core of not only what it means to be a person of faith, but to be a person at all. "Intimacy is the deepest quality of relation, the realization of ourselves, generically, as *humanity*—people of flesh and blood playing our separate parts in an absurd drama of loneliness." Living into this vision that we are constituted as one when we are most deeply human enables human beings to form communities that transgress the boundaries of loneliness and free human creativity. When we find one another in right-relation, "We will co-create the world, for in the beginning is the relation."[24]

Co-creating the world is a phrase echoed in the work of Philip Hefner, a theologian who has taught religion and science for many years at the Lutheran School of Theology. Hefner argues that the ability to significantly alter nature, as modern science offers, seems to give to humanity the ability to create as does divinity.[25] Hefner invented "created co-creator" to describe this ability and its limitations. "We humans, then, can claim no arrogant credit for being co-creators. Put in scientific terms, we did not evolve ourselves to this point; rather, the evolutionary process-under God's rule, I am arguing—evolved us as co-creators."[26]

While the language of co-creation is indeed similar to Heyward's in particular, the doctrine of God that accompanies this theological emphasis is still quite "top-down," as the Hefner quotation makes clear.

The term "rule" indicates that dominance and subordination is the paradigm in which a modicum of human freedom is preserved. Both Heyward and Brock use the deep encounter of human relationality to reconceive divinity itself and to move Christian theology away from the stifling strictures of classical monotheism.

Broadly speaking, those theologians who have most deeply assessed the impact of newer scientific developments such as the Human Genome Project—and these include Philip Hefner, Ted Peters, John Polkinghorne, and, to a lesser extent, James Gustafson—use process theology or at least process views. The term "process theology" denotes the influence of scientist and philosopher Alfred North Whitehead on a nineteenth-century Christian theology reeling from the implications of Charles Darwin and evolutionary theory.[27] Philosopher Ian Barbour describes the system that developed from Whitehead's thought: "The influence of biology and physics is evident in the process view of reality as a dynamic web of interconnected events. Nature is characterized by change, chance, and novelty as well as order. It is incomplete and still coming into being."[28]

A different theological anthropology emerged from the influence of Whiteheadian philosophy and a new dialogue with science. J. Robert Nelson compares a Whiteheadian view with that of Gustafson's normative understanding of the human being. "This [shift in theological anthropology] would have to be an alternative to the deeply etched idea of human nature as conventionally taught and believed by many people in the West: namely, the nonevolutionary, fixed, unchanging, and essentially dualistic concept of humans as split bodies and souls."[29]

While these theologians do challenge body/soul dualism and traditional Christian theologies' essentialist views of human nature, their work fails to appropriate the implications of the human genome. The failure occurs at a number of levels. There is an overemphasis on "persons and freedom," that is, a perspective both individualistic and romantic. There are allusions to relation and community, but relation is secondary to the individual and to the mind. Relationality is mentioned, as in Ted Peters's work, when he notes that "persons come in relationship: in relationship to themselves, to other selves, to the world around, to the world within, and to God." But when he plays his operative theological card of what counts the most, it is an argument couched in terms of "*the* self" "*the* soul"; indeed; it is practically a ballad. Its romantic optimism does not touch the ground.

Certainly the soul or self finds itself in a most precarious situation. It is utterly dependent upon its particular world for its very existence. Its particular world includes environmental determinants without and biological determinants within. Despite this precariousness, the human soul can dream dreams as yet undreamt and sing songs as yet unheard. It can draw its own world up into consciousness, and it can become conscious of this consciousness. Born on Earth its thoughts can soar toward heaven, and even beyond heaven to the stars and beyond the stars to infinite possibilities.[30]

Freedom is curiously lifted out of human history, and the romantic possibilities of the human imagination float away on a cloud. Completely absent is the capacity of human beings also to do extraordinary harm to one another—which, as was noted above, is concretely the case in the interactions of genes and various kinds of human-made environmental stressors; we explored this capacity, too, in the previous chapter considering violence. Given this capacity, and conversely, the way in which human community is deeply constitutive of human righteousness in a social sense, the implications of the new genetics are far more challenging to theology than even these creative theologians who have been struggling with these developments would allow. The way in which human bodiliness is constitutive of human nature is still subordinated to a free-floating rationality. Peters does not employ postmodernism in his philosophy of mind. There is a residual soul/body dualism that needs to be addressed.

Soul/Body Dualism

Dualism is not only oppositional thinking—this versus that. Dualism also implies that one of the two opposed factors is superior to the other. As noted in chapter 1, dualism of body/mind was enshrined in Western thought through the work of René Descartes. "Cartesian dualism" is the opposition of body and mind and the privileging of mind, construed as abstract reason.

Feminist bioethicists continue to be concerned that a Cartesian dualism predominates in their field. A preoccupation with principles or rules that presume an objective standpoint are a modern variant of this dualistic view. This objectivist stance precludes awareness of the social location of thought, the complexities of power, and newer critical perspectives that bring these issues into relief. Susan Wolf describes the layering of issues involved:

> Four features in particular seem responsible: a historical preference for abstract rules and principles that disregarded individual differences and context; an embrace of liberal individualism that obscured the importance of groups; the structure of bioethics as a field frequently serving government, medical schools, hospitals, and health professionals in a way that may have discouraged attention to the views of people lacking power inside and outside those institutions; and the frequent isolation of bioethics from major trends within the academy, including feminism, Critical Race Theory, and postmodernism.[31]

But the body can also become the dominant partner in the dualist equation; genetic determinism illustrates this risk. Women are particularly sensitive to the "anatomy is destiny" risks of such a view. It was the Enlightenment with its emphasis on human rights, equality, and the freedom of the mind that achieved greater social and political rights for women in the face of determinist interpretations of women's biology as destining them for childbearing and childrearing only.[32]

The implications of the new genetics for understanding human nature actually seem more to risk the latter, bio-determinist view, than to support a privileging of objective mind. The sociobiologists who posit that "the organism is only DNA's way of making more DNA"[33] have pushed this determinism to extremes. This is the so-called "selfish gene" thesis, depicting human beings as mere mechanisms created and maintained by genes to serve "their" ends. Richard Dawkins, in his book by that title, contends that genes "control the behaviour of *their* survival machines, not directly with their fingers on puppet strings, but indirectly like the computer programmer."[34] The anthropomorphism is obvious. Dawkins takes the "body" side of body/soul dualism to mean the complete obliteration of soul. As was noted in the previous chapter, from this perspective humanity is only a means and not an end, and sin becomes moot.

Modern Christian evangelicalism is no less wedded to determinism and body/soul dualism—though of the soul, not the body. Unlike Ted Jennings's depiction of Paul as the one who imagines that the "fundamental reorientation or transformation of the human being also entails the transformation of the whole creation as seen in the natural world (Romans 8),"[35] these evangelical scholars, such as John W. Cooper, posit a Pauline dualism of body and spirit.[36]

Dualism is scarcely a new problem for Christian theology. As Allen Verhey, in his chapter "The Body in the Bible: Life in the Flesh according to the Spirit," notes, the struggle of Christianity with Gnosticism is significant for the basic issues in theological anthropology.[37] Marcion was a second-century preacher who, as a Gnostic, saw the world as the work of an evil God. This God is roughly the God described in the Hebrew scriptures. The God of Jesus Christ is the God of spirituality and the nonmaterial. Marcion "(mis)understood Paul's contrast between 'flesh' and 'spirit' to entail an indifference, indeed an animosity, to the body."[38] This Gnosticism has not gone away, but remains in the evangelical biblical scholarship cited above.

Biblical scholars such as Ken Stone or Allen Verhey read the scriptures from a far more multivalent set of viewpoints than do the evangelical. Indeed, Verhey echoes Ken Stone's use of etiological analysis directly when he says, "Christians think about the body in the light of a story . . . the story of scripture. In the light of that story Christians struggle both to understand their embodiment and to shape their lives into something worthy of Paul's admonition, 'glorify God in your body' (1 Cor. 6:20)."[39] In a sense, Verhey is saying that the story of scripture, in this Pauline verse, is attempting to answer the question, "What is my body in relation to God?"

The Grace of Community

In chapter 7 we explored the way in which a different approach to human violence can reveal that human beings can sin with their rationality. This perspective challenges even the newer theological approaches to religion and science that are seeking to see the human being as a systemic whole, mind and body, without reducing the human to a host for his or her genes.

In the same way, we need to regard human physicality not simply as the drag of the material, that which must be overcome if we are to be deeply spiritual human beings. The physical and social bases of human life are connected under the doctrine of grace. As we can sin against one another through mind as well as body, so too can we grace one another through body as well as mind.

The Human Genome Project speaks graphically to human solidarity *in* creation as well as human solidarity *with* creation. But, as yet, neither science nor religion has acknowledged the depth to which we create one another or destroy one another as we form or deform our communities.

The human soul is as old as time. A concrete illustration of the way in which human beings have conceived their own ensoulment as dignity and well-being is in the Universal Declaration of Human Rights, issued in 1951. A project of the United Nations, those who worked on this declaration combed documents from earliest recorded human history. A striking concord exists, from century to century, in what human beings desire for themselves and their lives on this planet. Food, water, homes, safety, and the right to express one's self—these resound over and over in these documents as the definition of human well-being.[40]

This is what the biblical narratives call *shalom:* the human being under his or her own vine and fig tree, living in peace with the creation and with other human beings.

The desire of human beings to live in right relation with one another is not new. What *is* new is our realization that our very health depends on it. We are deeply embedded in this creation as individuals and as societies. We create and in turn are created by the fabric of our just or unjust relations with one another and with the planet.

Notes

Preface

1. The Report of the President's Council on Bioethics, *Human Cloning and Human Dignity* (New York: Public Affairs, 2002), 10-11.
2. See Syllabus in Appendix.

Introduction: Liberation Theology in Dialogue with the Human Genome Project

1. Stephen S. Hall, "James Watson and the Search for Biology's 'Holy Grail,'" *Smithsonian*, February 1990, 286.
2. Timothy Lenoir and Marguerite Hays, "The Manhattan Project for Biomedicine," in Philip R. Sloan, *Controlling Our Destinies: Historical, Philosophical, Ethical, and Theological Perspectives on the Human Genome Project* (Notre Dame, Ind: University of Notre Dame Press, 2000), 29.
3. Matt Ridley, *Genome: The Autobiography of a Species in 23 Chapters* (New York: HarperCollins, 2000), 7.
4. Ibid.
5. Ibid., 12.
6. Robert F. Weir, "Why Fund ELSI [Ethical, Legal, and Social Implications] Projects?" in Robert F. Weir, *Genes and Human Self-Knowledge* (Iowa City: University of Iowa Press, 1994), 189.
7. Audrey Chapman, *Unprecedented Choices: Religious Ethics at the Frontiers of Genetic Science* (Minneapolis: Fortress Press, 1999), 11ff.
8. Ibid.
9. Ibid., 181.
10. James Gustafson, "Genetic Engineering and the Normative View of the Human," in Preston Williams, *Ethical Issues in Biology and Medicine: Proceedings of a Symposium on the Identity and Dignity of Man* (Cambridge: Mass.: Schenkman, 1973), 46–58.
11. Ibid.
12. Sloan, *Controlling Our Destinies.*
13. John Polkinghorne, *Science and Theology: An Introduction* (Minneapolis: Fortress Press, 1998), 55–56.

14. Londa Schiebinger, *Has Feminism Changed Science?* (Cambridge, MA and London: Harvard University Press, 1999), 197–202.

15. *Plain Talk about the Human Genome Project: A Tuskegee University Conference on Its Promise and Perils . . . and Matters of Race,* ed. Edward Smith and Walter Sapp (Tuskegee, Ala.: Tuskegee University, 1997).

16. Ridley, *Genome,* 21.

17. Susan Griffin, *Pornography and Silence* (New York: Harper and Row, 1978), xvi.

18. Mary Daly, *Pure Lust* (Boston: Beacon, 1984), vii.

19. *Struggle to Be the Sun Again: Introducing Asian Women's Theology* (Maryknoll, N.Y.: Orbis, 1990).

20. "Possessing Different Allelles," in *Ethical Issues in Human Genetics,* ed. Bruce Hilton et al. (New York: Plenum, 1973), 430. See also glossary.

21. See chapter 4, "Theological Anthropology and the Human Genome Project," by Theodore W. Jennings Jr.

22. Naomi Goldenberg, *Returning Words to Flesh: Feminism, Psychoanalysis, and the Resurrection of the Body* (Boston: Beacon, 1990).

23. Gautam N. Allahbadia, "The 50 Million Missing Women," *Journal of Assisted Reproduction and Genetics* 19, no. 9 (2002): 411–16.

24. Ibid.

25. Ted Peters, *Playing God: Genetic Determinism and Human Freedom* (New York: Routledge, 1997), 98.

26. Ruth Hubbard and Elijah Wald, *Exploding the Gene Myth: How Genetic Information Is Produced and Manipulated by Scientists, Physicians, Employers, Insurance Companies, Educators, and Law Enforcers* (Boston: Beacon, 1993), 7.

1. Setting the Context: A Brief History of Science by a Sympathetic Theologian

1. See Michel Foucault, *The Archaeology of Knowledge,* trans. by A. M. Sheridan Smith (New York: Pantheon, 1982).

2. David Lindberg, *The Beginnings of Western Science: The European Scientific Tradition in Philosophical, Religious, and Institutional Context, 600 B.C. to A.D. 1450* (Chicago: University of Chicago Press, 1992), 27.

3. Charles Singer, *A Short History of Science to the Nineteenth Century* (Oxford: Oxford University Press, 1941), 32.

4. Jonathan Barnes, *Aristotle* (Oxford: Oxford University Press, 1982), 1.

5. Felix Grayeff, *Aristotle and His School: An Inquiry into the History of the Peripatos with a Commentary on Metaphysics ZHΛΘ* (London: Duckworth, 1974), 6.

6. Barnes, *Aristotle,* 21.

7. While Thomas's entire work can be summed up as an effort to explicate a "natural relation between all of the orders of creation," a specific discussion can be found in Questions 44–47 of the *Summa Theologica,* in *Introduction to St. Thomas Aquinas,* Modern Library (New York: Random House, 1948), 233–66.

8. Lindberg, *Beginnings,* 161.

9. *The Catholic Encyclopedia,* "Avicenna." See the website, http://www.newadvent.org/cathen/02157a.htm.

10. Contemporary historians of imperial Rome like Polybius and Plutarch and later historians note the popular dismissal of Greeks and Greek culture as effeminate. Despite a profound dependence on Greek thought and language, Romans regularly described their culture as "manly" in its militarism and emphasis on practice over thought, contrasting themselves to the conquered Greeks. See especially "The Expansion of Rome" by Elizabeth Rawson and "Cicero and Rome" by Miriam Griffin, both in *The Roman World,* ed. John Boardman, Jasper Griffin, and Oswyn Murray, Oxford History of the Classical World (Oxford: Oxford University Press, 1998).

11. Frances Bacon, "The New Organ on Aphorisms 31–36," in *The Scientific Background to Modern Philosophy: Selected Readings,* edited by Michael R. Matthews (Indianapolis: Hackett, 1989), 47–52.

12. See René Descartes, "Meditations 1 and 2" in *Meditations on the First Philosophy* (Indianapolis: Hackett, 1999).

13. Universalist notions of ultimate reality rely on a fundamental concept of cosmic unity. Such a concept does not presuppose the existence of a deity, but it is a theological notion in that all concepts of "ultimate reality" are pictures, or meaningful myths, stories even of reality. Such pictures, even if they do not possess resident gods as such, retain the mythic power that theology works to describe and explain.

14. Isaac Newton, "Preface to the First Edition," in *The Principia: Mathematical Principles of Natural Philosophy,* trans. by I. Bernard Cogen and Anne Whitman (Berkeley: University of California Press, 1999), 382–83.

15. See Stephen Hawking, *A Brief History of Time* (New York: Bantam, 1998).

16. For a discussion of Newton's views on the mechanical universe and God's role in it, see James Gleick, *Isaac Newton* (New York: Pantheon, 2003); and Isaac Newton, "General Scholium" in *Principia,* 939–44.

17. Newton, "The System of the World," *Principia,* 792.

18. Ibid.

19. Ibid., 793.

20. See David Hume, "Of Miracles," in *An Enquiry concerning Human Understanding* (Oxford: Oxford University Press, 1999), 169–86.

21. René Descartes, *Discourse on Method,* trans. John Veitch, in *The Rationalists* (New York: Anchor Doubleday, 1960), 52.

22. Peter J. Bowler, *Charles Darwin: The Man and His Influence* (Oxford: Blackwell, 1990).

23. Charles Darwin, *The Voyage of the Beagle,* Modern Library (New York: Random House, 2001) xxv–xxvi.

24. Ibid., 3.

25. Charles Darwin, *The Origin of Species* (New York: Prometheus, 1991).

26. For a fuller treatment of Freud's ideas on consciousness see, for example, *The Basic Writings of Sigmund Freud,* ed. A. A. Brill (New York: Modern Library, 1995). For a good secondary source that places Freud within the history of psychoanalysis, see Stephen Mitchell and Margaret Black, *Freud and Beyond: A History of Modern Psychoanalytic Thought* (New York: Basic Books, 1996). More specifically, see Freud's own *A General Introduction to Psychoanalysis* or *New Introductory Lectures on Psychoanalysis.*

27. "The Discovery of DNA's Structure." See the website: http://www.pbs.org/wgbh/evolution/library/06/3/1_063_01.html.

3. From Peapods to the Human Genome Project: Post-Mendelian Genetics

1. This karyotype was reproduced with permission from an article by Jeff Shaw, M.S., genetic counselor, entitled "Chromosome Deletion Outreach, Inc. Introduction to Chromosome Abnormalities." Last updated July 2000. The karyotypes in the articles were contributed by Century Health, Penrose–St. Francis Health Services, Cytogenetics Lab, Colorado Springs, Colo., and Shodair Children's Hospital, Cytogenetics Lab, Helena, Mont. The article is on the Chromosome Deletion Outreach (CDO) website. See www.chromodisorder.org/intro.htm.

2. This karyotype from the website www.downyn.com/whatisds.html is reproduced with permission. The arrow points to the extra chromosome 21.

3. Reproduced with permission from the CDO website (see n. 1 above). 21P refers to one end of the 21st chromosome; 21q to the other end.

4. The unbalanced translocation depicted below is an example of a zygote that inherited A and D from the balanced translocation above and a healthy chromosome 7 and 21 (E and F respectively) from another gamete. It is reproduced with permission from the CDO website (see n. 1 above).

5. On October 4, 2002, *The New York Times* reported that further gene therapy research on SCIDs had been suspended because the treatment that cured a three-year-old boy of his immune deficiency may have given him an illness similar to leukemia. This was another major setback for the gene therapy community. See Sheryl Gay Stolberg, "Trials Are Halted on a Gene Therapy," *New York Times*, October 4, 2002, A1, A21.

6. Diane Jean Schemo, "A Gift of Life Bridges Two Cultures and Families," *New York Times*, April 14, 2000, sec. B1.

4. Theological Anthropology and the Human Genome Project

1. Note the cautions suggested by David Botstein concerning what can be known and done, in "Of Genes and Genomes" in *Plain Talk about the Human Genome Project*, ed. Edward Smith and Walter Sapp (Tuskegee, AL: Tuskegee University Press, 1997), 207–14.

2. For an analysis of existentialism as gnosticism by the foremost interpreter of gnosticism, see Hans Jonas, *The Phenomenon of Life: Toward a Philosophical Biology* (New York: Dell, 1966).

3. See Owen Barfield, *Saving the Appearances: A Study in Idolatry* (New York: Harcourt, 1965). The corrective to this ignorance is most famously articulated in Thomas Kuhn, *The Structure of Scientific Revolutions* (Chicago: University of Chicago Press, 1962).

4. Gregory of Nyssa, "On the Making of Man," in *The Nicene and Post-Nicene Fathers*, second series, vol. 5, reprint (Grand Rapids: Eerdmans, 1954), 406.

5. Ibid., 393.

6. Ibid., 394.

7. Ibid., 395.

8. Ibid., 397.

9. Ibid., 399ff.

10. Ibid., chapter 7.

11. On modernity as the flourishing of gnosticism, see Eric Voegelin in *The Collected Works of Eric Voegelin,* edited and with an introduction by Ellis Sandoz, vol. 5 (Columbia: University of Missouri Press, 1989).

12. Anselm, *Cur Deus Homo?* Book 2, ch. 21. In *Why God Became Man. A Scholastic Miscellany: Anselm to Ockham,* ed. Eugene R. Fairweather (Philadelphia: Westminster, 1956), 182.

13. "Address on Religious Instruction," in *Christology of the Later Fathers,* ed. Edward R. Hardy (Philadelphia: Westminster, 1954), 293–94.

14. Ibid., ch. 25, 302.

15. Athanasius, "On the Incarnation," chap. 42, in *Christology of the Later Fathers,* 97.

16. Matt Ridley, *Genome: The Autobiography of a Species in 23 Chapters.* (New York: HarperCollins, 1999), 76.

17. In vol. 5 of *Nicene and Post Nicene Fathers* (Grand Rapids: Eerdmans, 1954), 428–70.

18. Ernst Käsemann, *Perspectives on Paul,* trans. Margaret Kohl (London: SCM, 1971).

19. Gregory, "On the Making of Man," 29.3, 421.

20. Irenaeus, "Against Heresies," in *Ante Nicene Fathers,* vol. 1 (Grand Rapids: Eerdmans, 1987), 531.

21. *The Koran* (surah) 75.

22. Gregory, "On the Making of Man," 27.8, 419.

23. Ibid., 26.1, 417.

24. Peter Brown, *The Cult of the Saints: Its Rise and Function in Latin Christianity* (Chicago: University of Chicago Press, 1981); Caroline Walker Bynum, *The Resurrection of the Body in Western Christianity, 200–1336,* (New York: Columbia University Press, 1995), 104–7, 201–13. See also Caroline Walker Bynum, *Fragmentation and Redemption: Essays on Gender and the Human Body in Medieval Religion* (New York: Zone, 1991).

25. There are also the possibilities associated with the blood-soaked imprint on Veronica's veil as explored by Leoncio A. Garza-Valdez in *The DNA of God? Newly Discovered Secrets of the Shroud of Turin* (New York: Berkeley, 1999).

26. Irenaeus, *Against Heresies,* book 3, chap. 14, no. 6, *Ante Nicene Fathers,* vol. 1, 443.

27. Rosemary Radford Ruether, "Can a Male Savior Save Women?" in *Sexism and God-Talk: Toward a Feminist Theology* (Boston: Beacon, 1983), 116–38.

28. Note in this connection Gregory's repeated reference to the restoration of all things in "On the Making of Man," 412, 414, 418.

29. See Gordon Kaufman, *Theology for a Nuclear Age* (Philadelphia: Westminster, 1985).

30. Matt Ridley's discussion of this material is helpful. See Matt Ridley, *Genome: The Autobiography of a Species in 23 Chapters* (New York: HarperCollins, 1999), 122–35. Ted Peters discusses this from a theological point of view in *Playing God? Genetic Determinism and Human Freedom* (New York: Routledge, 1997), 39–46.

31. Incidentally, these suppositions of sexual conflict may at least help in thinking through the implication of feminist theologians that "sin" is different for males and females. See Judith Plaskow, *Sex, Sin and Grace: Women's Experience and the Theologies of Reinhold Niebuhr and Paul Tillich* (New York: University Press of America, 1980).

32. For Augustine's views on this, see *The City of God*, book 14, and *The Literal Interpretation of Genesis*, book 9 in *Ancient Christian Writers* 41 (New York: Newman, 1982).

33. For important questions about the presumed bias of the genome project and the difficulties facing the Human Genome Diversity Project see *Plain Talk about the Human Genome Project*, ed. Edward Smith and Walter Sapp (Tuskegee, Ala.: Tuskegee University, 1997), 51–104.

34. Ibid.

35. "Biotech's Traffic Cop," in the *Chicago Tribune Magazine*, October 7, 2001, points to the patenting gold rush for genes. One specific illustration: "'A genetic test for breast cancer would be about $50,' Andrews says, 'Licensing fees make it $2,500.'"

36. Gregory, "On the Making of Man," 390.

37. Ibid., 392.

38. For Barth's reflections on this theme, see *Church Dogmatics III, 2* (Edinburgh: T. & T. Clark, 1960), 222ff.

39. Gregory, "On the Making of Man," 391.

40. Ibid.

5. Adam, Eve, and the Genome

1. See, for example, Ken Stone, *Sex, Honor, and Power in the Deuteronomistic History* (Sheffield: Sheffield Academic Press, 1996), especially 27–49; Thomas W. Overholt, *Cultural Anthropology and the Old Testament* (Minneapolis: Fortress Press, 1996); and Paula McNutt, *Reconstructing the Society of Ancient Israel* (Louisville: Westminster John Knox, 1999).

2. See, for example, D. Andrew Kille, *Psychological Biblical Criticism* (Minneapolis: Fortress Press, 2001); Ilona N. Rashkow, *Taboo or Not Taboo: Sexuality and Family in the Hebrew Bible* (Minneapolis: Fortress Press, 2000); The Bible and Culture Collective, *The Postmodern Bible* (New Haven: Yale University Press, 1995), 187–224.

3. The term *culture* is itself a much-disputed concept. For an excellent discussion of the term that both summarizes recent theories of "culture" and attempts to relate those theories to theology, see Kathryn Tanner, *Theories of Culture: A New Agenda for Theology* (Minneapolis: Fortress Press, 1997).

4. Sherry Ortner, "Generation X: Anthropology in a Media-Saturated World," in George E. Marcus, ed., *Critical Anthropology Now: Unexpected Contexts, Shifting Constituencies, Changing Agendas* (Santa Fe: School of American Research Press, 1999), 83.

5. For introductions to lesbian and gay studies and queer theory, see Henry Abelove, Michèle Aina Barale, and David M. Halperin, eds., *The Lesbian and Gay Studies Reader* (New York: Routledge, 1993); Annamarie Jagose, *Queer Theory: An Introduction* (New York: New York University Press, 1996); and William B. Turner, *A Genealogy of Queer Theory* (Philadelphia: Temple University Press, 2000). See also Laurel C. Schneider, "Queer Theory"; and Ken Stone, "Sexuality," in A. K. M. Adam,

ed., *Handbook of Postmodern Biblical Interpretation* (St. Louis: Chalice, 2000). For examples of the use of such perspectives in biblical interpretation see, for example, Ken Stone, "Biblical Interpretation as a Technology of the Self: Gay Men and the Ethics of Reading," in Danna Nolan Fewell and Gary A. Phillips, eds., *Bible and Ethics of Reading, Semeia* 77 (Atlanta: Scholars, 1997); Robert E. Goss and Mona West, eds., *Take Back the Word: A Queer Reading of the Bible* (Cleveland: Pilgrim, 2000); Ken Stone, ed., *Queer Commentary and the Hebrew Bible* (Cleveland: Pilgrim, 2001); and Stephen D. Moore, *God's Beauty Parlor: And Other Queer Spaces in and around the Bible* (Stanford: Stanford University Press, 2001).

6. See, e.g., Sherry Ortner and Harriet Whitehead, eds., *Sexual Meanings: The Cultural Construction of Gender and Sexuality* (Cambridge: Cambridge University Press, 1981); Carole Vance, "Anthropology Rediscovers Sexuality: A Theoretical Comment," *Social Science and Medicine* 33/8 (1991), 875–84; Steven Seidman, ed., *Queer Theory/Sociology* (Cambridge and Oxford: Blackwell, 1996); Roger N. Lancaster and Micaela di Leonardo, eds., *The Gender/Sexuality Reader* (New York: Routledge, 1997); Peter M. Nardi and Beth E. Schneider, eds., *Social Perspectives in Lesbian and Gay Studies* (New York: Routledge, 1998); Ellen Lewin and William L. Leap, *Out in Theory: The Emergence of Lesbian and Gay Anthropology* (Urbana, Ill.: University of Illinois Press, 2002).

7. Matt Ridley, *Genome: The Autobiography of a Species in 23 Chapters* (New York: HarperCollins, 1999), 7.

8. Ted Peters, *Playing God? Genetic Determinism and Human Freedom* (New York: Routledge, 1997), xiii. The phrase "gene myth" recurs throughout Peters's discussion.

9. Peters, *Playing God*? 96; emphasis in original.

10. Norman K. Gottwald, *The Hebrew Bible: A Socio-Literary Introduction* (Philadelphia: Fortress Press, 1985), 98, 156. I am working in this article with a broad rather than a narrow understanding of biblical etiological discourse. It is not my intention to address such narrow questions as the form-critical identification of specific phrases that might be used to identify etiological narrative, or the process by which explicit etiological connections might have been added to older narratives. For one influential example of a more narrowly defined approach to biblical etiologies, see Burke O. Long, *The Problem of Etiological Narrative in the Old Testament* (Berlin: Verlag Alfred Töpelmann, 1968).

11. W. R. M. Lamb, trans., *Plato V: Lysis, Symposium, Gorgias*, Loeb Classical Library (Cambridge: Harvard University Press, 1961), 132–47.

12. See, e.g., the different implications drawn from this text by John Boswell, "Revolutions, Universals, and Sexual Categories," in Martin Duberman, Martha Vicinus, and George Chauncey, eds., *Hidden from History: Reclaiming the Gay and Lesbian Past* (New York: Penguin, 1989), 25–26; and David M. Halperin, *One Hundred Years of Homosexuality: And Other Essays on Greek Love* (New York and London: Routledge, 1990), 18–21.

13. See, for example, Simon LeVay, *The Sexual Brain* (Cambridge: MIT Press, 1992); idem, *Queer Science: The Use and Abuse of Research into Homosexuality* (Cambridge: MIT Press, 1996); Dean Hamer with Peter Copeland, *The Science of Desire* (New York: Simon and Schuster, 1994).

14. See especially Simon LeVay, *Queer Science*, 273–95.

15. See, for example, Edward Stein, *The Mismeasure of Desire: The Science, Theory, and Ethics of Sexual Orientation* (Oxford: Oxford University Press, 1999).

16. Hermann Gunkel, *The Legends of Genesis: The Biblical Saga and History,* trans. W. H. Carruth (New York: Schocken, 1964 [1901]), 25.

17. The etiological dimensions of this story are widely acknowledged in biblical scholarship but are discussed in an especially clear and helpful way by Carol Meyers, *Discovering Eve: Ancient Israelite Women in Context* (Oxford: Oxford University Press, 1988), 72–121.

18. All biblical quotations in this chapter are, for convenience, taken from the *New Revised Standard Version.*

19. See also Meyers, *Discovering Eve,* 88.

20. For a clear recognition of ways in which this story lends itself to justifications of the subordination of women to men, see Pamela J. Milne, "The Patriarchal Stamp of Scripture: The Implications of Structuralist Analysis for Feminist Hermeneutics," with a new afterword in Athalya Brenner, ed., *A Feminist Companion to Genesis* (Sheffield: Sheffield Academic Press, 1993), 146–72.

21. For one attempt to do so, see Mieke Bal, *Lethal Love: Feminist Literary Readings of Biblical Love Stories* (Bloomington: Indiana University Press, 1987), 104–30.

22. Anne Fausto-Sterling, *Sexing the Body: Gender Politics and the Construction of Sexuality* (New York: Basic, 2000).

23. In anthropology see, e.g., Roger N. Lancaster, *Life Is Hard: Machismo, Danger, and the Intimacy of Power in Nicaragua* (Berkeley: University of California Press, 1992), 235–78; Gilbert Herdt, *Same Sex, Different Cultures: Exploring Gay and Lesbian Lives* (Boulder, Colo.: Westview, 1997); and sources cited in note 6 above. For more historically oriented analyses, see, for example, Jeffrey Weeks, *Coming Out: Homosexual Politics in Britain, from the Nineteenth Century to the Present* (London: Quartet, 1977); John D'Emilio, "Capitalism and Gay Identity," in Ann Snitow, Christine Stansell, and Sharon Thompson, eds., *Powers of Desire: The Politics of Sexuality* (New York: Monthly Review Press, 1983); George Chauncey, *Gay New York: Gender, Urban Culture, and the Making of the Gay Male World, 1890-1940* (New York: Basic, 1994); and David M. Halperin, *How to Do the History of Homosexuality* (Chicago: University of Chicago Press, 2002).

24. Simon Parker, "Ammonite, Edomite, and Moabite," in John Kaltner and Steven McKenzie, eds., *Beyond Babel: A Handbook for Biblical Hebrew and Related Languages* (Atlanta: Society of Biblical Literature, 2002), 51.

25. Randall Bailey, "They're Nothing but Incestuous Bastards: The Polemical Use of Sex and Sexuality in Hebrew Canon Narratives," in Fernando F. Segovia and Mary Ann Tolbert, eds., *Reading from This Place: Volume 1: Social Location and Biblical Interpretation in the United States* (Minneapolis: Fortress Press, 1995), 132.

26. See, for example, Meyers, *Discovering Eve,* 11–13.

27. See, for example, Jennifer Terry, *An American Obsession: Science, Medicine, and Homosexuality in Modern Society* (Chicago: University of Chicago Press, 1999). Cf. Janice M. Irvine, *Disorders of Desire: Sex and Gender in Modern American Sexology* (Philadelphia: Temple University Press, 1990).

28. David M. Halperin, *Saint Foucault: Towards a Gay Hagiography* (Oxford: Oxford University Press, 1995), 42.

6. Dreaming the Soul: African American Skepticism Encounters the Human Genome Project

1. Daniel J. Kevles, "Out of Eugenics: The Historical Politics of the Human Genome," in Daniel J. Kevles and Leroy Hood, eds., *The Code of Codes: Scientific and Social Issues in the Human Genome Project* (Cambridge, Mass.: Harvard University Press, 1992), 3–36, at 5.

2. F. J. Ayala, "The Myth of Eve: Molecular Biology and Human Origins," Science 270 (1995): 1930–36.

3. Erik Erikson, *Dimensions of a New Identity* (New York: Norton, 1974), 17.

4. Sidney E. Mead, *History and Identity* (Atlanta: Scholars, 1979), 11.

5. See Winthrop Hudson and John Corrigan, *Religion in America*, 5th ed. (New York: Macmillan, 1992).

6. C. G. Jung, "On the Nature of Dreams," *Dreams* (Princeton: Princeton University Press, 1974), 68.

7. Ibid., 73.

8. "The 1998 DNA test results identify a chromosomal link between Eston Hemings and the male Jefferson line. Thomas Jefferson is included among the twenty-five possible fathers, but he is eliminated because of the lack of admissible evidence. It is surprising that the sources and the nature of the information that make up the Tom and Sally myth has put the academic community into such a quandary. It is a tale which should return to its status as no more than a footnote to the Jefferson legacy" (Richard E. Dixon, "Thomas Jefferson—Sally Hemings, Trial Analysis, Evidence on Paternity, the Case against Thomas Jefferson," retrieved June 2000 from www.angelfire.com /va/TJTruth).

9. In 1517, Bartolomé de Las Casas, also known as the Apostle to the Indies, after watching thousands of natives dying in corrals and burned alive, returned to Spain and pleaded with Charles V to spare the natives. Las Casas begged the King, as an act of mercy toward the natives, to import Africans to be slaves, twelve for each colonist. In 1518, Charles V of Spain granted license *(asiento)* for importation of 4,000 African-born people to be enslaved each year to the Indies. The license was sold to the Portuguese. This was the beginning of the enslavement of West Africans and the Atlantic slave trade. See Edward Reynolds, *Stand the Storm: A History of the Atlantic Slave Trade* (London: Allen, 1989), 58–62.

10. Excerpt from "I've Been to the Mountain Top" sermon, April 3, 1968, Memphis, Tenn.

7. A Gene for Violence? Genetic Determinism and Sin

1. See Reinhold Niebuhr, *The Nature and Destiny of Man,* vol. 1 (New York: Scribers, 1941), 228. "But this definition of sin as pride, which history and experience have verified . . ." (228).

2. Augustine, *Confessions,* intro. and notes by Maria Boulding (Hyde Park, N.Y.: New York City Press, 1997), 32.

3. F. Schleiermacher, *The Christian Faith,* ed. H. R. Mackintosh and J. S. Stewart (Edinburgh: T. & T. Clark, 1968).

4. George Albert Coe, *Religion of a Mature Mind* (Chicago and London: Revell, 1902).

5. Reinhold Niebuhr, *Moral Man and Immoral Society: A Study in Ethics and Politics* (Louisville: Westminster John Knox, 2001).

6. Gustavo Gutierrez, *A Theology of Liberation* (Maryknoll, N.Y.: Orbis, 1973), 21–42.

7. James Cone, *A Black Theology of Liberation* (Maryknoll, N.Y.: Orbis, 1990).

8. Valerie Saiving in *Weaving the Visions: New Patterns in Feminist Spirituality,* eds. Carol Christ and Judith Plaskow (San Francisco: Harper and Row, 1989).

9. Emily Townes, *A Troubling in My Soul: Womanist Perspectives on Evil and Suffering,* (Maryknoll, N.Y.: Orbis, 1993).

10. Kenneth Stone, ed., *Queer Commentary and the Hebrew Bible* (Cleveland: Pilgrim, 2001).

11. Edward O. Wilson, *Sociobiology: The New Synthesis* (Cambridge: Harvard University Press, 1975).

12. Richard Dawkins, *The Selfish Gene* (Oxford: Oxford University Press, 1976).

13. Ibid., 3.

14. Ibid.

15. Ibid., 2.

16. Ibid., 207.

17. Jonathan Marks, *What It Means to Be 98% Chimpanzee: Apes, People, and Their Genes* (Berkeley: University of California Press, 2002), 123–27.

18. Randy Thornhill and Craig Palmer, *A Natural History of Rape: Biological Bases of Sexual Coersion* (Cambridge: Massachusetts Institute of Technology, 2000).

19. Ibid., ix.

20. Ibid., 124–31.

21. Ibid., 144.

22. Ibid., 149.

23. Ibid., x.

24. *Webster's Third New International Dictionary* (Chicago: Encyclopedia Britannica, 1961).

25. Thornhill and Palmer, *Natural History of Rape,* 8.

26. Ruth Hubbard and Elijah Wald, *Exploding the Gene Myth* (Boston: Beacon, 1993), 6, citing Richard Saltus, "Medical Notebook," *Boston Globe* (10 October 1991), 3.

27. Robert M. Grant, A Sourcebook of Heretical Writings from the Early Christian Period (New York: Harper, 1961), 96.

28. Warren S. Brown, H. Newton Malony, Nancey Murphy, eds., *Whatever Happened to the Soul? Scientific and Theological Portraits of Human Nature* (Minneapolis: Fortress Press, 1998), 24; describing the work of Daniel Dennett.

29. Ibid., 25.

30. Ibid., 55.

31. Ibid., 179, citing Thomas F. Torrance, *Divine and Contingent Order* (Oxford: Oxford University Press, 1981), 129.

32. For a complete survey of all these documents, see the excellent overview in Audrey Chapman, *Unprecedented Choices: Religious Ethics at the Frontiers of Genetic Science* (Minneapolis: Fortress, 1999), 31–48.

33. The other such initiative was in response to the development of nuclear weaponry. See Peter Goodchild Jr., *Robert Oppenheimer: Shatterer of Worlds* (Boston: Houghton Mifflin, 1981), chap. 1.

34. Letter from Dr. Claire Randall, General Secretary, National Council of Churches; Rabbi Bernard Mandelbaum, General Secretary, Synagogue Council of America; and Bishop Thomas Kelly, General Secretary, U. S. Catholic Conference to President Carter, 20 June 1980. Reproduced in the President's Commission for the Study of Ethical Problems in Medicine and Behavioral Research, *Splicing Life: The Social and Ethics Issues of Genetic Engineering with Human Beings* (Washington, D.C.: U.S. Government Printing Office, 1982), App. B, 95, cited in Chapman, *Unprecedented Choices*, 27.

35. Ibid., 34ff.

36. Thornhill et al., *A Natural History*, 145.

37. Ibid., 122, citing W. Marshall and S. Barrett, *Criminal Neglect: Why Sex Offenders Go Free* (Westminster, Md.: McClelland-Banton, 1990, 105–6.

38. The classic in this area is Susan Brownmiller, *Against Our Will: Men, Women, and Rape* (New York: Bantam, 1976).

39. Susan Brooks Thistlethwaite and Mary Potter Engel, eds., *Lift Every Voice: Constructing Christian Theologies from the Underside* (Maryknoll, N.Y.: Orbis, 2001), 161–62.

40. The term "hermeneutic of suspicion" was first used by Juan Luis Segundo in his book *The Liberation of Theology* (Maryknoll, N.Y.: Orbis, 1976). It has come to mean a questioning of the universality of the experience of those in the first world and an attempt to see the world "from below." See Thistlethwaite and Engel, *Lift Every Voice*, 299.

41. WCC, *Biotechnology: Its Challenges to the Churches and the World* (Geneva: World Council of Churches, 1989), 7, 11.

42. *Faith and Science in an Unjust World: Report of the World Council of Churches' Conference on Faith, Science and the Future. Volume 2: Reports and Recommendations* (Geneva: World Council of Churches, 1980), 135–36.

43. Ibid., vol. 1, 267.

44. Ibid., 270–71.

45. Ibid., 272–77.

8. The Chemistry of Community

1. Boston: Beacon, 1993, 63–64.

2. Adrienne Asch and Gail Geller, "Feminism, Bioethics, and Genetics," in Susan M. Wolf, ed., *Feminism and Bioethics: Beyond Reproduction* (New York and London: Oxford University Press, 1996), 321, citing Ruth Hubbard and Elijah Wald, *Exploding the Gene Myth* (Boston: Beacon, 1993), particularly chapter 4, for a discussion of the variability of expression of genes linked with dominant disorders as well as multifactorial disorders. Neil A. Holtzman, *Proceed with Caution: Predicting Genetic Risks in the Recombinant DNA Era* (Baltimore: Johns Hopkins University Press, 1989), 81. See also Barton Childs and Charles R. Scriver, "Age at Onset and Causes of Disease," *Perspectives in Biology and Medicine* 29 (1986): 437–60. Eliot Marshall, "Search for a Killer: Focus Shifts from Fat to Hormones," *Science* 259 (1993): 618–21.

3. See "Part I: The Relationship of Feminism and Bioethics," in Susan M. Wolf,

Feminism and Bioethics: Beyond Reproduction (New York and Oxford: Oxford University Press, 1996), 47–162, for an exhaustive discussion of this important debate.

4. Edward Smith and Walter Sapp, eds., *Plain Talk about the Human Genome Project: A Tuskegee University Conference on Its Promise and Perils . . . and Matters of Race* (Tuskegee, Ala.: Tuskegee University, 1997), ix.

5. Michael Klug et al., "The Association of Skin Color with Blood Pressure in U.S. Blacks with Low Socioeconomic Status," in *Journal of the American Medical Association* 265 (5): 599–602.

6. Ibid., 32.

7. Ibid.

8. Ibid., 34.

9. Ibid., 35.

10. Ibid., 42.

11. CNN news program, 21 October 2002.

12. Wolf, ed., *Feminism and Bioethics*, 332, citing Mary-Claire King, Sarah Rowell, and Susan M. Love, "Inherited Breast and Ovarian Cancer: What Are the Risks? What Are the Choices?" *Journal of the American Medical Association* 269 (1993): 1975–1980.

13. Ibid., 332.

14. John C. Avise, *The Genetic Gods: Evolution and Belief in Human Affairs* (Cambridge, Mass.: Harvard University Press, 1998), 73.

15. Ibid., 73.

16. Hubbard, *Exploding the Gene Myth*, 90.

17. See K. A. Lochner et al., "Social Capital and Neighborhood Mortality Rates in Chicago," *Social Science Medicine* 56, no. 8 (April 2003): 1797–805.

18. D. Levenson, "Poverty Is a Major Factor in African American Breast Cancer Deaths," repr. *Medical Guide Outcomes* 13, no.21 (November 1, 2002): 9–10, 12.

19. Dorothy E. Roberts, "Reconstructing the Patient: Starting with Women of Color," in Wolf, ed., *Feminism and Bioethics*, 123, citing Alexandra Dundas Todd, *Intimate Adversaries: Cultural Conflict between Doctors and Women Patients* (Philadelphia: University of Pennsylvania Press, 1989), 77.

20. Gary Gunderson, *Deeply Woven Roots: Improving the Quality of Life in Your Community* (Minneapolis: Fortress Press, 1997), 3.

21. Beverly Harrison, *Making the Connections: Essays in Feminist Social Ethics,* ed. Carol Robb (Boston: Beacon, 1985), 186.

22. Leonardo Boff, *Liberating Grace,* trans. John Drury (Maryknoll, N.Y.: Orbis, 1979), 3.

23. Rita Nakashima Broch, *Journeys by Heart: A Christology of Erotic Power* (New York: Crossroad, 1988), 17.

24. Carter Heyward, *The Redemption of God: A Theology of Mutual Relation* (Washington, DC: University Press of America, 1982), xix.

25. Philip Hefner, *The Human Factor: Evolution, Culture, and Religion* (Minneapolis: Fortress Press, 1993).

26. Philip Hefner, "The Evolution of the Created Co-Creator," in *Cosmos as Creation: Theology and Science in Consonance,* ed. Ted Peters (Nashville: Abingdon, 1989), 227.

27. John Polkinghorne, *Science and Theology: An Introduction* (Minneapolis: Fortress Press, 1998), 55–56.

28. Ian Barbour, *Religion in an Age of Science,* 28, cited in J. Robert Nelson, *On the New Frontiers of Genetics and Religion* (Grand Rapids: Eerdmans, 1994), 18.

29. J. Robert Nelson, *On the New Frontiers of Genetics and Religion* (Grand Rapids: Eerdmans, 1994), 18.

30. Ted Peters, *Playing God: Genetic Determinism and Human Freedom* (New York: Routledge, 1997), 163–65.

31. Wolf, *Feminism and Bioethics,* 14–15.

32. Ibid., 325ff.

33. Edward O. Wilson, *Sociobiology: The New Synthesis* (Cambridge, MA: Harvard University Press, 1978), 3.

34. Richard Dawkins, *The Selfish Gene* (Oxford: Oxford University Press, 1976). Italics added.

35. See above, chapter 4.

36. Robert H. Gundry, *Soma in Biblical Theology with Emphasis on Pauline Anthropology,* Society of New Testament Studies Monograph Series 29 (Cambridge: Cambridge University Press, 1976), and John W. Cooper, *Body, Soul and Life Everlasting: Biblical Anthropology and the Monism-Dualism Debate* (Grand Rapids: Eerdmans, 1989).

37. Allen Verhey, ed., *Religion and Medical Ethics: Looking Back, Looking Forward* (Grand Rapids: Eerdmans, 1996), 196.

38. Lisa Cahill and Margaret Farley, eds., *Embodiment, Morality, and Medicine* (Dordrecht: Kluwer Academic Publishers, 1995), 9.

39. Ibid., 10.

40. *The United Nations Universal Declaration on Human Rights.* The U.N. Department of Social Affairs (New York: United Nations, ST/SOA/5, 11 July 1951).

Glossary

alleles. Alternate forms or varieties of a gene. The alleles for a trait occupy the same locus or position on homologous chromosomes and thus govern the same trait. However, because they are different, their action may result in different expressions of that trait.

amino acids. Organic molecules that are building blocks of proteins. There are twenty different kinds of amino acids in living things. Proteins are composed of different combinations of amino acids assembled in chain-like molecules. Amino acids are primarily composed of carbon, oxygen, hydrogen, and nitrogen.

analogues. Likenesses found in humans and animals.

chromosomes. Thread-like, gene-carrying bodies in the cell nucleus. Chromosomes are composed primarily of DNA and protein. They are visible only under magnification during certain stages of cell division. Humans have forty-six chromosomes in each somatic cell and twenty-three in each sex cell.

diploid number. The full component of chromosomes normally found in somatic cells. In humans, the number is forty-six. See also haploid number.

DNA (deoxyribonucleic acid). A large organic molecule that stores the genetic code for the synthesis of proteins. DNA is composed of sugars, phosphates, and bases arranged in a double helix-shaped molecular structure. Segments of DNA in chromosomes correspond to the specific genes.

dominant allele. An allele that masks the presence of a recessive allele.

double helix. The twisted ladder shape that is characteristic of DNA molecules.

ethics. The principle of right and wrong and good conduct.

fertilization. Conception; the process of sexual reproduction by which the chromosomes from a sperm cell enter the nucleus of an ovum and combine with its chromosomes.

gametes. Reproductive cells—sperm or unfertilized ovum cells—produced in the testes and ovaries of animals. Gametes are produced by meiosis. They normally have half the number of chromosomes found in somatic cells.

genes. Units of inheritance usually occurring at specific locations, or loci, on a chromosome. Physically, a gene is a sequence of DNA bases that specify the order of amino acids in an entire protein, or, in some cases, a portion of a protein. A gene may be made up of hundreds of thousands of DNA bases. Genes are responsible for hereditary characteristics in plants and animals.

genetic coding. The genetic makeup of humans and other species.

genome. An organism's gene makeup.

genotype. The genetic makeup of an individual. Genotype can refer to an organism's entire genetic makeup or to the alleles at a particular locus. See phenotype.

haploid number. The number of chromosomes in gametes. Human sperm and ova normally contain only twenty-three chromosomes, which is the result of the halving of chromosome pairs in meiosis. See diploid number.

hemophilia. An X-linked genetically inherited recessive disease in which one or more of the normal blood clotting factors is not produced. This results in prolonged bleeding from even minor cuts and injuries. Hemophilia most often afflicts males.

heterozygous. A genotype consisting of two different alleles of a gene for a particular trait (Aa). Individuals who are heterozygous for a trait are referred to as heterozygotes. See homozygous.

homologous chromosomes. Chromosomes that are paired during meiosis. Such chromosomes are alike with regard to size and also position of the centromere. They also have the same genes, but not necessarily the same alleles, at the same locus or location.

homozygous. Having the same allele at the same locus on both members of a pair of homologous chromosomes. Homozygous also refers to a genotype consisting of two identical alleles of a gene for a particular trait. An individual may be homozygous dominant (AA) or homozygous recessive (aa). Individuals who are homozygous for a trait are referred to as homozygotes. See heterozygous.

Huntington's disease. A severe genetically inherited fatal degenerative nerve disorder. The symptoms usually do not appear until early middle age. There is a progressive loss of muscle control that inevitably leads to paralysis and death.

individuation. The distinctiveness or uniqueness of an individual.

interrelatedness. To come into mutual relationship.

living species. Animals other than humans.

meiosis. Cell division in specialized tissues of ovaries and testes that results in the production of sperm or ova. Meiosis involves two divisions and results in four daughter cells, each containing only half the original number of chromosomes—twenty-three in the case of humans. These cells can develop into gametes. See mitosis.

mitosis. The simple cell division process that occurs in somatic cells. One cell divides into two offspring cells that are identical to each other in their chromosome complement. Mitosis produces cells with diploid numbers of chromosomes—forty-six in the case of humans. See meiosis.

moral. Judgment of the goodness or badness of human actions.

mutation. An alteration of genetic material such that a new variation is produced. For instance, a trait that has only one allele (A) can mutate to a new form (a). This is the only mechanism of evolution that can produce new alleles of a gene. Technically, mutation refers to changes in DNA bases as well as changes in chromosome number and/or structure.

nucleic acids. The largest type of molecule in living organisms. It is composed of a chain of nucleotides that code for the synthesis of specific proteins. DNA and RNA are types of nucleic acids.

nucleotide. The basic building block of nucleic acid. It consists of any one of four specific purine or pyrimidine bases attached to a ribose or deoxyribose sugar and phosphate group.

ovum (plural: ova). A female sex cell or gamete.

phenotype. The observable or detectable characteristics of an individual organism; the detectable expression of a genotype.

polymorphism. A genetic trait controlled by more than one allele, each of which has a frequency of 1 percent or greater in the population gene pool.

population. A more or less distinct group of individuals within a species who tend to restrict their mate selection to members of their group. Members of a population tend to have similar genetic characteristics due to generations of interbreeding.

proteins. Any of a large number of complex organic molecules that are composed of one or more chains of amino acids. Proteins can serve a wide variety of functions through their ability to bind to other molecules. Proteins may be enzymes, hormones, antibodies, structural components, or gas-transporting molecules.

recessive allele. An allele that is masked in the phenotype by the presence of a dominant allele. Recessive alleles are expressed in the phenotype when the genotype is homozygous recessive (aa).

recombination. The exchange of genetic material between homologous chromosomes at the beginning of meiosis. This results in sperm and ova with greater genetic diversity. Specifically, a portion of a chromosome is broken and reattached on another chromosome. Recombination is also referred to as crossing-over.

retinal atrophy. This concerns the wasting away of the inner living of the eye.

RNA (ribonucleic acid). A type of nucleic acid that is found in both the nucleus and the cytoplasm of cells. Unlike DNA, RNA is single stranded. Messenger RNA (mRNA) carries the genetic code from the DNA in the chromosomes and translates it with the help of transfer RNA (tRNA) at the site of the ribosomes in the cytoplasm in order to assemble, or synthesize, proteins.

sex cell. A gamete, either a sperm or an ovum. Sex cells are produced by the meiosis process. See somatic cell.

sex-linked. Referring to a gene that is part of a sex chromosome. Since all of the genes on a chromosome are inherited as a package, they are essentially linked together.

sickle-cell trait. A genetically inherited recessive condition in which red blood cells are distorted resulting in severe anemia and related symptoms that are often fatal in childhood.

somatic cell. Basically, all the cells in the body except those directly involved with reproduction. Most cells in multicellular plants and animals are somatic cells. They reproduce by mitosis and have a diploid number of chromosomes. See sex cell.

species. The largest natural population of organisms that can interbreed to produce fertile offspring. Members of one species are reproductively isolated from members of all other species (i.e., they cannot mate with them to produce fertile offspring).

sperm. A male sex cell or gamete.

Tay-Sachs disease. An inherited metabolic abnormality that is fatal in early childhood. Eastern European Jews have an unusually high frequency of this harmful recessive allele in their population; however, it can occur in any human group.

transgenic. The moving of genes.

X-linked. Referring to a gene that is carried by an X chromosome. See sex-linked gene.

zygote. A "fertilized" ovum. More precisely, this is a cell that is formed when a sperm and an ovum combine their chromosomes at conception. A zygote contains the full complement of chromosomes (in humans 46) and has the potential of developing into an entire organism.

Index

achondroplastic dwarfism, 62–63
adenosine deaminase deficiency
    (ADA), 79–80
African American culture,
    129–44; American history and,
    132–37; communality and
    relationships in, 138–39,
    141–43; dreaming and, 131,
    135–41; freedom and, 133,
    139–41; Human Genome Pro-
    ject and, 129–31, 143–44; as
    resistance culture, 137–38,
    140–41; and scientific racism,
    129–31, 141, 143–44, 163–65
African American theologies, 6, 147
African Americans: breast cancer
    and, 167; hypertension in,
    163–65
Angelman syndrome, 75
Anselm, 100
Aquinas, Thomas, 28–29, 32
Aristotle, 18–24, 25, 27–28, 45–46
Athanasius, 100–101
Atwood, Margaret, 6
Augustine of Hippo, 31, 107, 145
autosomal dominant conditions,
    54, 61–63, 80–81
autosomal recessive conditions,
    54–61, 69, 75–76
Averroes, Ibn Roschd, 28
Avicenna, 28

Bacon, Francis, 34
Barbour, Ian, 170
Barnes, Jonathan, 19
Barth, Karl, 110
Basil "the Great," 96
biblical studies: and etiology,
    112–13, 117–20, 121–26; inter-
    disciplinary approaches in,
    112–15. *See also* etiological dis-
    course
Boff, Leonardo, 168
breast cancer, 4, 80, 165–67
Brock, Rita Nakashima, 168–69,
    170
Brown, Peter, 104
Brown, Warren S., 153
Butler, Lee H., Jr., 8. *See also*
    African American culture
Bynum, Carolyn Walker, 104

cardiovascular disease (CVD),
    73–74
Carter, Jimmy, 154–55
Chinese Human Genome Diversity
    Project (CHGDP), 8–9
Chodorow, Nancy, 6–7
Christ, Carol, 6
chromosomal variations, 70–77;
    chromosomal translocation,
    72–73; imprinting and, 75–76;
    karyotype images of, 70–73;

multifactorial disorders, 73–74; and novel mechanisms of inheritance, 74–76; triplet repeat expansions, 76–77; uniparental disomy and, 74–75

chromosomes, 53. *See also* chromosomal variations

Chung, Hyun Kyung, 7

clinical genetics, 77–83; alternative therapies and, 80; DNA fingerprinting and, 9, 101; ethical and policy issues of, 4, 9, 10–11, 78–80, 83–89, 153–54; gene therapy, 11, 79–80, 178n. 5; genetic testing, 77–83; insurance issues and, 4, 83; pediatric testing and, 82–83; predictive testing and, 80–83; scientific racism and, 129–31; sin and, 107

Coe, George Albert, 146

community. *See* relationality

Cooper, John W., 173

Cooper, Richard S., 163–65

Copernicus, Nicolaus, 29

Crick, Francis, 50, 53

cystic fibrosis (CF), 54–55, 58, 75–76, 78, 80, 81, 82–83

Daly, Mary, 6

Darwin, Charles, 43–47, 146, 148

Dawkins, Richard, 148, 149, 172

Descartes, René, 33–36, 41–42, 103, 171

determinism. *See* genetic determinism

DNA (deoxyribonucleic acid): discovery of, 50, 53–54; fingerprinting and, 9, 101; genetic determinism and, 148–49, 172; Mendelian genetics and, 53–54

Down syndrome, 70, 71

dualism, 171–73; in bioethics field, 171–72; in doctrines of sin and grace, 152–53, 157; feminist/liberation theologies and, 6, 162–63; genetic determinism and, 172; gnostic worldview and, 94, 102, 106, 152, 173; process-oriented theologies and, 170–71; relationality in place of, 6, 162–63; in sex and gender research, 121; traditional genetic science and, 161–62; traditional theology and, 94, 102, 106, 172–73

Duchenne muscular dystrophy (DMD), 64, 83, 86–89

Eaves, Lincoln, 151–52

Einstein, Albert, 50

Engel, Mary Potter, 156–57

environment and gene expression, 74, 161–67

Erikson, Erik, 132

ethical challenges of genetics: and etiology of sexual orientation, 10–11, 117, 120–21; genetic testing and, 4, 9, 10–11, 78–79, 83–89; and ideological contexts of science, 158–59; insurance issues and, 4, 83; racist potential of Human Genome Project, 107–8, 129–31, 141, 143–44; theological anthropology and human dignity, 3–4, 153–55

etiological discourse, 112–26; biblical texts and, 112–13, 117–20, 121–26; confusion of etiological and ethical questions, 116–17, 120–21; cultural assumptions and questions in, 119–20, 121–26; defining, 115–16; the "gay gene" and homosexuality, 11, 114–17, 120–21; "gene myth" and determinism, 114–15; Genesis stories and, etiological discourse *(continued)* 117–20, 121–26; and the genome as "text," 112–15; and modern dialogue between religion and science, 125–26; negative evaluations and, 118–19

eugenics, 108

evolutionary psychology/sociobiology, 148–51, 155–56, 172

evolutionary theory, 44, 46–47, 146

feminist theologies: and doctrine of sin, 147, 159; grace and restoration in, 168–69; human uniqueness and, 9–10; relationality/connectedness and, 4, 5–7, 162, 168. *See also* liberation theologies

fragile X, 76–77

Franklin, Rosalind, 50

Freud, Sigmund, 43, 47–51, 135

fundamentalism, 94–95

Galen, 27–28

Galileo, 17, 32, 41

gay and lesbian theologians, 147–48

"gay gene," 10–11, 114–17, 120–21

"Gene myth," 114–15

gene therapy, 11, 79–80, 178n. 5. *See also* clinical genetics

genes. *See* clinical genetics; environment and gene expression; genetic determinism; Mendelian genetics; post-Mendelian genetics

Genesis stories: of Adam and Eve, 117–20; of Ammonites and Moabites, 121–26

genetic determinism: criminality and, 107, 149–51, 155–56; dualism and, 172; as flawed science, 151–52; "gene myth" and, 114–15; and role of race in science, 163–65; sin and, 148–52, 155–56; and sociobiology/evolutionary psychology, 148–51, 155–56, 172

genetic testing. *See* clinical genetics

Genome (Ridley), 1–2, 101–2, 108

Gilligan, Carol, 6–7

Gnostic worldview, 94, 102, 106, 152, 173

Goldenberg, Naomi, 10

grace: dualism and doctrines of, 152–53, 157; relationships and, 168–69, 173–74

Greenham Common, 6

Gregory of Nyssa, 96–98, 99, 100, 102–3, 109–10

Griffin, Susan, 6

Gunderson, Gary, 167

Gunkel, Hermann, 117

Gustafson, James, 170

Gutiérrez, Gustavo, 147, 156

Hamer, Dean, 10, 11, 116, 126

Harrison, Beverly, 168

Hefner, Philip, 169, 170

Hemings, Sally, 136

hemophilia, 64, 67

Heyward, Carter, 169–70

Hippocrates, 27

history of science, 17–51; Aquinas and, 28–29, 31; Aristotle and, 18–24, 25, 27–29, 45–46; Augustine and, 31; classification and, 22–23; consciousness and, 48–49; Darwin and, 43–47, 146, 148; Descartes and, 33–36, 41–42; Freud and, 43, 47–51; idealism and, 18–19, 20–21, 22–24, 35–36, 42; Islamic science and, 25–28, 29; Latin thought and, 30–31, 177n. 10; logic and, 21–22; mechanistic model and, 37–39, 49, 50; medical science and, 27–28, 37–38; medieval science, 28–31; Newton and, 33–34, 36–43, 46, 48–49; parsimony principle and, 39–40, 42, 46; Plato and, 18–24, 35–36, 42; Ptolemaic geocentrism and, 29–31; rationality and, 38–39, 42, 48–49; Reformation and Luther, 31–33; and relationship of science and religion, 17, 33–35, 44, 46–47, 50–51; Renaissance and, 31–33; scientific method and, 39–43; scientific revolution and, 32, 33–43; and search for certainty, 34–35, 50–51; theological anthropology and, 33, 44, 46–47; twentieth-century science and, 50–51, 146–48; universalism and, 36–38, 40–41, 42, 46, 177n. 13

Hubbard, Ruth, 12, 151–52, 161–62, 166

Human Genome Diversity Project (HGDP), 8–9, 108

Human Genome Project (HGP): African American culture and, 129–31, 143–44; budget for, 3; human variation and, 8, 108–9; original sin and, 107–9; racist potential of, 107–9, 129–31, 141, 143–44; research of, 53–54

Hunayn Ibn Ishaq, 27

Huntington's disease, 76, 78, 80–81

hypertension, 163–65

Imago Dei: human reason as, 42, 159–60; and theological anthropology, 5, 98, 109–10, 153–55, 159–60

individuation, 9–12, 98, 101–2, 103–5

insurance issues, 4, 83

Irenaeus, 31, 102, 105, 109

Islamic science, 25–28, 29

Jefferson, Thomas, 132, 136, 143–44, 183n. 8

Jennings, Theodore, Jr., 5, 8, 144, 172–73. *See also* theological anthropology

Jung, Carl, 131, 135

Kant, Immanuel, 38

Käsemann, Ernst, 102

Kevles, Daniel, 129

King, Jonathan, 158–59

King, Martin Luther, Jr., 139–41

Lactantius, 31

Las Casas, Bartolomé de, 137, 183n. 9

Lebacqz, Karen, 159

LeVay, Simon, 116

liberation theologies: and alternative approaches to genetics and bioethics, 159–60; and doctrine of sin, 147, 159; and epistemology of the oppressed, 4; and human uniqueness, 9–10; and relationality, 162, 168. *See also* feminist theologies

Lucretius, 29

Luther, Martin, 32–33, 168

Malony, H. Newton, 153

Marcion, 173

mechanistic model, 37–39, 49, 50

medieval science, 28–31

Mendel, Gregor, 52, 69

Mendelian genetics, 52–68; autosomal dominant conditions and, 54, 61–63, 80–81; autosomal recessive conditions and, 54–61, 69, 75–76; and discovery of

Mendelian genetics (*continued*)
DNA, 53–54; and discovery of
hereditary traits, 52; post-
Mendelian genetics and, 62, 69;
x-linked conditions and, 54,
63–68. *See also* post-Mendelian
genetics
Miller, Jean Baker, 6–7
Muhammad, 25
Murphy, Nancey, 153

National Institutes of Health
(NIH), 3, 8, 10, 79–80, 107–8
A Natural History of Rape (Thorn-
hill and Palmer), 149–51
Nelson, J. Robert, 170
Newton, Isaac, 33–34, 36–43, 46,
48–49
Niebuhr, Reinhold, 9–10, 99
Nietzsche, Friedrich, 149

Palmer, Craig T., 149–51, 155–56
Peters, Ted, 11, 114–15, 116–17,
120, 170–71
Plaskow, Judith, 9
Plato, 18–24, 35–36, 42, 116
Polkinghorne, John, 170
post-Mendelian genetics, 69–89;
autosomal dominant conditions
and, 62, 80–81; autosomal
recessive conditions and, 69,
75–76; chromosomal variations
and, 70–77; clinical genetics
and, 77–83; environment and
expression of diseases in, 74,
80–81; ethical and policy issues
raised by, 83–89; multifactorial
disorders and, 73–74; and novel
mechanisms of inheritance,
74–76. *See also* chromosomal
variations; clinical genetics; ethical challenges of genetics
postmodernism, 22, 148

Prader-Willi syndrome, 75
pre-implantation genetic diagnosis
(PGD), 67
Process theology, 3, 4, 170–71
Protestantism: history of slavery
and, 137; Reformation and, 34,
168; and statements on genetic
engineering, 153–54; theological
anthropology and, 3
Ptolemaic geocentrism, 29–31

rape, 149–51, 155–56
Razi, Abu Bakr Mohammad Ibn
Zakariya al-, 28
reason/rationality: in history of science, 38–39, 42, 48–49; as Imago
Dei, 42, 159–60; sin and, 157;
theological anthropology and,
97, 98, 159–60
Reformation, 31–33, 168
relationality: African American culture and, 138–39, 141–43; dualism and, 6, 162–63;
feminist/liberation theologies
and, 4, 5–7, 162, 168; grace and,
168–69, 173–74; and interaction
of genes and environment, 74,
161–67; theological anthropology and, 167–71
Renaissance, 31–33
Ridley, Matt: on genome as text,
1–2, 4, 114; on human variability, 101–2, 108–9
Roberts, Dorothy, 167
Romans, Paul's letter to, 110–11
Ross, Lainie Friedman, 7, 11, 161.
See also Mendelian genetics;
Post-Mendelian genetics
Ruether, Rosemary Radford, 5, 156

Saiving, Valerie, 9
Schneider, Laurel C., 6, 7. *See also*
history of science

scientific method, 39–43; parsimony principle in, 39–40, 42, 46;
rule of causes and, 40; rule of
refutability and, 41–43; rule of
universality and, 40–41, 42, 46
scientific revolution, 32, 33–43;
Descartes and, 33–36, 41–42;
mechanistic universe and,
37–39; Newton and, 33–34,
36–43, 46, 48–49; scientific
method and, 39–43; universalism and, 36–38, 40–41, 42
The Selfish Gene (Dawkins), 148, 172
severe combined immunodeficiency syndrome (SCID),
79–80, 178n. 5
sickle-cell anemia (SCA), 54, 55,
58, 80, 81, 82
sin, 145–60; dualism and doctrines
of, 152–53, 157; feminist theologies and, 9–10; genetic determinism and, 148–52, 155–56;
genetics and human freedom,
152–53; grace and, 152–53, 157;
history of doctrine of, 145–48;
and human dignity/image of
God, 153–55, 159–60; and negative aspects of genetic science,
107–8, 153–55, 158–59; origi-
nal/universal, 106–9; rational,
157; redemption and, 106–7;
social construction of, 9,
147–48, 156–57; theological
anthropology and, 106–9,
145–48
Singer, Charles, 18–19
Sociobiology: The New Synthesis
(Wilson), 148
sociobiology/evolutionary psychology, 148–51, 155–56, 172
Starhawk, 6
Stone, Ken, 11, 145, 149, 173. *See
also* etiological discourse

Sturtevant, Alfred, 69
Symposium (Plato), 116

Tay-Sachs disease, 11
Tertullian, 31
text, genome as, 1–2, 4, 112–15. *See
also* etiological discourse
theological anthropology: bodiliness and, 102–3; Darwin and,
44, 46–47, 146, 148; and doctrine of sin, 106–9, 145–48; ethical challenges of, 3–4, 153–55;
fundamentalism and, 94–95;
gnosticism and, 94, 102, 106,
152, 173; of Gregory of Nyssa,
96–98, 99, 100, 102–3, 109–10;
history of science and, 33, 44,
46–47, 145–48; human dignity
and, 3–4, 153–55, 159–60;
human freedom and, 152–53;
Human Genome Project and,
3–4, 5, 93–111; Imago Dei and,
5, 98, 109–10, 153–55, 159–60;
individuation and, 9–12, 98,
101–2, 103–5; of Luther, 33; and
negative aspects/risks of genetic
science, 107–9, 153–55, 158–59;
and Paul's letter to the Romans,
110–11; process theology and, 3,
4, 170–71; reason/rationality
and, 97, 98, 159–60; redemption
and resurrection in, 102–9; rela-
tionality/communality and,
167–71; and relationship of science and religion, 33, 44, 46–47,
94–98; resurrection of the body
and, 102–5; species solidarity
and, 5–6, 98–99, 110–11; species
unity and, 6–9, 98, 99–101
Thistlethwaite, Susan Brooks. *See*
relationality; sin
Thornhill, Randy, 149–51, 155–56
Tillich, Paul, 94, 99

Torrance, Thomas, 153
Tubman, Harriet, 139–40
Turner syndrome, 70–71
Tuskegee Syphilis Study, 163
Tuskegee University, conference on
    Human Genome Project, 108–9,
    163

Universal Declaration of Human
    Rights (1951), 174
universalism, 36–38, 40–41, 42, 46,
    177n. 13

Verhey, Allen, 173

Wald, Elijah, 161–62
Watson, James, 50, 53
Whatever Happened to the Soul?
    (Brown, Murphy, Malony, eds.),
    153, 155
Whitehead, Alfred North, 3, 170
Wilson, Edward O., 148
Wolf, Susan, 172
World Council of Churches,
    157–59

X-linked conditions, 54, 63–68, 83,
    86–89